PISA

Are Students Ready to Take on Environmental Challenges?

OECD

BETTER POLICIES FOR BETTER LIVES

Please cite this publication as:
OECD (2022), *Are Students Ready to Take on Environmental Challenges?*, PISA, OECD Publishing, Paris, https://doi.org/10.1787/8abe655c-en.

ISBN 978-92-64-51202-3 (print)
ISBN 978-92-64-93358-3 (pdf)

PISA
ISSN 1990-8539 (print)
ISSN 1996-3777 (online)

Photo credits:
Cover:
© LuminaStock/iStock
© Dean Mitchell/iStock
© bo1982/iStock
© karandaev/iStock
© IA98/Shutterstock
© Tupungato/Shutterstock

Corrigenda to publications may be found on line at: www.oecd.org/about/publishing/corrigenda.htm.

Foreword

"Never before have the stakes been so high for the role of science education in shaping how people interact with the environment. Human activities such as the generation of greenhouse gases, the accumulation of waste, the fragmentation or destruction of ecosystems, and the depletion of resources are having a substantial impact on the global environment." These were the opening sentences of a report from one of the first PISA assessments, carried out back in 2006.

PISA 2006 offered the first international assessment on what students know about the environment. The results showed that fewer than one in five 15-year-olds on average across OECD countries could thoroughly explain environmental processes and phenomena. This included using evidence to compare and differentiate among competing explanations. Close to two-thirds of 15-year-olds had at least a fair understanding of the science underpinning environmental issues. For example, they could interpret the relationship between two charts showing carbon dioxide emissions and the average temperature of the Earth's atmosphere. But that figure ranged from 80% in Finland to below 20% in Qatar, Azerbaijan and Kyrgyzstan.

Importantly, students with poorer knowledge and skills around environmental science often reported an almost naïve optimism that the environmental challenges would go away by themselves. That is not surprising. A better science education enables students to more realistically assess the magnitude of the challenges that lie ahead. It helps them apply ethical reasoning in relation to science and to consider consequences and evaluate externality in relation to experimental design and problem analysis. And a good science education helps students accept that science does not give direct answers for decision making or 'what one should do' but requires ethical and value-driven considerations.

The world demands bold action to meet the global goal of net zero emissions by 2050. Education has a pivotal role in preparing us for a greener future, fostering sustainability, and keeping the world we know in ecological balance. Education can also build our resilience, helping us live in an increasingly imbalanced world. It can help us make better trade-offs between the present and the future, and between situational values – 'I will do whatever the current situation allows me to do' – and sustainable values that better align individual and collective well-being.

Beyond providing people with the scientific knowledge and skills that underpin a green economy, education can shape individual behaviour that influences political commitments, whether that is financing political parties or social activism. It can shape behaviour that impacts local communities – through volunteering or community services – and business practices, the latter through changes in consumption and lifestyle patterns, and personal investment and employment choices.

However, results from PISA 2015, which was the last time science was the assessment's main domain, show little progress in 15-year-olds' environmental knowledge and understanding compared to PISA 2006. When there is need for a better understanding of the science of the environment and more active engagement on this issue but little progress in learning outcomes, we should ask ourselves what we can do differently. This is why PISA 2018 took this agenda up again.

Human nature should be our ally in this – we are all born scientists. Children love to understand nature, to compare and contrast, to try things out and test new ideas, to figure out cause and effect. They take nothing for granted, always ready not just to learn but to unlearn and relearn when new paradigms emerge. And when they discover something new, they immediately take ownership of it and are eager to tell the whole world.

But as children grow older, many turn away from this early love, considering science to be an abstract world of formulas and equations unrelated to their lives and dreams. A lot of that has to do with how we learn and teach science. What students learn in school science is often a mile wide but just an inch deep, quickly memorised and then forgotten, and unrelated to the environment. Amid all the facts and figures learned in school, it is easy to lose sight of what it means to think like a scientist – to build a hypothesis, design an experiment, and distinguish questions that are scientifically investigable from those that are not.

Educating for the environment needs to not just equip young people with the decision-making skills to navigate through life but empower and support them to take action. As this report shows, pro-environmental attitudes and science proficiency tend to reinforce each other. Pro-environmental attitudes can foster curiosity and motivation for learning science; at the same time, scientific understanding of the environment lays the foundation for pro-environmental attitudes.

Findings in this report also reveal that scientific knowledge and skills do not automatically lead to action: in 2018, the share of students who performed well in science but did not act for the environment was considerable. If schools help students develop pro-environmental attitudes, this can mobilise their knowledge and propel them into action. Students with an environmental sense-of-purpose are more likely to carry out environmental actions. This is good news because, on average, some 8 out of 10 students reported that they care about the environment.

As the report shows, students who are enthusiastic about the environment have a greater propensity to take action when they are in close contact with parents or school peers who are involved in environmental action – especially school peers. The results also show that students are more likely to take part in environmental actions if they are enrolled in schools where other students are also involved in environmental actions. At school, friends and peers form social networks that share information on environmental issues and encourage students to actively participate in environmental initiatives. Environmental activities at school that motivate not only the individual but groups of students and the entire student community are promising. Environmental education initiatives should target school communities as a whole.

So, education needs to do better in helping students develop a sense of self-efficacy, agency and responsibility. Only in this way can young people unleash their knowledge and energy to build sustainable cities, start sustainable businesses, push the innovation frontier for green technologies, rethink individual lifestyles, back ecologically responsible policy making, and, most importantly, strike the right balance between meeting the needs of the present and safeguarding the ability of future generations to meet their own needs.

When young people create new value, they ask questions, collaborate, and try to 'think outside the box'. They approach problems using a range of strategies, reflect on what has and has not worked, and have the resilience and agility to try out new solutions. In doing so they become more prepared and resilient in the face of uncertainty and change.

Some will say the climate challenge is far too urgent to place all our hopes on the next generation. And yes, that is true. But the sluggish progress we are seeing in public awareness of and adults' behaviour about climate change shows how much harder it is to unlearn comfortable beliefs and habits than to get it right from the start. An excellent education in environmental science, built on a foundation of education science, will serve the hopes and aspirations of people, economies and nations. It will improve and save many lives, and is one of the great investments a society can make in its people and its future. Today's school students are just a small share of our populations, but they are 100% of our future.

Acknowledgements

This report is the product of a collaborative effort between the countries and economies participating in PISA and the OECD Secretariat. The development of the report was guided by Miyako Ikeda. The report was drafted by Daniel Salinas, with contributions from Giannina Rech. Francesco Avvisati contributed to Chapter 2. Analytical and statistical support was provided by Choyi Whang and Kartika Herscheid. Clara Young edited the report. Andreas Schleicher and Yuri Belfali provided valuable feedback at various stages of the report. This report also benefited from the input and expertise of Young Chang, Esther Ferreira Dos Santos, Mario Piacentini, Anna Pons and Miho Taguma. Production was co-ordinated by Stephen Flynn and Della Shin laid out the publication. Administrative support was provided by Thomas Marwood. The development of the report was steered by the PISA Governing Board, chaired by Michele Bruniges (Australia), with Peggy Carr (United States) and Carmen Tovar Sánchez (Spain) as vice-chairs.

PISA

Table of Contents

BOXES

FIGURES

TABLES

Executive Summary

How prepared are students to take on environmental challenges? In a climate-changing world, readiness means having the knowledge, skills, attitudes, and values to take action on rising carbon emissions, diminishing biodiversity and other environmental degradation. This report posits that proficiency in science, particularly on environmental and sustainability issues, is a facet of this readiness as are young people's awareness of climate-change dynamics; confidence that they understand them, sense of responsibility about the state of the planet; and taking action to protect it. It looks at how economic status; gender; parents' environmental attitudes and behaviours; school peers' involvement in environmental actions; students' growth mindset; and school characteristics play into students' environmental science performance, attitudes and actions, and how schools can help propel students to act.

Chapter 1 lays out the conceptual and analytical framework. The report uses two sources of PISA data: data on 15-year-old students' science performance collected from PISA 2006 and PISA 2015 when science was the assessment's main domain; and data on environmental sustainability and pro-environmental attitudes and actions collected within the Global Competence framework in PISA 2018. Through these data, PISA 2018 measured student agency vis-à-vis the environment.

Chapter 2 zooms in on the evolution of student performance in environmental science from PISA 2006 to PISA 2015. It also looks at student performance in environmental sustainability test items in PISA 2018. The reports finds that students' performance in environmental science decreased slightly between PISA 2006 and PISA 2015 on average across OECD countries.

Performance on environmental sustainability test units in PISA 2018 revealed students' need for a more nuanced and complex grasp of climate-change science: students in 20 out of the 26 countries/economies with available data had more difficulties identifying short-term than long-term solutions to climate change: that is, distinguishing between combatting climate change and adapting to its effects. Environmental science performance in PISA 2006 and PISA 2015, and environmental sustainability performance in PISA 2018 are related to overall science performance.

Chapter 3 turns to students' environmental attitudes and values. The report focuses on their awareness of climate-change issues; their sense-of-purpose or feeling of responsibility towards the planet; and their self-efficacy in environmental understanding – that is – students' confidence that they are knowledgeable about climate-change science. Some three out of four students are environmentally aware; almost four in five students have an environmental sense-of-purpose; and six out of ten students display self-efficacy in environmental understanding.

Nearly half of students have all three values of awareness, sense-of-purpose and self-efficacy in environmental understanding, making them "environmentally enthusiastic". Some 6% have none and are "environmentally indifferent". Environmentally enthusiastic students also scored about 80 points higher in science than environmentally indifferent students, on average, after accounting for student socio-economic status. In fact, environmentally enthusiastic students are not only more proficient in science but tend to have parents who are environmentally aware and take part in environmental actions. They also tend to believe in a growth mindset, come from advantaged backgrounds and to be girls.

Chapter 4 looks at young people taking action on environmental issues. It uses PISA data to elucidate the relationship between both science performance and environmental actions, and pro-environmental attitudes and environmental actions. What is sobering is that while half of students who sat PISA 2018 have "environmentally enthusiastic" values and attitudes, only a fifth of students were "actively involved" in environmental actions and a fifth did not take any action on climate change at all. The environmental actions PISA 2018 asked students about included reducing energy consumption at home; choosing certain products for environmental or ethical reasons regardless of price; boycotting products or companies for environmental or other reasons; signing environmental or social petitions online; and participating in activities to protect the environment. The climate activism spearheaded by young people such as #FridaysForFuture and Extinction Rebellion Youth would have fallen in the last category, but PISA data was collected in most countries before the eruption of these movements in the fall of 2018.

Students' reported environmental actions in 2018 showed interesting differences across countries and economies. In 14 countries/economies, the percentage of students who did not participate in any environmental action at the time was 25% or more; among this group are large OECD countries/economies such as France, Germany, Italy and Scotland

(United Kingdom). In Indonesia, Jordan, Thailand and Türkiye, however, 40% or more of students participated in four or five environmental actions, and in Viet Nam, almost nine in ten students did.

What also stands out in Chapter 4 is that it is students' environmental sense-of-purpose – their feeling of responsibility towards the planet – that is key to their activism. And, in no country or economy was the share of students who displayed environmental sense-of-purpose in 2018 lower than two-thirds of the student population.

Chapter 5 focuses on ways in which education can better prepare students to take action on climate change and environmental issues. In terms of academic performance, the share of students who are strong in science but do not act for the environment is considerable. Still, better performers have on average more environmental sympathies and values than lower-performing students, and students with pro-environmental attitudes are more likely to act for the environment. Education should try to foster not just students' science proficiency but their pro-environmental convictions as well: together, scientific knowledge and environmental values can better galvanise young people's action on climate change.

To develop students' sense of environmental purpose, which is crucial to their acting on climate change, schools that are the most successful are those that are themselves environmentally active. Schools can encourage students to carry out climate action projects either in the classroom or after regular school hours. They can work together with the surrounding community on local environmental initiatives, making them more real and relatable to young people. Involving family members in school-activated climate projects potentially strengthens students' resolve that they should do something about climate change. And enriching environmental curriculum and projects with growth-mindset interventions nudges young people into taking action on climate change all the more. What the report finds is that a "universal" intervention for all kinds of environmental action does not work. It depends on what kind of students they are and what kind of environmental actions are desired. Understanding these differences is important if schools are to mobilise responsible student participation in climate and environmental action.

As for environmental pedagogy, merely covering climate change in school curriculum is not enough: more attention needs to be paid to how it is being implemented. Educators should focus on students developing a more complex, nuanced understanding of the timeline of climate-change responses. Schools should consider a more holistic approach to environmental education such as UNESCO's Whole-School pedagogy, which embeds classroom learning within the overall environmental values of the school and the immediate community.

And, finally, urgent attention needs to be paid to building good science proficiency and pro-environmental attitudes among socio-economically disadvantaged students and in countries/economies where student performance in science needs boosting. This is especially true for lower-income countries/economies. More often than not, they are the ones who bear the brunt of extreme climate-change effects.

Reader's Guide

Data underlying the figures

The data referred to in this report are presented in Annex B and, in greater detail, including additional tables, on the PISA website (www.oecd.org/pisa).

Three symbols are used to denote missing data:

c There were too few observations to provide reliable estimates (i.e., there were fewer than 30 students or fewer than 5 schools with valid data).

m Data are not available. There was no observation in the sample; these data were not collected by the country; or these data were collected but subsequently removed from the publication for technical reasons.

Country coverage

This publication features data on 66 countries and economies in total. Chapter 2 (section 2.1) features data from the 26 countries and economies that administered the PISA 2018 Global Competence cognitive test (12 OECD and 14 partner countries/economies[1]). Chapter 2 (section 2.2) features data from 51 countries and economies (37 OECD and 14 partner countries/economies[2]) that participated in PISA 2006 and PISA 2015 cycles. Chapter 3 features data from 66 countries and economies (30 OECD and 36 partner countries/economies[3]). Chapter 4 features data for 63 countries and economies (27 OECD and 36 partner countries/economies[4]). In figures, OECD countries/economies are indicated in black and partner countries and economies are indicated in blue.

The statistical data for Israel are supplied by and under the responsibility of the relevant Israeli authorities. The use of such data by the OECD is without prejudice to the status of the Golan Heights, East Jerusalem and Israeli settlements in the West Bank under the terms of international law.

Two notes apply to the statistical data related to Cyprus:

- **Footnote by Turkey:** The information in this document with reference to "Cyprus" relates to the southern part of the Island. There is no single authority representing both Turkish and Greek Cypriot people on the Island. Türkiye recognises the Turkish Republic of Northern Cyprus (TRNC). Until a lasting and equitable solution is found within the context of the United Nations, Türkiye shall preserve its position concerning the "Cyprus issue".
- **Footnote by all the European Union Member States of the OECD and the European Union:** The Republic of Cyprus is recognised by all members of the United Nations with the exception of Türkiye. The information in this document relates to the area under the effective control of the Government of the Republic of Cyprus.

Hong Kong (China), Netherlands, Portugal and United States: Data did not meet the PISA technical standards but were accepted as largely comparable (see Annexes A2 and A4 from (OECD, 2019$_{[1]}$)).

In 2018, some regions in Spain conducted their high-stakes exams for tenth-grade students earlier in the year than in the past, which resulted in the testing period for these exams coinciding with the end of the PISA testing window. Because of this overlap, a number of students were negatively disposed towards the PISA test and did not try their best to demonstrate their proficiency. Although the data of only a minority of students show clear signs of lack of engagement (see Annex A9 from (OECD, 2019$_{[1]}$)), the comparability of PISA 2018 data for Spain with those from earlier PISA assessments cannot be fully ensured.

PISA collects reliable and comparable data from participating countries and territories. Following OECD data regulations, a visual separation between countries and territories has been used in all charts to reduce the risk of data misinterpretation.

International averages

The OECD average corresponds to the arithmetic mean of the respective country estimates. The overall average corresponds to the arithmetic mean of the respective country/economy estimates. These averages were calculated for all indicators presented in this report.

In this publication, the overall average is used in most chapters when the focus is on comparing performance across education systems. The OECD average is used in Chapter 2.

In analyses involving data from multiple years, the OECD average is always reported on consistent sets of OECD countries, and several averages may be reported in the same table. For instance, the "OECD average-38" refers to the average across all 38 OECD countries and is reported as missing if fewer than 38 OECD countries have comparable data; the "OECD average-30" includes only 30 OECD countries that have non-missing values across all the assessments for which this average itself is non-missing. This restriction allows for valid comparisons of the OECD average over time.

The number in the label used in figures and tables indicates the number of countries included in the average:

- **OECD average**: Arithmetic mean across all OECD countries with available data.
- **OECD average-33 (Chapter 2)**: Arithmetic mean across all OECD countries, excluding Colombia, Costa Rica, Iceland, Japan and Norway.
- **OECD average-30 (Chapter 3)**: Arithmetic mean across all OECD countries, excluding Czech Republic, Denmark, Finland, Japan, Luxembourg, Norway, Sweden and the United States.
- **OECD average-27 (Chapter 4)**: Arithmetic mean across all OECD countries, excluding Belgium, Czech Republic, Denmark, Finland, Israel, Japan, Luxembourg, the Netherlands, Norway, Sweden and the United States.

If data from subnational entities are reported for some countries in an indicator, the subnational data are included in the calculation of the OECD average.

Rounding figures

Because of rounding, some figures in tables may not add up exactly to the totals. Totals, differences and averages are always calculated on the basis of exact numbers and are rounded only after calculation.

All standard errors in this publication have been rounded to one or two decimal places. Where the value 0.0 or 0.00 is shown, this does not imply that the standard error is zero, but that it is smaller than 0.05 or 0.005, respectively.

Reporting student data

The report uses "15-year-olds" as shorthand for the PISA target population. PISA covers students who are aged between 15 years 3 months and 16 years 2 months at the time of assessment and who are enrolled in school and have completed at least 6 years of formal schooling, regardless of the type of institution in which they are enrolled, and whether they are in full-time or part-time education, whether they attend academic or vocational programmes, and whether they attend public or private schools or foreign schools within the country.

Reporting school data

The principals of the schools in which students were assessed provided information on their schools' characteristics by completing a school questionnaire. Where responses from school principals are presented in this publication, they are weighted so that they are proportionate to the number of 15-year-olds enrolled in the school.

Focusing on statistically significant differences

This volume discusses only statistically significant differences or changes. These are denoted in darker colours in figures and in bold font in tables. Unless otherwise specified, the significance level is set to 5%. See Annex A2 for further information.

Abbreviations used in this report

% dif.	Percentage-point difference
Score dif.	Score-point difference
Dif.	Difference
ESCS	PISA index of economic, social and cultural status
S.D.	Standard deviation
S.E.	Standard error

Further documentation

For further information on the PISA assessment instruments and the methods used in PISA, see the *PISA 2018 Technical Report* (OECD, 2020[2]).

StatLink

This report has *StatLinks* at the bottom of tables and graphs. To download the matching Excel® spreadsheet, just type the link into your Internet browser, starting with the *https://doi.org* prefix, or click on the link from the e-book version.

Notes

1. For Chapter 2 (section 2.1), the 12 OECD countries/economies are: Canada, Chile, Colombia, Costa Rica, Greece, Israel, Korea, Latvia, Lithuania, Scotland (United Kingdom), the Slovak Republic and Spain. The 14 partner countries/economies are: Albania, Brunei Darussalam, Croatia, Hong Kong (China), Indonesia, Kazakhstan, Malta, Morocco, Panama, Philippines, Serbia, Singapore, Chinese Taipei and Thailand.

2. Chapter 2 (section 2.2), the 37 OECD countries are: Australia, Austria, Belgium, Canada, Chile, Colombia, the Czech Republic, Denmark, Estonia, Finland, France, Germany, Greece, Hungary, Iceland, Ireland, Israel, Italy, Japan, Korea, Latvia, Lithuania, Luxembourg, Mexico, the Netherlands, New Zealand, Norway, Poland, Portugal, the Slovak Republic, Slovenia, Spain, Sweden, Switzerland, Türkiye, the United Kingdom and the United States. The 14 partner countries/economies are: Brazil, Bulgaria, Croatia, Hong Kong (China), Indonesia, Jordan, Macao (China), Montenegro, Qatar, Romania, Chinese Taipei, Thailand, Tunisia and Uruguay.

3. For Chapter 3, the 30 OECD countries/economies are: Australia, Austria, Belgium, Canada, Chile, Colombia, Costa Rica, Estonia, France, Germany, Greece, Hungary, Iceland, Ireland, Israel, Italy, Korea, Latvia, Lithuania, Mexico, the Netherlands, New Zealand, Poland, Portugal, Scotland (United Kingdom), the Slovak Republic, Slovenia, Spain, Switzerland and Türkiye. The 36 partner countries/economies are: Albania, Argentina, Baku (Azerbaijan), Bosnia and Herzegovina, Brazil, Brunei Darussalam, Bulgaria, Croatia, Cyprus, the Dominican Republic, Hong Kong (China), Indonesia, Jordan, Kazakhstan, Kosovo, Lebanon, Macao (China), Malaysia, Malta, Moldova, Montenegro, Morocco, North Macedonia, Panama, Peru, Philippines, Romania, Saudi Arabia, Serbia, Singapore, Chinese Taipei, Thailand, Ukraine, the United Arab Emirates, Uruguay and Viet Nam.

4. For Chapter 4, the 27 OECD countries/economies are: Australia, Austria, Canada, Chile, Colombia, Costa Rica, Estonia, France, Germany, Greece, Hungary, Iceland, Ireland, Italy, Korea, Latvia, Lithuania, Mexico, New Zealand, Poland, Portugal, Scotland (United Kingdom), the Slovak Republic, Slovenia, Spain, Switzerland and Türkiye. The 36 partner countries/economies are the same as Chapter 3: Albania, Argentina, Baku (Azerbaijan), Bosnia and Herzegovina, Brazil, Brunei Darussalam, Bulgaria, Croatia, Cyprus, the Dominican Republic, Hong Kong (China), Indonesia, Jordan, Kazakhstan, Kosovo, Lebanon, Macao (China), Malaysia, Malta, Moldova, Montenegro, Morocco, North Macedonia, Panama, Peru, Philippines, Romania, Saudi Arabia, Serbia, Singapore, Chinese Taipei, Thailand, Ukraine, the United Arab Emirates, Uruguay and Viet Nam.

References

OECD (2020), *PISA 2018 Technical Report*, https://www.oecd.org/pisa/data/pisa2018technicalreport/. [2]

OECD (2019), *PISA 2018 Results (Volume I): What Students Know and Can Do*, PISA, OECD Publishing, Paris, https://dx.doi.org/10.1787/5f07c754-en. [1]

PISA

1

Introduction and Conceptual Framework

INTRODUCTION

In September 2015, the world's leaders set ambitious goals for the future of the global community, the Global Goals or the 2030 Agenda for Sustainable Development. The 17 Sustainable Development Goals (SDGs) adopted by the 70th General Assembly of the United Nations in 2015 are a universal call for action to end poverty, protect the planet and ensure that all people enjoy peace and prosperity. The Sustainable Development Goals on education (Goal 4) and climate change (Goal 13) recognise the importance of education for sustainable development and education's role in climate change responses (Box 1.1).

About a year later, in November 2016, the Paris Agreement, a legally binding international treaty to reduce global greenhouse gas emissions and foster global collaboration to adapt to the impacts of climate change, entered into force. By 2022, 192 countries had joined the Agreement[1], a convergence that reflects the growing scientific and international consensus on the urgency of addressing climate change and global warming (IPCC, 2022[1]). OECD estimates show that the potential consequences of inaction on climate for human well-being are dramatic: for example, if average global temperature continues to rise at current rates ("business-as-usual scenario"), melting polar ice caps will cause a rise in global sea levels, which, in turn, will produce major destructive effects in coastal cities by 2070 (OECD, 2012[2]). Furthermore, human activity is causing a wide range of environmental disruptions that include more frequent wild fires, biodiversity loss, water scarcity and declining quality, waste pollution, and deforestation, among others (Ruckelshaus et al., 2020[3]).

In the face of this environmental crisis, agency and resilience are fundamental to humankind's response (OECD, 2021[4]; Feder et al., 2019[5]; Mirzaei Rafe et al., 2019[6]). Renewable energy sources (Panwar, Kaushik and Kothari, 2011[7]), circular economies (Corona et al., 2019[8]), the creation, restoration and improved management of existing habitats to capture carbon and protect wildlife (Stafford et al., 2020[9]) as well as new ways of understanding the relationship between nature and human society (Fraser, Mabee and Slaymaker, 2003[10]) are examples of the ways scientists, activists and communities are reducing the negative impacts of human lifestyles on Earth.

Education also has a role to play. Scientific knowledge and skills on environmental issues drive the innovation climate mitigation and adaptation strategies so critically depend upon. Building a sustainable society and tackling the climate crisis also requires behavioural changes in all populations, including young people. This report examines 15-year-old students' readiness to address environmental challenges. Based on the PISA data, both from PISA 2018 and earlier assessments, it provides international comparative perspectives on students' environmental competencies and attitudes – in their capacity to reflect and act responsibly on environmental issues. This report particularly focuses on student agency, which is rooted in students' ability and willingness to positively influence their own lives and the world around them. The report also suggests potential roles educators and parents can play. The following three aspects will be covered: students' knowledge and skills on environmental issues (Chapter 2); students' attitudes regarding environmental issues (i.e. awareness, self-efficacy in environmental understanding and sense-of purpose) (Chapter 3), and students' involvement in actions regarding environmental issues (Chapter 4).

CONCEPTUAL FRAMEWORK

Young people have a crucial role in tackling environmental challenges. They will experience the consequences of climate and environmental change more directly during their lifetime than any previous generation in recent history (Thiery et al., 2021[11]). Are students prepared and ready to actively address environmental challenges? And, how can education prepare students with the knowledge, skills and the environmentally-related attitudes they need?

Figure 1.1 shows how student readiness for environmental challenges is examined in this report. The report has been designed with the hypothesis that students' preparedness for today's environmental challenges requires (i) scientific knowledge and skills, including proficiency in environmental science and sustainability; (ii) pro-environmental attitudes and values, including environmental awareness and sense-of-purpose, and self-efficacy in environmental understanding[2]; and (iii) taking part in environmentally responsible actions. Students with a science-based understanding of climate change and ways to solve and adapt to it, and the belief that it is important and possible for them to make a difference are likelier to respond actively and responsibly to environmental challenges.

The report also considers contexts that can influence student readiness for environmental challenges. These contexts include student characteristics such as socio-economic status (for a definition of socio-economic status in PISA, see Box 1.2), gender, growth mindset and fear of failure; parents' environmental attitudes and behaviours; and school characteristics, including the coverage of environmental issues in the curriculum and the degree of involvement in environmental actions among other students in the school.

Figure 1.1 **Conceptual and analytical framework**

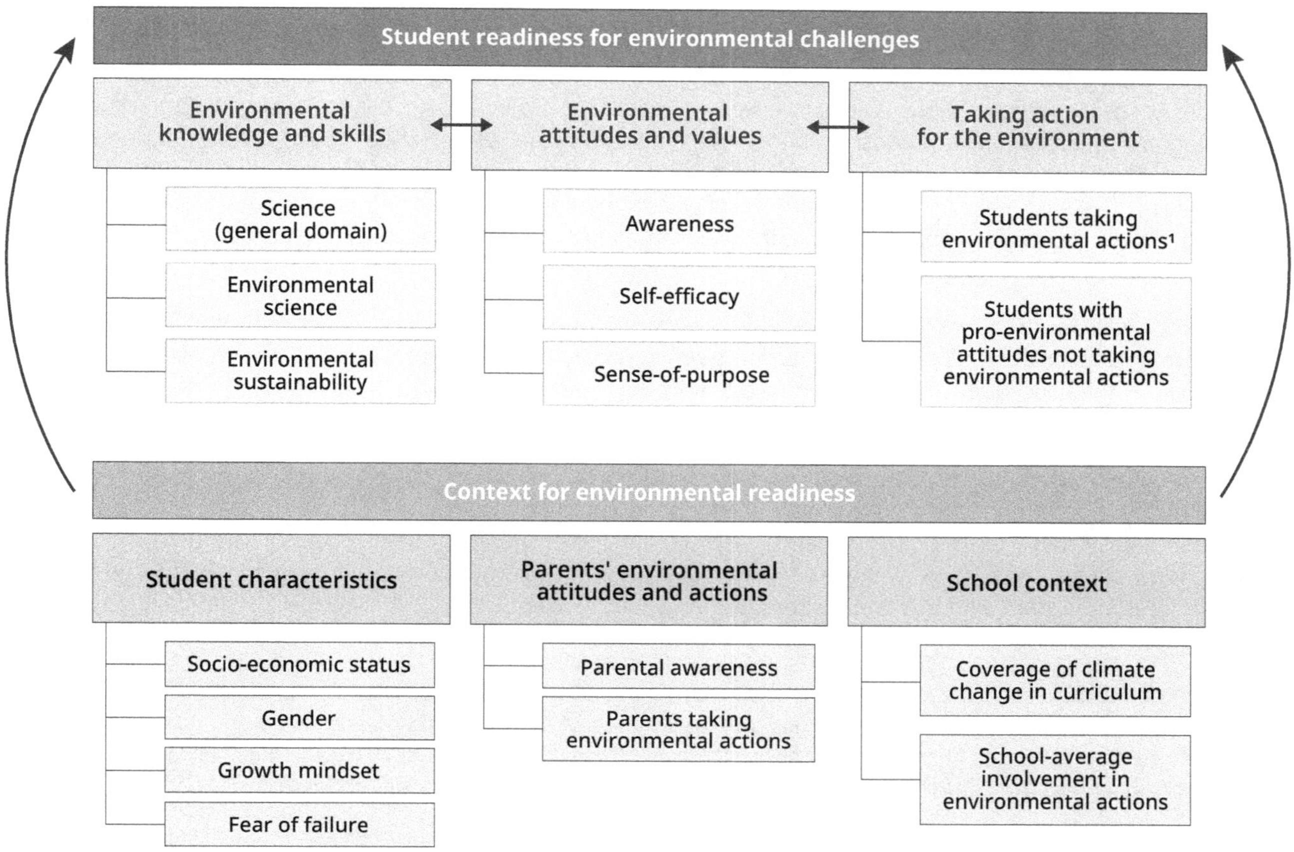

1. The environmental actions examined in this report are the following: 1) Reducing the energy used at home (e.g. by turning the heating down or turning the air conditioning down or by turning off the lights when leaving a room) to protect the environment; 2) Choosing certain products for ethical or environmental reasons, even if they are a bit more expensive; 3) Signing environmental or social petitions online; 4) Boycotting products or companies for political, ethical or environmental reasons; 5) Participating in activities in favour of environmental protection.

To measure environmentally- related concepts, this report uses two sources of PISA data: data collected through instruments (e.g. test items and contextual questionnaires) developed for the Science Framework since 2006, and data collected through instruments developed for the Global Competence framework in PISA 2018.

ENVIRONMENTAL ISSUES IN THE PISA SCIENCE ASSESSMENT FRAMEWORK

PISA has collected data on environmental issues since its beginning. The PISA science framework, upon which the PISA science assessment is based, has considered environmental science topics to be a part of scientific literacy since PISA 2000. In PISA 2000, biodiversity (species, gene pool, evolution) and ecosystems (food chains, sustainability) were defined as major scientific themes for the assessment of scientific literacy; in addition, the maintenance of and sustainable use of species, interdependence of physical/biological systems, pollution, production and loss of soil, and weather and climate were included as topics in the science assessment (OECD, 2000$_{[12]}$).

In PISA 2006, when science became the major domain of the PISA assessment for the first time, the PISA science framework defined the environment as one of the key contexts (i.e. life situations that involve science and technology) used to frame items of the science assessment. Examples of the environmental contexts used in PISA 2006 science assessment are the following: environmentally friendly behaviour; use and disposal of materials; disposal of waste; environmental impact; local weather; biodiversity; ecological sustainability; control of pollution; and the production and loss of soil. Climate change and species extinction are also contexts for the PISA 2006 science assessment (OECD, 2006$_{[13]}$).

Furthermore, in PISA 2006 the science framework defined that attitudes towards science played an important part of scientific literacy: "a person's scientific literacy includes certain attitudes, beliefs, motivational orientations, sense of self-efficacy, values, and ultimate actions" (OECD, 2006[13]). The group of attitudes towards science defined as "responsibility towards resources and environments" included three attitudes: show a sense of personal responsibility for maintaining a sustainable environment; demonstrate awareness of the environmental consequences of individual actions; and, demonstrate willingness to take action to maintain natural resources.

The report *Green at Fifteen* (OECD, 2009[14]), based on data from PISA 2006, analysed what students knew about environmental issues, what attitudes students held towards the environment, and where students gained environmentally-related knowledge from. The report showed that the great majority of students in most countries participating in PISA 2006 are proficient at some level of environmental science and geoscience, but proficiency is unevenly distributed across the population. Students with disadvantaged socio-economic backgrounds and girls, on average, showed significantly lower proficiency.

The *Green at Fifteen* report also showed that student awareness of environmental issues tends to go hand-in-hand with their performance in environmental science. Students who reported the greatest familiarity with complex environmental phenomena (i.e. the consequences of clearing forests for other land use; acid rain; the increase of greenhouse gases in the atmosphere; nuclear waste; and use of genetically modified organisms) tend also to have high levels of proficiency.

Furthermore, the report found that while students' environmental awareness is related to their socio-economic background, those with more disadvantaged socio-economic status are no less likely to report a sense of responsibility for environmental issues (i.e. students were asked "Do you see the environmental issues below as a serious concern for yourself and/or others?" with issues being the following: air pollution; energy shortages; extinction of plants and animals; clearing of forests for other land use; water shortages; and nuclear waste).

The PISA 2015 results showed that students' environmental awareness had increased since 2006 on average across OECD countries (Echazarra, 2018[15]). This was the second time science was the major domain in the PISA assessment. For example, on average across OECD countries, the percentage of students who stated they were informed about the increase of greenhouse gases in the atmosphere rose from 57% in 2006 to 64% in 2015, and a similar percentage-point increase was observed when students were asked about the use of genetically modified organisms.

However, during the same period, students did not become more optimistic about resolving these problems. In general, environmentally aware students are more pessimistic about the future of Earth. For instance, on average, 15-year-old students who claimed to be informed about the increase of greenhouse gases were 43% more likely to consider that this problem would get worse over the next 20 years than students who claimed to not be informed about this.

Fifteen-year-old students are, in general, more optimistic about environmental issues than their parents, according to the PISA 2015 results (Avvisati, 2019[16]). Beliefs are influenced by knowledge and life experiences. Parents may have more knowledge than students about environmental issues. It is also possible that parents may have tried to bring about environmental change but repeated actions had not led to any improvements , resulting in a feeling of helplessness. This suggests that it is important to make sure that realistic pessimism does not result in a sense of futility.

What can make students informed optimists? While PISA cannot prove cause and effect, two factors showed a strong association with both awareness about environmental problems and a belief that these problems would be ameliorated over the next 20 years: the number of science activities in which students participate and students' exposure to enquiry-based teaching (Echazarra, 2018[15]).

ENVIRONMENTAL ISSUES IN THE PISA 2018 GLOBAL COMPETENCE ASSESSMENT

PISA 2018 sheds light on an important new aspect for climate change action: student agency. Agency involves undertaking critical appraisal and evaluation of evidence regarding complex systemic issues; setting goals to bring about change; deciding how to take responsible action; and making decisions by examining evidence (OECD, 2019[17]; Environmental Science Expert Group, 2022[18]).The PISA 2018 assessment of Global Competence defined agency regarding global issues as "a worldview in which one sees oneself as connected to the world community and feels a sense of responsibility for its members" (OECD, 2020[19]). A person who exhibits agency in global issues has concerns for people in other parts of the world and a moral responsibility to try to improve others' living condition. And, because they care about future generations, they will act to preserve Earth's environmental integrity.

In the context of the Global Competence assessment, PISA 2018 created an index of student agency regarding global issues. It includes a measure of how much students care about the environment: i.e. students were asked the extent to which they agree with the statement "Looking after the environment is important to me" (item st219q03 in the student questionnaire).

Because item st219q03 is part of a larger set of items measuring student agency, by itself it captures only a partial dimension of what student agency means. For this reason, in this report, the construct measured by item st219q03 will be referred to as environmental sense-of-purpose. This reframing of the item's original construct is based on the concept of student agency developed by the OECD's Future of Education and Skills 2030 project (OECD, 2019[20]). It defines student agency as the capacity to set a goal, reflect and act responsibly to effect change, and underscores that student agency requires the ability to frame a guiding purpose and identify actions to achieve a goal. The development of a sense of purpose during adolescence is part of a person's search for meaning and their desire to make a difference in the world (Damon, Menon and Cotton Bronk, 2003[21]).

In this report, students for whom looking after the environment is important are students who can find a sense of identity, motivation and purpose in acting for the environment. These students are also conveying a personal commitment to environmental action – this is corroborated in the analyses included in this report, which show a strong correlation between students' environmental sense-of-purpose and involvement in environmental actions. From now on, in Chapters 3 and 4, where data on student attitudes towards the environment are examined, students with an environmental sense-of-purpose are those who reported that looking after the global environment is important to them.

Another reason why the PISA 2018 study on Global Competence is important for examining environmental agency is that it measures whether students took part in environmental actions. These include: saving energy at home; choosing "green" products; signing online environmental petitions; boycotting products for environmental reasons; and participating in activities in favour of environmental protection. In this report, these data will be analysed in Chapter 4. Research on social movements and environmental movements is used in the report to better frame and understand student participation in environmental actions (Klandermans, 2007[22]; Snow and Soule, 2010[23]).

Box 1.1. **The role of education for sustainable development and climate change in the United Nations' Sustainable Development Goals**

Sustainable development was originally defined as "development that meets the needs of the present without compromising the ability of future generations to meet their own needs" (WCED, 1987[24]). Since then, it has been subject to discussion and revisions (Shah, 2008[25]; Holden, Linnerud and Banister, 2014[26]). In the context of the UN's Sustainable Development Goals, there are two goals that address directly the role of education in sustainable development and climate change.

The first one is Goal 4, "Ensure inclusive and equitable quality education and promote lifelong learning opportunities for all", which includes the following target:

- **Target 4.7**: By 2030, ensure that all learners acquire the knowledge and skills needed to promote sustainable development, including, among others, through education for sustainable development and sustainable lifestyles, human rights, gender equality, promotion of a culture of peace and non-violence, global citizenship and appreciation of cultural diversity and of culture's contribution to sustainable development.

The second goal, Goal 13, "Take urgent action to combat climate change and its impacts", includes the following target:

- **Target 13.3**: Improve education, awareness-raising and human and institutional capacity on climate change mitigation, adaptation, impact reduction and early warning.

This target aims at expanding the extent to which global citizenship education (GCED) and education for sustainable development (ESD) are mainstreamed in national education policies; curricula; teacher education; and student assessment. As defined by the United Nations, GCED and ESD nurture respect for all, build a sense of belonging to a common humanity, foster responsibility for a shared planet, and help learners become responsible and active global citizens and proactive contributors to a more peaceful, tolerant, inclusive, secure and sustainable world. They aim to empower learners of all ages to face and resolve local and global challenges and to take informed decisions and actions for environmental integrity, economic viability and a just society for present and future generations, while respecting cultural diversity.

Source: https://unstats.un.org/sdgs

Box 1.2. Definition of socio-economic status in PISA

The PISA index of economic, social and cultural status (ESCS)

Socio-economic status is a broad concept that aims to reflect the financial, social, and cultural resources available to students and the social position of the student's family/household.

In PISA, a student's socio-economic status is estimated by the PISA index of economic, social and cultural status (ESCS), a composite measure that combines into a single score the financial, social and cultural resources available to students (see PISA 2018 Technical Report (OECD, 2020[27])). In practice, it is derived from several variables related to students' family background that are then grouped into three components: parents' education, parents' occupations, and an index summarising a number of home possessions that can be taken as proxies for material wealth or cultural capital, such as possession of a car, the existence of a quiet room to work, access to the Internet, the number of books and other educational resources available in the home.

Definition of socio-economically advantaged and disadvantaged students

In this report, socio-economically disadvantaged students are defined as those whose value on the PISA index of economic, social and cultural status (ESCS) is among the bottom 25% of students within their country or economy.

Similarly, socio-economically advantaged students as those whose ESCS is among the top 25% of students within their country or economy.

Source: OECD (2020), *PISA 2018 Technical Report*, https://www.oecd.org/pisa/data/pisa2018technicalreport/

Notes

1. https://treaties.un.org/doc/Publication/MTDSG/Volume%20II/Chapter%20XXVII/XXVII-7-d.en.pdf

2. Self-efficacy is the extent to which individuals believe in their own ability to engage in certain activities and perform specific tasks. PISA has traditionally asked students to judge their capabilities in specific content areas, such as mathematics or science. In 2018 PISA asked students about their ability to explain environmentally-related phenomena. In this report, students displaying self-efficacy in environmental understanding are students who reported that they could explain how carbon-dioxide emissions affect global climate change easily or with a bit of effort. See Box 3.1 in Chapter 3 for additional details.

References

Avvisati, F. (2019), "Is there a generational divide in environmental optimism?", *PISA in Focus*, No. 95, OECD Publishing, Paris, https://dx.doi.org/10.1787/04677bea-en. [16]

Corona, B. et al. (2019), "Towards sustainable development through the circular economy — A review and critical assessment on current circularity metrics", *Resources, Conservation and Recycling*, Vol. 151, p. 104498, https://doi.org/10.1016/j.resconrec.2019.104498. [8]

Damon, W., J. Menon and K. Cotton Bronk (2003), "The Development of Purpose During Adolescence", *Applied Developmental Science*, Vol. 7/3, pp. 119-128, https://doi.org/10.1207/s1532480xads0703_2. [21]

Echazarra, A. (2018), "Have 15-year-olds become "greener" over the years?", *PISA in Focus*, No. 87, OECD Publishing, Paris, https://dx.doi.org/10.1787/6534cd38-en. [15]

Environmental Science Expert Group (2022), *Agency in the Anthropocene. Supporting Document to PISA 2025 Science Framework.* [18]

Feder, A. et al. (2019), "The Biology of Human Resilience: Opportunities for Enhancing Resilience Across the Life Span", *Biological Psychiatry*, Vol. 86/6, pp. 443-453, https://doi.org/10.1016/j.biopsych.2019.07.012. [5]

Fraser, E., W. Mabee and O. Slaymaker (2003), "Mutual vulnerability, mutual dependence", *Global Environmental Change*, Vol. 13/2, pp. 137-144, https://doi.org/10.1016/S0959-3780(03)00022-0. [10]

Holden, E., K. Linnerud and D. Banister (2014), "Sustainable development: Our Common Future revisited", *Global Environmental Change*, Vol. 26, pp. 130-139, https://doi.org/10.1016/j.gloenvcha.2014.04.006. [26]

IPCC (2022), *Climate Change 2022: Impacts, Adaptation, and Vulnerability. Contribution of Working Group II to the Sixth Assessment Report of the Intergovernmental Panel on Climate Change.* [1]

Klandermans, B. (2007), "The Demand and Supply of Participation: Social-Psychological Correlates of Participation in Social Movements", in *The Blackwell Companion to Social Movements*, Blackwell Publishing Ltd, Oxford, UK, https://doi.org/10.1002/9780470999103.ch16. [22]

Mirzaei Rafe, M. et al. (2019), "The application of critical realism as a basis for agency in environmental education: The case of Roy Bhaskar", *Australian Journal of Environmental Education*, Vol. 35/3, pp. 230-238, https://doi.org/10.1017/aee.2019.21. [6]

OECD (2021), "Building resilience: New strategies for strengthening infrastructure resilience and maintenance", *OECD Public Governance Policy Papers*, No. 05, OECD Publishing, Paris, https://doi.org/10.1787/354aa2aa-en. [4]

OECD (2020), *PISA 2018 Results (Volume VI): Are Students Ready to Thrive in an Interconnected World?*, PISA, OECD Publishing, Paris, https://dx.doi.org/10.1787/d5f68679-en. [19]

OECD (2020), *PISA 2018 Technical Report*, https://www.oecd.org/pisa/data/pisa2018technicalreport/. [27]

OECD (2019), *OECD Future of Education and Skills. OECD Learning Compass 2030. A Series of Concept Notes.* [20]

OECD (2019), *Student Agency for 2030. Concept Note*, OECD Future of Education and Skills 2030, http://www.oecd.org/education/2030-project/teaching-and-learning/learning/student-agency/Student_Agency_for_2030_concept_note.pdf. [17]

OECD (2012), *OECD Environmental Outlook to 2050*, OECD Publishing, http://dx.doi.org/10.1787/9789264122246-en. [2]

OECD (2009), *Green at Fifteen?: How 15-Year-Olds Perform in Environmental Science and Geoscience in PISA 2006*, PISA, OECD Publishing, Paris, https://dx.doi.org/10.1787/9789264063600-en. [14]

OECD (2006), *Assessing Scientific, Reading and Mathematical Literacy: A Framework for PISA 2006*, PISA, OECD Publishing, Paris, https://doi.org/10.1787/9789264026407-en. [13]

OECD (2000), *Measuring Student Knowledge and Skills: The PISA 2000 Assessment of Reading, Mathematical and Scientific Literacy*, PISA, OECD Publishing, Paris, https://doi.org/10.1787/9789264181564-en. [12]

Panwar, N., S. Kaushik and S. Kothari (2011), "Role of renewable energy sources in environmental protection: A review", *Renewable and Sustainable Energy Reviews*, Vol. 15/3, pp. 1513-1524, https://doi.org/10.1016/j.rser.2010.11.037. [7]

Ruckelshaus, M. et al. (2020), "The IPBES Global Assessment: Pathways to Action", *Trends in Ecology and Evolution*, Vol. 35/5, pp. 407-414, https://doi.org/10.1016/j.tree.2020.01.009. [3]

Shah, M. (2008), "Sustainable Development", in *Encyclopedia of Ecology*, Elsevier, https://doi.org/10.1016/b978-008045405-4.00633-9. [25]

Snow, D. and S. Soule (2010), *A primer on social movements*, WW Norton. [23]

Stafford, R. et al. (2020), "Evaluating optimal solutions to environmental breakdown", *Environmental Science & Policy*, Vol. 112, pp. 340-347, https://doi.org/10.1016/j.envsci.2020.07.008. [9]

Thiery, W. et al. (2021), "Intergenerational inequities in exposure to climate extremes", *Science*, Vol. 374/6564, pp. 158-160, https://doi.org/10.1126/science.abi7339. [11]

WCED, S. (1987), *World commission on environment and development. Our common future.* [24]

2

Student knowledge of and skills in environmental issues

What the data tell us

- Student performance on environmental sustainability was measured in PISA 2018 with five test units. About 1 in 4 students responded correctly to items in the Palm Oil and Rising Sea Levels test units on average across countries/economies. About 4 in 10 responded correctly on average to questions in the three remaining test unites. Singapore performed the best in three out of the five environmental sustainability test units; Hong Kong (China) and Korea performed the best in one test unit. The Philippines showed the lowest levels of performance in four out of the five test units considered in this chapter, and Indonesia, Kazakhstan and Panama in one test unit.
- In 20 out of 26 countries/economies with available data, students had more difficulty identifying a short-term response to sea level rise caused by global warming than a long-term response. The share of students who correctly identified a long-term response was more than 15 percentage points greater than the share of students who correctly identified a short-term response in Brunei Darussalam, Chile, Hong Kong (China), Malta, Thailand and Singapore. In five countries/economies the difference was not statistically significant and in Serbia more students correctly identified a short-term response than a long-term response.
- Between PISA 2006 and PISA 2015, the percentage of students who answered correctly on average across 11 environmental science trend items decreased by 0.5 percentage point on average across OECD countries. Performance in environmental science improved the most in Portugal, Qatar and Romania, and declined the most in Hong Kong (China) and the Slovak Republic over this period.
- The socio-economic gap in environmental science in favour of advantaged students did not, on average, widen or narrow between 2006 and 2015. However, in Luxembourg and Finland the socio-economic gap across the 11 environmental science trend items widened whereas in Thailand and the United States it narrowed.
- Both the environmental sustainability performance measured in PISA 2018 and environmental science performance assessed between PISA 2006 and PISA 2015 are related to science performance. In Estonia, Italy, Poland, Portugal, Romania and Qatar, performance on both environmental and non-environmental science items improved between PISA 2006 and PISA 2015. In Australia, Belgium, the Czech Republic, Finland, Greece, the Netherlands, New Zealand and the Slovak Republic, performance on the environmental and non-environmental science items declined.

This chapter explores student proficiency in environmental science and sustainability as measured by PISA. In the first section, the chapter examines student performance in environmental sustainability items in PISA 2018. The second section looks at the evolution of student performance in environmental science between PISA 2006 and 2015.

The conceptual basis for the environmental sustainability items examined in the first section is the PISA 2018 Global Competence assessment, which measures students' competence in various global issues, including environmental sustainability (OECD, 2019[1]). Students' competence in environmental sustainability encompasses their knowledge of the demand for and use of natural resources; their understanding of the main forces that deplete the planet's natural environment; and their awareness of how improvements in the quality of life should be pursued without damaging the planet for future generations. The environmental sustainability domain is split into two subdomains: natural resources and environmental risks; and policies, practices and behaviours for environmental sustainability. The subdomain on natural resources and environmental risks looks at students' competence in the main environmental challenges facing the planet and ecological interdependence in society. The subdomain on policies, practices and behaviours for environmental sustainability covers students' attitudes towards management practices when facing these environmental challenges.

With regards to the environmental science items (examined in the second section of this chapter), their conceptual basis is the PISA science framework that was developed in PISA 2006 (OECD, 2006[2]), used for the PISA science assessment in 2006, 2009 and 2012, and updated in PISA 2015 (OECD, 2017[3])[1]. Furthermore, the PISA report *Green at Fifteen?* (OECD, 2009[4]) built on the PISA science framework to develop a definition of student proficiency in environmental science that includes the following competences:

- *Scientific knowledge and use of that knowledge to identify questions, acquire new knowledge, explain biological and geoscience phenomena related to the environment, and draw evidence-based conclusions about the environment.* For example, when individuals read about global warming, can they separate environmental scientific-related from non-scientific aspects of the text, and can they apply knowledge and justify personal decisions?
- *Understanding of the characteristic features of environmental science as a form of human knowledge and inquiry.* For example, do individuals know the difference between evidence-based explanations and personal opinions about the environment?
- *Awareness of how environmental science can shape our use of Earth's resources, policies about environmental sustainability, and future responsibility towards environmental quality.* For example, are individuals aware of environmental changes and the effects of those changes on economic and social stability?
- *Willingness to engage with environmental science and ideas of environmental science as a reflective citizen and consumer of geological and biological resources.* This addresses the value students place on environmental science both in terms of topics, scientific approach to understanding the earth's environment and solving environmental issues.

Figure 2.1 **How student knowledge of and skills in environmental issues are measured in this report**

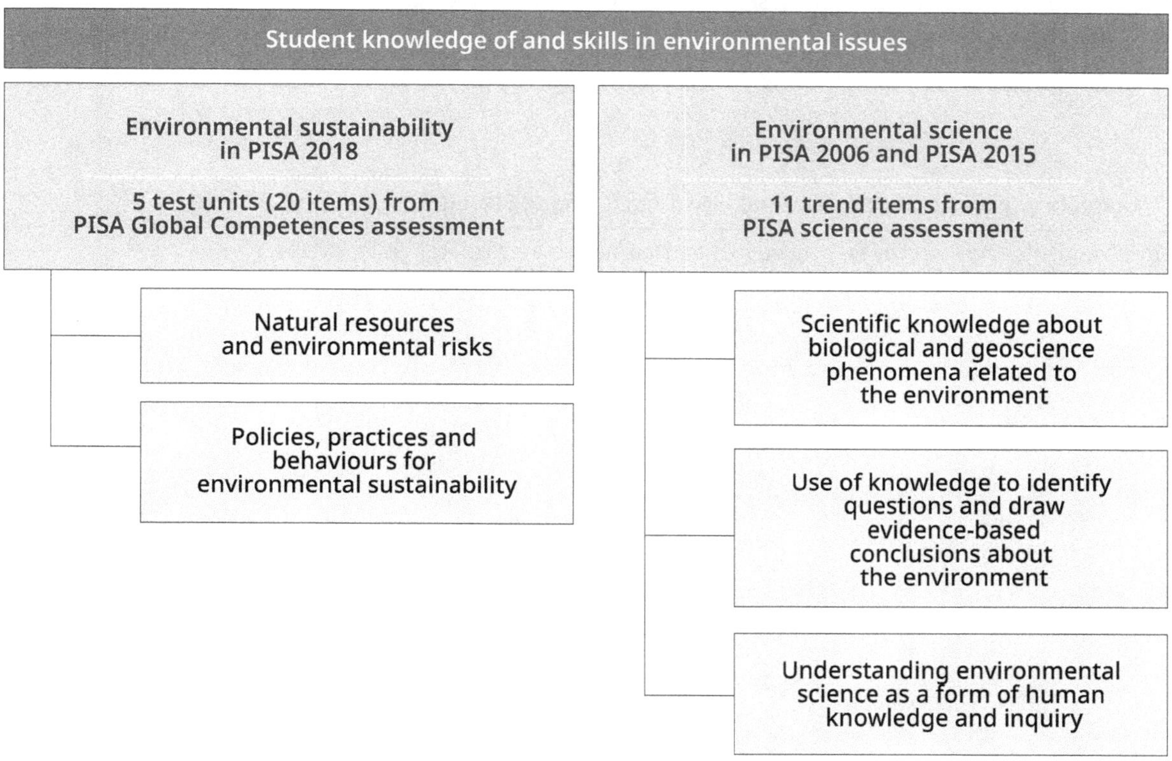

ENVIRONMENTAL SUSTAINABILITY: STUDENT PERFORMANCE IN 2018

PISA 2018 Global Competence assessment included 20 items about "Natural resources and environmental risks" and "Policies, practices and behaviours for environmental sustainability" (hereafter, environmental sustainability items). These items were organised in five test units: "Rising Sea Levels", "Ethical Clothing", "Oil Exploration", "Palm Oil" and "Blue River Dam". The "Rising Sea Levels" unit was publicly released. It is examined in some detail in the next section.

Analysis included in this section cover the 26 countries and economies that administered the Global Competence cognitive test[2]. Because data is only available for 12[3] out of the 38 OECD countries, the average across all 26 countries and economies with available data will be used instead of the OECD average throughout this section.

Student performance in environmental sustainability: Rising sea levels test unit

The "Rising Sea Levels" unit focuses on the effects of rising temperatures on sea levels. The introduction sets the stage for the items within the unit, which explores the effects of rising sea levels on individuals who live in areas of low elevations, such as islands and coastal areas.

This unit has five items. The final item asks students to consider a set of proposals and identify which ones represent a short-term response to a more immediate need and which ones represent a long-term response to more systemic causes of rising sea levels. To respond to this item, students need to apply their knowledge of environmental issues (i.e. possible solutions to sea-level rise), and consider and distinguish between ex-post remedies to various problems caused by rising sea levels and interventions to tackle the source of the problem.

For example, a proposal of «Building sea defences such as dams and sea walls» is a short-term response as it resolves the issue of flooding but not that of rising sea levels itself. In contrast, proposals of "Reducing greenhouse gases that are warming the planet" is a long-term response as it responds to the cause of rising sea levels.

Responses to these items provide some information about students' ability to distinguish between short- and long-term responses to climate change; yet, interpreting these results requires considering rising sea levels as one particular aspect of the problem: additional measures would be required to fully capture students' ability to distinguish between short- and long-term responses to climate change.

Over 70% of students responded that "Reducing greenhouse gases that are warming the planet» is a long-term response on average across the 26 countries/economies that implemented this item. This shows that it is common knowledge to 15-year-old students that reducing greenhouse gases is a long-term solution to global warming, which causes rising sea levels. However, it varies across countries/economies. In Canada, Hong Kong (China), Korea, Singapore and Chinese Taipei, around 85% or more of students responded correctly, identifying that this is a long-term response (Figure 2.2). In contrast, from 41 to 49% of students responded it is a short-term response in Brunei Darussalam, Indonesia, Kazakhstan and Panama (Table B.2.30).

Figure 2.2 **Example of environmental sustainability item: Rising sea levels**

Percentage of students who correctly responded to the following sub-items of Rising sea levels

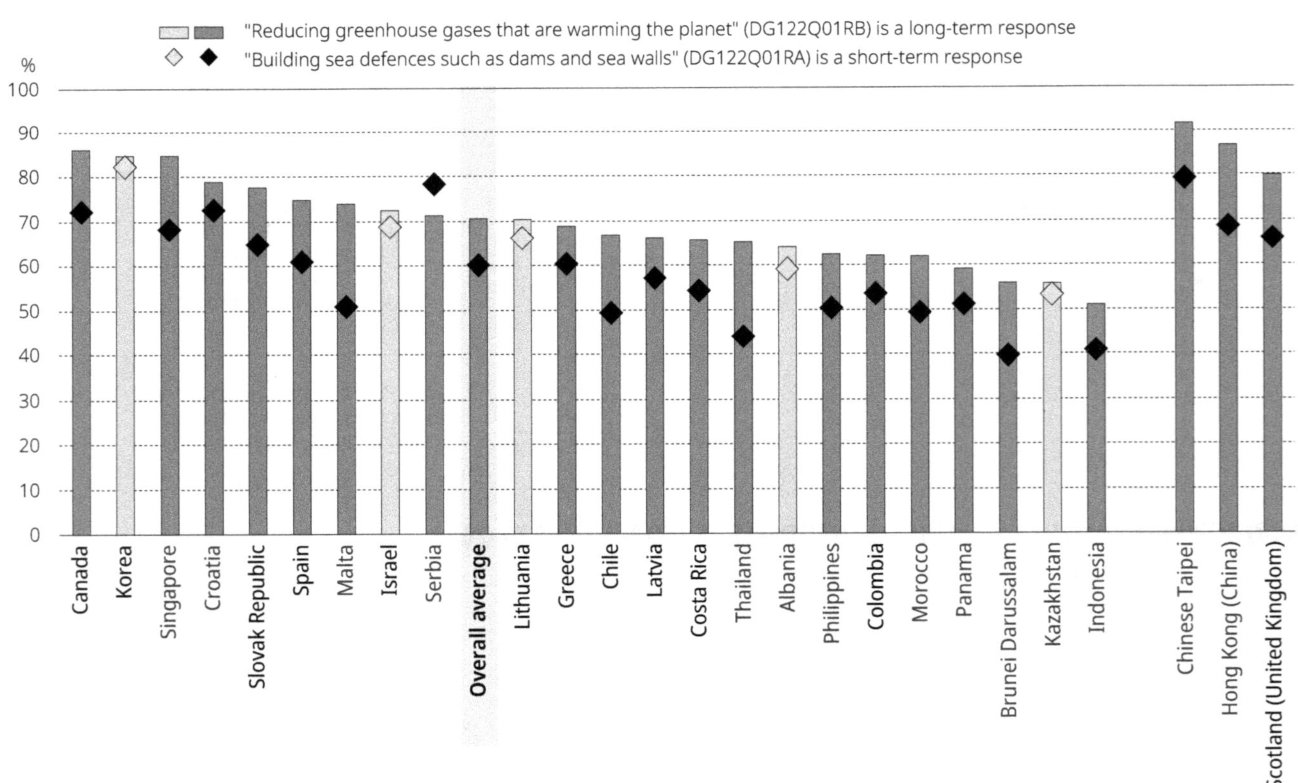

Note: Statistically significant differences between the percentage of students who correctly responded to item DG122Q01RA and those to item DG122Q01RB are shown in a darker tone.

Countries and economies are ranked in descending order of the percentage of students who correctly identified the sub-item DG122Q01RB as a long-term response.

Source: OECD, PISA 2018 Database, Table B.2.31.

StatLink https://stat.link/2f1tev

Socio-economically disadvantaged students were more likely to respond to this question incorrectly than advantaged students in all countries/economies with available data except Albania, Greece and Hong Kong (China). Overall, 79% of advantaged students responded correctly on average across countries/economies compared to 64% of disadvantaged students (Table B.2.33).

Fifteen-year-old students seem to have more difficulty identifying short-term proposals that do not provide a long-term solution to the issue of rising sea levels. On average across 26 countries/with available data, 60% of students responded that "Building sea defences such as dams and sea walls" is a short-term response. This means that 40% of students did not recognise that this is not a long-term solution to the problem of rising sea levels, which is global warming. In Korea, Serbia and Chinese Taipei, over three in four students recognised the short-term nature of this proposal while less than 45% of students did in Brunei Darussalam, Indonesia, and Thailand (Table B.2.30).

Socio-economically disadvantaged students were more likely to respond to this question incorrectly than advantaged students in half of countries/economies with available data. While 66% of advantaged students responded correctly on average across countries/economies, 56% of disadvantaged students responded correctly (Table B.2.33).

In 20 out of 26 countries/economies with available data, students had more difficulty identifying a short-term a response to the rise in sea levels caused by global warming than a long-term a response. The share of students who correctly identified a proposal as a long-term response was more than 15 percentage points higher than the share of students who correctly identified a proposal as a short-term response in Brunei Darussalam, Chile, Hong Kong (China), Malta, Thailand and Singapore (Figure 2.2). In five countries/economies the difference was not statistically significant and in Serbia more students correctly identified a short-term response than a long-term response.

Performance in environmental sustainability units

At the test unit level, the average percentage correct across items in a test unit was about a quarter in test units Palm Oil (28%) and Rising Sea Levels (28%); about 40% in the Oil Exploration and Ethical Clothing test units; and about half (44%) in test unit Blue River Dam, on average across countries and economies (Tables B.2.10-14).

Figure 2.3 shows variation in the average percentage correct in test units related to environmental sustainability across countries/economies. Singapore had the highest average percentage correct in three out of the five test units considered in this chapter: 65% in the Ethical Clothing unit, 48% in the Rising Sea Levels unit and 58% in the Blue River Dam unit. Hong Kong (China) had the highest average percentage correct in the Oil Exploration unit (56%). Korea had the highest average percentage correct in the Palm Oil unit (46%). By contrast, the Philippines showed the lowest levels of performance in four out of the five environmental sustainability test units, and Indonesia, Kazakhstan and Panama showed the lowest levels of performance in the Palm Oil unit (less than 20% correct) (Tables B.2.10-14).

Performance in environmental sustainability units, by gender and socio-economic status

In terms of socio-economic status, performance in environmental sustainability was better among socio-economically advantaged than disadvantaged students in each of the 20 environmental sustainability items on average across countries and economies. The difference between the average percentage of advantaged and disadvantaged students who correctly responded to an item ranged from three percentage points (item 5 of the Blue River Dam test unit) to 23 percentage points (item 2 of the Ethical Clothing test unit) (Tables B.2.20-24).

In most of the 20 environmental sustainability items, there is a socio-economic gap in performance in most or all countries and economies. However, in 5 out of the 20 environmental sustainability items[4], the percentage of advantaged and disadvantaged students who correctly responded to an item was no different in most countries.

In terms of gender, performance in environmental sustainability was better among girls than boys in 14 out of the 20 environmental sustainability items on average across countries and economies[5]. In these items, the average difference between the percentage of girls and the percentage of boys who correctly responded to the item ranged from two percentage points (item 2 of test unit Rising Sea Levels) to eight percentage points (item 2 of test unit Oil Exploration) (Tables B.2.20-24). However, the cross-country averages do not reflect the fact that in the majority of countries/economies performance in environmental sustainability items was not different between girls and boys. In 13 out the 14 items where girls outperformed boys on average[6] as well as in the other six items where no gender differences were found on average across countries and economies, performance in environmental sustainability items was not different between girls and boys in most countries and economies (Tables B.2.20-24).

Figure 2.3 **Average percentage of students who correctly answered environmental sustainability items, across test units**

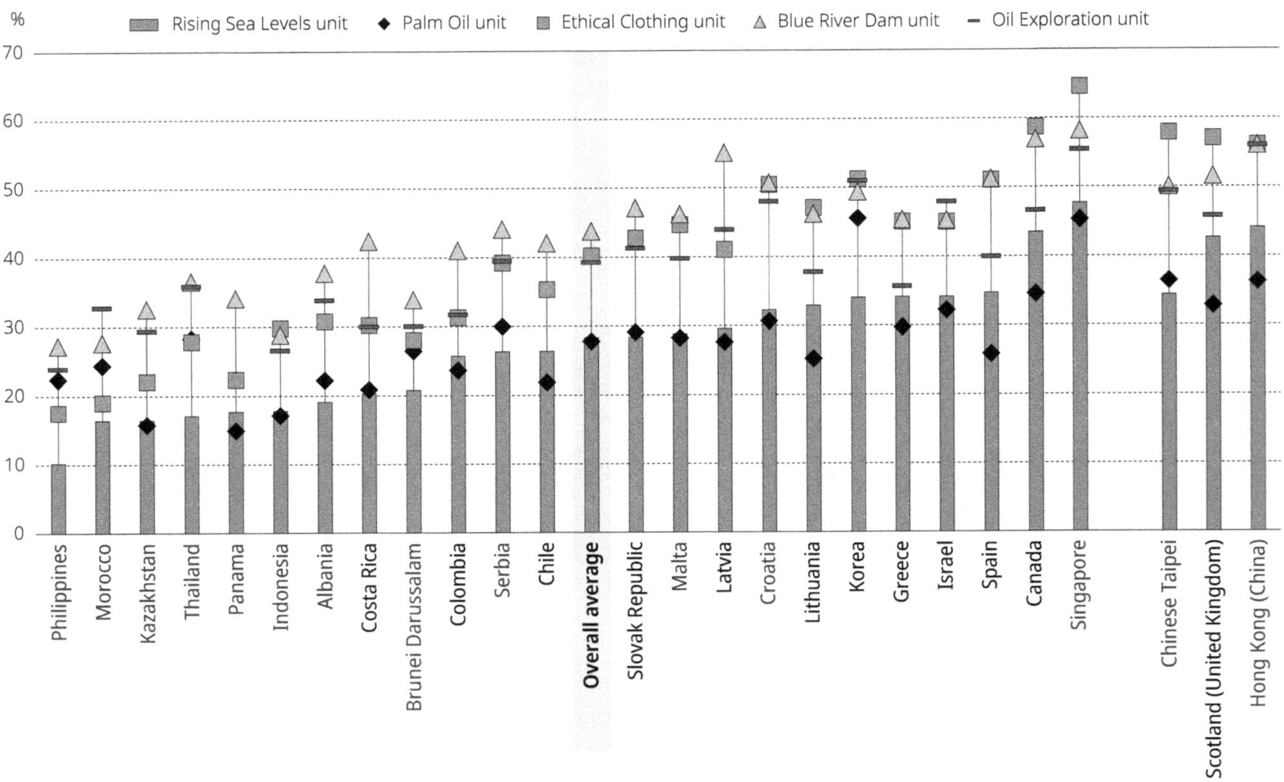

Countries and economies are ranked in ascending order of the percentage of students who correctly responded the items in the Rising Sea Levels unit.
Source: OECD, PISA 2018 Database, Tables B.2.10 to B.2.14.
StatLink https://stat.link/npiv7h

Performance in environmental sustainability units, and general science performance

Students who performed well on environmental sustainability items also scored higher in the PISA 2018 science test. In each environmental sustainability item measured in PISA 2018 the mean score in science was higher for students who got full credit for the items as opposed to those who answered the items incorrectly on average across countries and economies (Tables B.2.15-19).

Furthermore, in 11 out of the 20 environmental sustainability items examined in this report, the mean score in science was higher for students who got full credit in every country/economy with available data. In the remaining 9 environmental sustainability items, the mean score in science was higher for students who got full credit in the majority of countries and economies but not in all of them. The number of countries/economies where the difference in the mean score in science between students who got full credit and no credit in environmental sustainability items was not statistically significant ranged from one country (Indonesia in item 1 of test unit Rising Sea Levels; Latvia in item 3 of the Ethical Clothing unit; Costa Rica in item 1 of the Oil Exploration unit) to 14 countries/economies (in item 5 of test unit Blue River Dam) (Tables B.2.15-19).

The association between performance in environmental sustainability and performance in the general science test is also observed at the system level. Figure 2.4 depicts the mean score in science for each country and economy in the x-axis and percentage of items with correct response in each test unit on the y-axis. Results show that countries/economies where the mean score in science is higher tend to perform better on the environmental sustainability test units.

ENVIRONMENTAL SCIENCE: STUDENT PERFORMANCE BETWEEN 2006 AND 2015

This section provides an overview of trends in student performance in environmental science, focusing on 11 science items in the PISA 2006 and 2015 when science was the main focus of the assessment. These science trend items are part of the following test units of the PISA science assessment: Algae, Different Climates, Earth Temperature, Extinction of the Dinosaurs, Penguin Island, Solar Power Generation, Water and Wild Oat Grass. See Annex A4 for information on PISA data available for analysis of trends in environmental science performance.

Figure 2.4 **Mean score in science and average percentage correct across items in environmental sustainability test units**

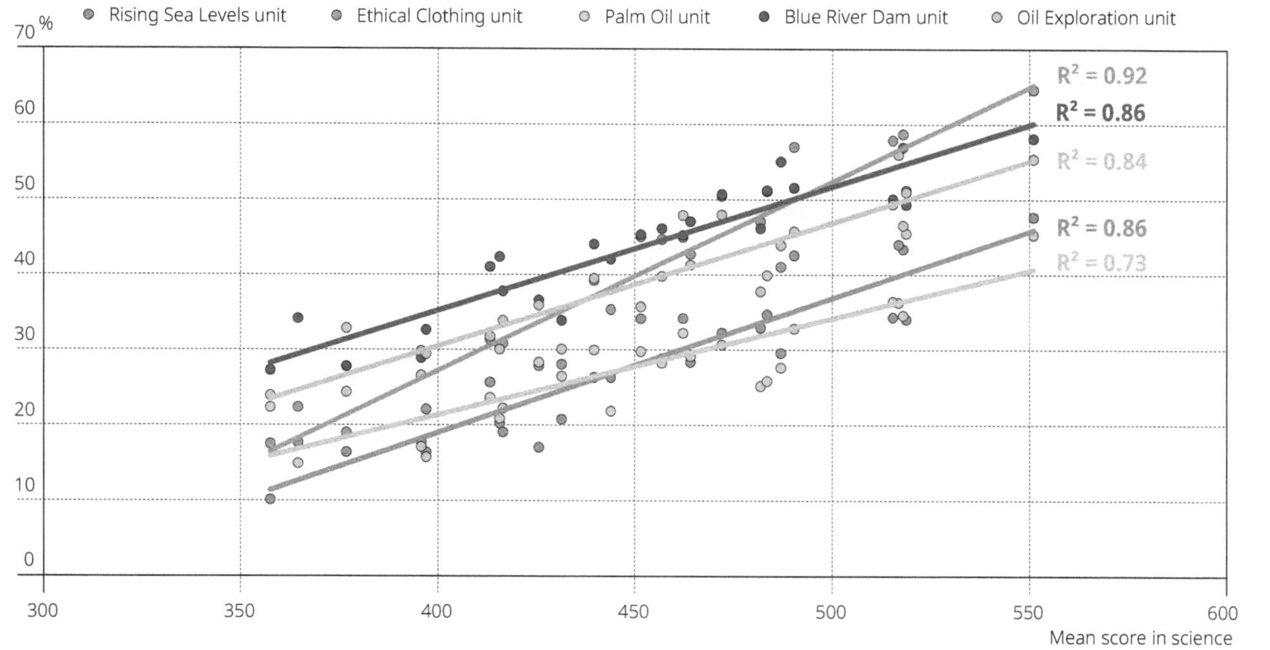

Note: Each dot represents a country/economy.
Source: OECD, PISA 2018 Database, Tables B.2.10 to B.2.14.
StatLink https://stat.link/9413wt

Student performance in environmental science items

On average across 11 environmental science trend items, the percentage of students who answered items correctly decreased by 0.5 percentage points between PISA 2006 and PISA 2015 on average across OECD countries with comparable data[7] (Figure 2.5). A similar moderate decline is also observed for non-environmental science items. Across the 47 non-environmental science items which allow for comparing performance across paper- and computer-based administration, the proportion of correct responses declined by 0.9 percentage points on average (Table B.2.3). Furthermore, mean score in the science assessment (which includes environmental and non-environmental trend items) declined by 6 score points during the period, on average across OECD countries (Figure 2.5). In other words, the slight decline in average performance between 2006 and 2015 is not specific to environmentally related science items but also observed across non-environmental science items and science performance in general.

Performance in environmental science improved the most between PISA 2006 and PISA 2015 in Qatar, Romania and Portugal (Figure 2.5). In Qatar, student performance improved in all 11 environmental science items considered in this analysis. In Romania performance improved in seven environmental science items and declined in one only. Both of these countries were among the lowest-performing countries in these items in PISA 2006; thus, their improvement in performance brings them closer to, yet does not reach, the average of performance observed in OECD countries in PISA 2015 (Tables B.2.1, B.2.2 and B.2.3). In addition, both countries improved their mean science performance between 2006 and 2015(Figure 2.5). In the case of Qatar, mean science performance increased by 68 points, the largest increase for this period among all countries and economies with available data. In Romania, mean science performance improved by 16 points between 2006 and 2015.

In Portugal, the percentage of students who answered correctly increased in 6 items and declined in none (Table B.2.3). Portugal was the OECD country where mean science performance increased the most between PISA 2006 and PISA 2015 (27 score-point increase) (Figure 2.5).

Countries/economies where performance in environmental science declined markedly include the Slovak Republic, where the percentage of students who correctly answered environmental science items declined in five out of the 11 items and increased in only one; and Hong Kong (China), where performance declined in 6 items and improved in none. The Slovak Republic performed around the OECD average in PISA 2006 (average percentage correct across environmental science items was 42% in the Slovak Republic), and the negative trend brought it below the OECD average in PISA 2015.

Hong Kong (China) was the country/economy with the highest average percentage correct across environmental science items in PISA 2006 (together with Finland). Despite the decline during this period, it remained above the average performance observed across OECD countries in PISA 2015 (Tables B.2.1, B.2.2 and B.2.3).

In the Slovak Republic a decline of 4 percentage points is observed in the average percentage of students who answered non-environmental science items correctly (average across 47 non-environmental science items). In Hong Kong (China), no change is observed in the average percentage of students who answered non-environmental science items correctly between PISA 2006 and 2015 (Table B.2.3).

Figure 2.5 **Change between PISA 2006 and PISA 2015 in student performance in environmental science items and in science**

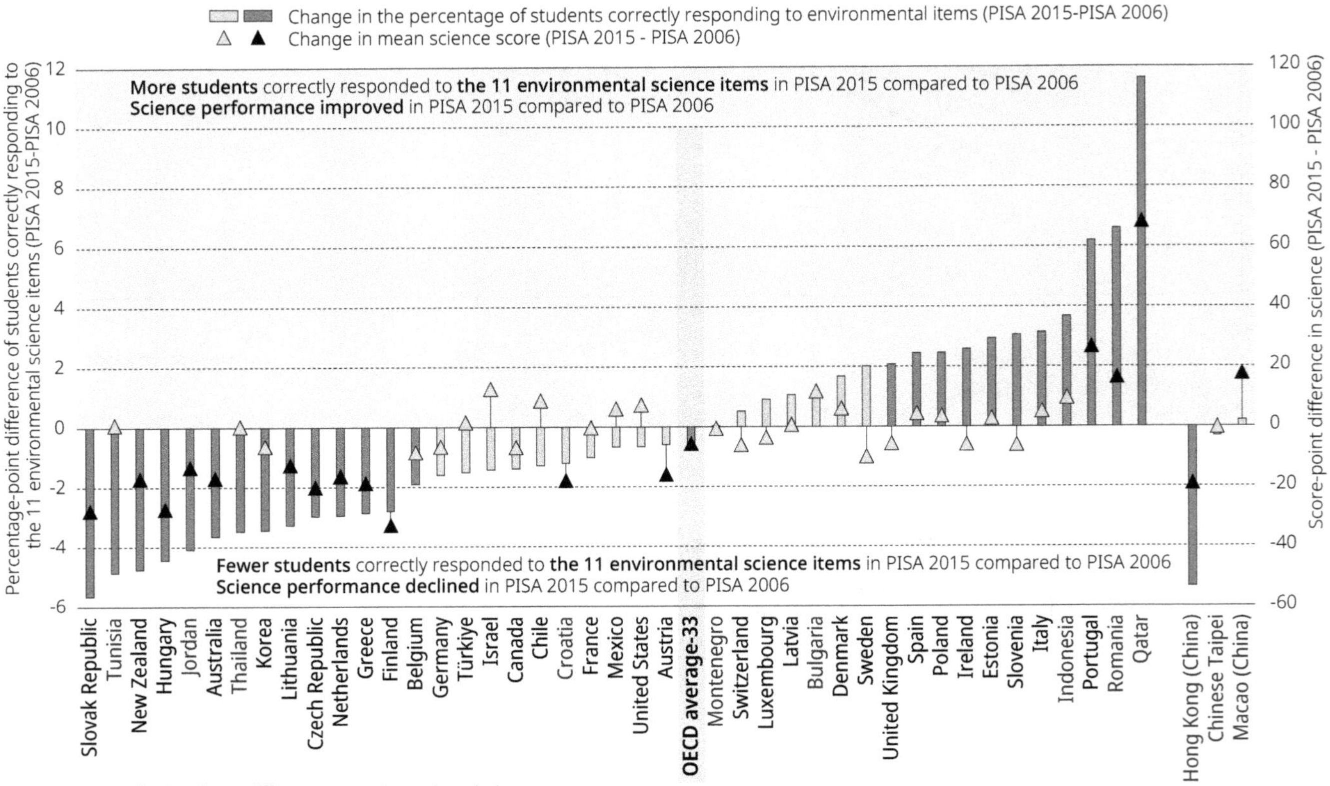

Note: Statistically significant differences are shown in a darker tone.

Countries and economies are ranked in ascending order of the percentage-point difference of students correctly responding to science items between PISA 2006 and PISA 2015.

Source: OECD, PISA 2006 and PISA 2015 Databases, Table B.2.3.

StatLink https://stat.link/i7k03u

Student performance in environmental science items and student socio-economic background

As in other cognitive domains measured in PISA, student performance in environmental science is, on average, higher among socio-economically advantaged students than disadvantaged ones. On average across OECD countries in PISA 2006, the percentage of students who answered environmental science items correctly was higher among advantaged than disadvantaged students on average across all environmental science items and for each environmental science item considered in this analysis (Table B.2.4).

Yet, the performance difference in a single point of time does not necessarily remain the same over time. Were changes in environmental science performance between PISA 2006 and PISA 2015 different for advantaged and disadvantaged students? And did the socio-economic gap in environmental performance widen or narrow?

Socio-economic gap in environmental science performance stayed constant over time between 2006 and 2015. On average across OECD countries, performance (i.e. average percentage correct across all environmental science items) declined by 0.7 percentage points among disadvantaged students (a significant decline) and by 0.3 percentage points among advantaged students (a non-significant decline); the difference between the two trends is, however, not significant, meaning that it is not possible to conclude that disadvantaged students experienced a steeper decline (Figure 2.6 and Table B.2.6).

Figure 2.6 **Change between PISA 2006 and PISA 2015 in the percentage of students who correctly answered the 11 environmental science items, by student socio-economic background**

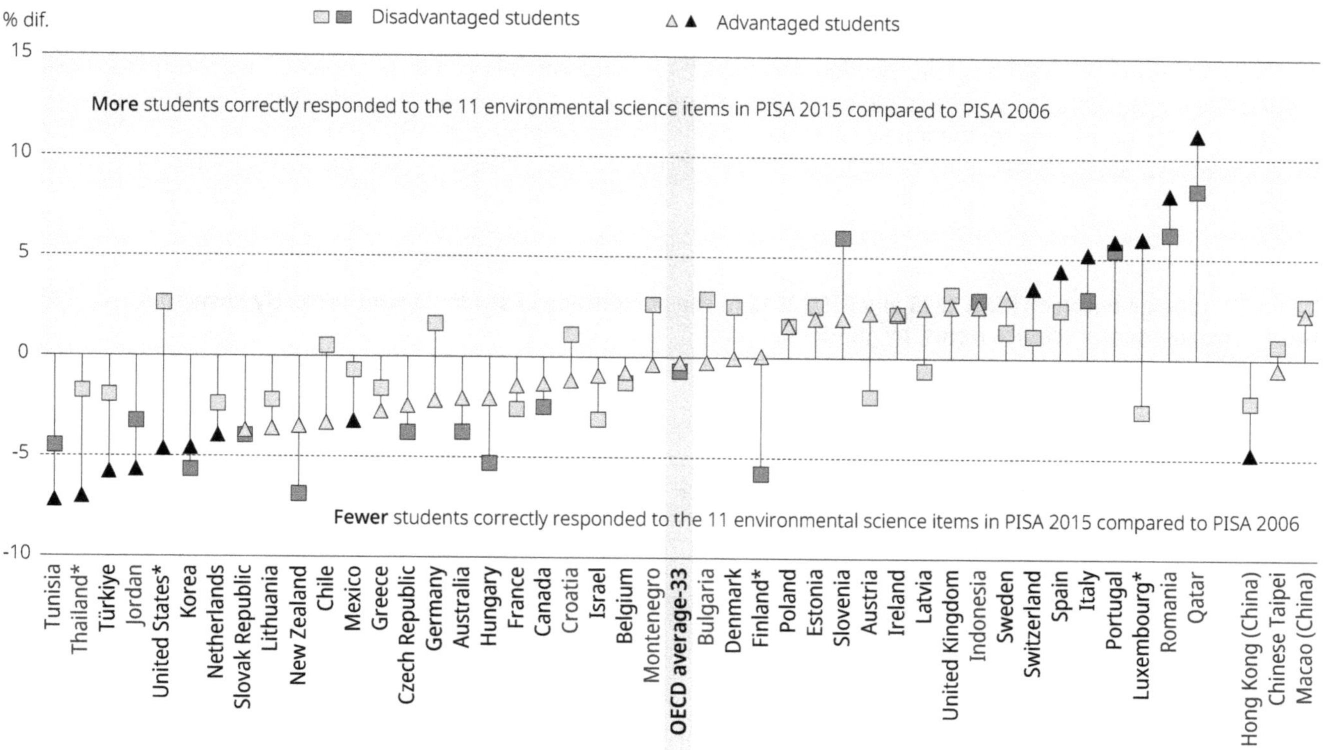

Notes: Statistically significant differences between PISA 2006 and PISA 2015 are shown in a darker tone.
Statistically significant difference between socio-economic advantaged and disadvantaged students (between PISA 2006 and PISA 2015) is shown with an asterisk next to the country/economy name.
Countries and economies are ranked in ascending order of the percentage-point difference of advantaged students responding correctly to science items between PISA 2006 and PISA 2015.
Source: OECD, PISA 2006 and PISA 2015 Databases, Table B.2.6.
StatLink https://stat.link/sp9ltw

In Thailand and the United States, advantaged students experienced a steeper decline in their performance than disadvantaged students; as a result, the socio-economic gap in environmental science performance shrank between PISA 2006 and 2015 (Figure 2.6). In Thailand, performance declined by 7 percentage points among advantaged students and did not change for disadvantaged students; in the United States performance declined by 5 percentage points among advantaged students and did not change for disadvantaged students (Table B.2.6).

By contrast, the socio-economic gap in environmental science performance grew in Luxembourg and Finland between PISA 2006 and 2015 (Figure 2.6). In Luxembourg, performance improved by 6 percentage points among advantaged students and did not change for disadvantaged students; in Finland, performance declined by 6 percentage points among disadvantaged students and did not change for advantaged students (Table B.2.6).

Student performance in environmental science items and gender

Student performance in environmental science is, on average, slightly higher among boys than girls. On average across OECD countries in PISA 2006, the percentage of students who answered environmental science items correctly (i.e. average across all 11 items) was 45% among boys and 43% among girls (a statistically significant difference). In 25 countries and economies, however, the performance in environmental science was no different between boys and girls (Table B.2.7). In PISA 2015, the percentage of students who answered environmental science items correctly was 44% among boys and 42% among girls (Table B.2.8). Performance declined by nearly 1 percentage point in both groups and, as a result, the slight gender difference in environmental science performance stayed the same over time between 2006 and 2015 (Figure 2.7 and Table B.2.9).

In five countries (Finland, Indonesia, the Slovak Republic, Sweden, and the United Kingdom) the gender gap in environmental science performance changed over time. In Finland, performance declined by 5 percentage points among boys and did not change for girls. In the Slovak Republic, performance declined by 7 percentage points among boys and by 4 percentage points among girls. In Finland, the gender gap in environmental science performance was not statistically significant in 2006 but it became significant in favour of girls in PISA 2015. In the Slovak Republic, boys performed better than girls in 2006 but the difference became null in PISA 2015 (Figure 2.7 and Tables B.2.7-9).

As shown in Figure 2.7, in Indonesia, Sweden and the United Kingdom, performance improved among girls (between around 4 and 5 percentage points) and did not change among boys. In Sweden and the United Kingdom, this trend meant that the gender gap in environmental science performance in favour of boys in PISA 2006 became null in PISA 2015. In Indonesia, where boys and girls performed similarly in PISA 2006, girls performed better than boys in PISA 2015 (Tables B.2.7-9).

Figure 2.7 **Change between PISA 2006 and PISA 2015 in the percentage of students who correctly answered the 11 environmental science items, by gender**

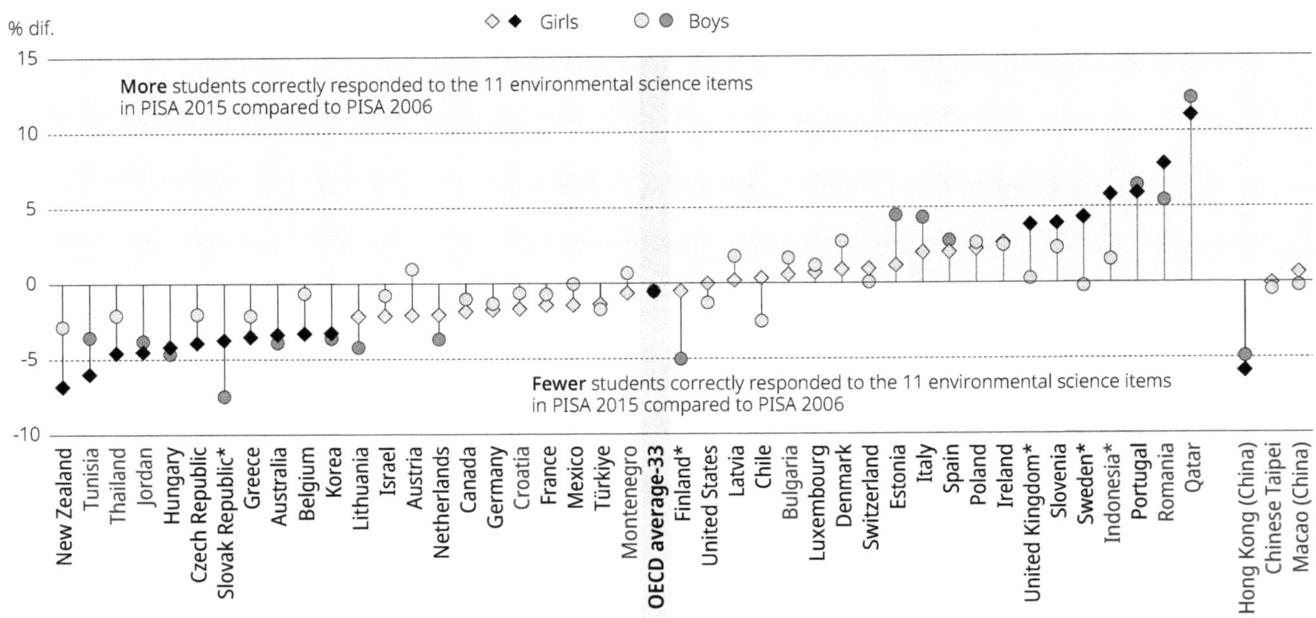

Notes: Statistically significant differences between PISA 2006 and PISA 2015 are shown in a darker tone.

Statistically significant difference between girls and boys (between PISA 2006 and PISA 2015) is shown with an asterisk next to the country/economy name.

Countries and economies are ranked in ascending order of the percentage-point difference of girls responding correctly to science items between PISA 2006 and PISA 2015.

Source: OECD, PISA 2006 and PISA 2015 Databases, Table B.2.9.

StatLink https://stat.link/mwq2at

Student performance in environmental science items and general science performance

Performance in environmental science is closely related to science performance in general. Across countries and economies and considering only those items administered in both PISA 2006 and 2015 which can be compared across paper- and computer-based administration, the proportion of correct responses on the 11 environmental science items is very strongly related to the proportion of correct responses on the 47 non-environmental science items (Pearson's correlation is 0.97 in 2006 across 48 countries/economies, and 0.96 in 2015 across 41 countries/economies).

In general, trends in performance on environmental science items are matched by trends in the same direction across non-environmental science items. Figure 2.8 contrasts the trends across the two sets of items in 38 countries/economies and they are similar in most cases. A more positive trend on environmental science items is observed in seven countries and economies: in Spain, Ireland, Slovenia and the United Kingdom, performance on environmental science items improved while performance on the non-environmental items remained stable; in Canada, Croatia and Germany, performance on environmental science items remained stable while performance on the non-environmental items declined. In contrast, a more negative trend in environmental science items is observed in six countries/economies: in Hong Kong (China), Jordan, Thailand, and Lithuania, performance on environmental science items declined while performance on the non-environmental items remained stable; in Latvia and Macao (China), performance on environmental science items remained stable while performance on non-environmental items improved.

Figure 2.8 **Change between PISA 2006 and PISA 2015 in the percentage of students answering correctly environmental and non-environmental science items**

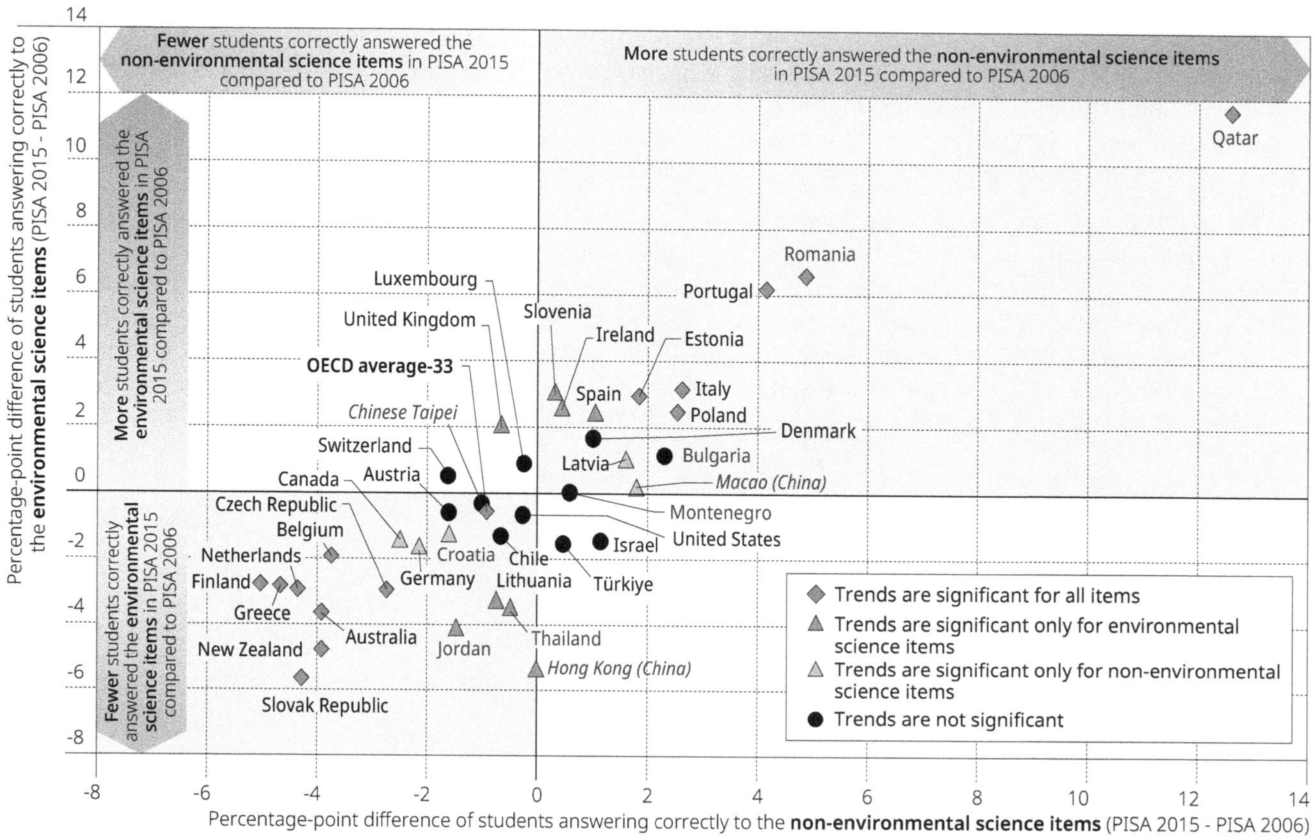

Note: Only countries and economies that have comparable data between 2006 and 2015 are shown in this figure.
Source: OECD, PISA 2006 and PISA 2015 Databases, Table B.2.3.
StatLink https://stat.link/smnec9

POLICY IMPLICATIONS FOR THE CHAPTER

This chapter shows that student knowledge of and skills in environmental issues varies markedly across countries and economies. Whereas in some countries/economies half or more of students were able to respond correctly to a variety of questions on environmental sustainability, in others only a minority of students were able to do so. Furthermore, analysis of student performance in environmental science items shows that it has not improved over time between 2006 and 2015. Students need to be better prepared on environmental issues, especially in countries where student performance tends to be lower.

One area educators could focus on is students' understanding of different responses to climate change. This chapter shows that many students could not adequately distinguish between short-term and long-term responses to the rise in sea levels caused by climate change, for example. While it is common knowledge to 15-year-old students that reducing greenhouse gases is a long-term solution to global warming, students misidentifying building sea defences as a long-term solution reveals a need for more complex and nuanced differentiation between combatting climate change and adaptation to its effects.

Regarding socio-economic and gender disparities, the socio-economic gap in environmental science performance is pervasive across countries and economies, and persistent over time. In terms of gender, environmental science performance is, on average, slightly higher among boys than girls but in many countries/economies boys and girls perform at similar levels. To help weaker groups gain better environmental science understanding, special attention needs to be paid to disadvantaged students in countries/economies with a widening socio-economic gap such as Finland and Luxembourg; girls in countries/economies that show a significant gender gap in favour of boys such as Chile, Denmark, the Slovak Republic and the United Kingdom, and boys in countries such as Jordan and Qatar whose gap is in favour of girls.

In general, students who perform well in science also do so on environment-related items. Trends in performance on environmental science at the education-system level are matched by trends in the same direction across non-environmental science items. Thus, providing high quality science education might strengthen students' ability to understand the science behind environmental issues. However, in some countries/economies, general science and environmental science performance show different patterns. Further research is needed to better understand why such different patterns are observed in order to effectively prepare students to tackle climate change and environmental issues.

The results presented in this chapter are part of an on-going effort by the OECD to provide high-quality information about student knowledge and skills in environmental science. PISA has collected data on student performance in environmental science since 2000. Building on what has been learned from analyses of past PISA data, PISA continues its efforts to collect relevant data that will contribute to students' preparedness for environmental challenges. PISA 2025 will feature an updated Science Framework, making student performance on environmental issues and environmental agency a central focus. In addition, further test items will be publicly released after 2025 to concretely describe what PISA is measuring and what students know and are able to do about climate change and the environment.

Notes

1. A new update of the science framework for PISA 2025 is currently under development.

2. Countries and economies that administered the Global Competence cognitive test are the following: Albania, Brunei Darussalam, Canada, Chile, Colombia, Costa Rica, Croatia, Greece, Hong Kong (China), Indonesia, Israel*, Kazakhstan, Korea, Latvia, Lithuania, Malta, Morocco, Panama, Philippines, Scotland (United Kingdom), Serbia, Singapore, the Slovak Republic, Spain, Chinese Taipei and Thailand. *The statistical data for Israel are supplied by and under the responsibility of the relevant Israeli authorities. The use of such data by the OECD is without prejudice to the status of the Golan Heights, East Jerusalem and Israeli settlements in the West Bank under the terms of international law.

3. Scotland (United Kingdom) is included in the count of 12.

4. These 4 items are the following: item 5 in the Rising Sea Levels unit; item 3 in the Ethical Clothing unit; items 4 and 5 in the Palm Oil unit; and item 5 in the Blue River Dam unit.

5. These 14 items are the following: items 1, 2, 3 and 4 in the Rising Sea Levels unit; all items in the Ethical Clothing unit; item 5 in the Palm Oil unit; items 1, 3 and 4 in the Blue River Dam unit; and items 1 and 2 of the Oil Exploration unit.

6. In item 4 of the Rising Sea Level unit, the difference in performance was greater among girls than among boys in 15 out of the 26 countries and economies with available data.

7. From the 38 member OECD countries, only 33 have comparable data between PISA 2006 and PISA 2015 cycles.

References

OECD (2019), "PISA 2018 Global Competence Framework", in *PISA 2018 Assessment and Analytical Framework,* OECD Publishing, Paris, https://doi.org/10.1787/043fc3b0-en. [1]

OECD (2017), *PISA 2015 Assessment and Analytical Framework: Science, Reading, Mathematic, Financial Literacy and Collaborative Problem Solving*, PISA, OECD Publishing, Paris, https://doi.org/10.1787/9789264281820-en. [3]

OECD (2009), *Green at Fifteen?: How 15-Year-Olds Perform in Environmental Science and Geoscience in PISA 2006,* PISA, OECD Publishing, Paris, https://doi.org/10.1787/9789264063600-en. [4]

OECD (2006), *Assessing Scientific, Reading and Mathematical Literacy: A Framework for PISA 2006,* PISA, OECD Publishing, Paris, https://doi.org/10.1787/9789264026407-en. [2]

PISA

3

Students' attitudes and beliefs regarding environmental issues

What the data tell us

- Almost four in five students displayed environmental sense-of-purpose (i.e. looking after the global environment is important to them); some three out of four students displayed environmental awareness (i.e. they know something about or are very familiar with climate change); and three out of five students displayed self-efficacy in environmental understanding (i.e. they could explain how carbon-dioxide emissions affect global climate change) on average across countries/economies.
- About half of students are "environmentally enthusiastic", i.e. they displayed the three pro-environmental attitudes considered in this report on average across countries/economies. By contrast, about 6% of students are "environmentally indifferent", i.e. do not display any of the pro-environmental attitudes considered in this report.
- Students who have one, two or three environmental attitudes performed better in science than students who do not display any environmental attitude. Environmentally enthusiastic students scored about 80 points higher than environmentally indifferent students, on average, after accounting for student socio-economic status.
- There are multiple factors that can shape students' environmental attitudes. In terms of background, the likelihood of being an environmentally enthusiastic student is, on average, greater among students who come from socio-economically advantaged families and among girls. In terms of factors that are amenable by education policy and practice, the likelihood of being an environmentally enthusiastic students is, on average, greater among students who are proficient in science; have parents who are environmentally aware and take part in environmental actions; believe in a growth mindset and attend schools where climate change is included in the formal curriculum.

To what extent do 15-year-old students embrace and display the kinds of environmental attitudes required to face environmental challenges? This chapter aims to answer this question by looking at three environmental attitudes and beliefs measured in PISA 2018: sense-of-purpose regarding environmental issues, awareness of environmental issues and self-efficacy or confidence in their knowledge of environmental issues (see Box 3.1). The chapter looks at the number of environmental attitudes displayed by students and different possible combinations among them. In addition, the chapter examines how student environmental attitudes/beliefs (henceforth expressed as "environmental attitudes") vary by: student performance in science, gender and socio-economic status; student growth mindset; schools covering climate change in their formal curriculum; and parents' environmental attitudes and actions.

Box 3.1. **How students' pro-environmental attitudes are measured in PISA**

Environmental sense-of-purpose

PISA 2018 asked students the extent to which they agreed with the following statement: "Looking after the global environment is important to me". Four response categories were offered to them. Students who selected "strongly agree" or "agree" are considered to have environmental sense-of-purpose. Students who selected "strongly disagree" or "disagree" are considered as not displaying environmental sense-of-purpose. In other words, in this report, students with an environmental sense-of-purpose are students who reported that looking after the global environment is important to them.

Environmental awareness

PISA 2018 asked students how informed they were about climate change and global warming and offered four response categories. Students who selected the categories "I am familiar with this and I would be able to explain this well" or "I know something about this and could explain the general issue" are considered as displaying environmental awareness. Students who selected "I have never heard of this" or "I have heard about this but I would not be able to explain what it is really about" are considered as not displaying environmental awareness. In other words, in this report, environmentally aware students are students who reported that they know something about or are very familiar with climate change and global warming.

Self-efficacy in environmental understanding

PISA 2018 asked students how easy they thought it would be for them to perform the following task: "Explain how carbon-dioxide emissions affect global climate change". Four response categories were offered to them. Students who selected "I could do this easily" or "I could do this with a bit of effort" were considered to have self-efficacy in their knowledge and understanding of environmental issues. Students who selected "I would struggle to do this on my own" or "I could not do this" were considered as not displaying self-efficacy in environmental understanding. In other words, in this report, students displaying self-efficacy in environmental understanding are students who reported that they could explain how carbon-dioxide emissions affect global climate change easily or with a bit of effort.

Data limitations and interpretation

Each of the three pro-environmental attitudes considered in this report is measured using a single questionnaire item. This means they are proxy measures that capture part of each construct but do not cover every aspect of it. For example, environmental awareness and self-efficacy use questions asking about climate change, but more robust measures might want to include topics such as bio-diversity loss, pollution, invasive species, genetic modification, etc. The same is true for sense-of-purpose, which could ask about care for the local environment, not just the global environment as it currently stands. PISA will improve its measurement of pro-environmental attitudes in the context of the new PISA 2025 Science Framework, which will include "scientific identity" as a new dimension of the assessment (OECD, 2020[1]).

In addition, environmental attitudes are not observed but are based on students' self-reports. Care must be taken when comparing these self-reported attitude results as they may be influenced by cultural norms. Also notice that in the text of the report students are sometimes described as "displaying" or "having" environmental attitudes. This is done for economy of language, with the understanding that these attitudes are self-reported and thus it is more precise to say that students reported having environmental attitudes.

Data availability

Data on students' environmental sense-of-purpose is available for 27 OECD countries and 35 partner countries and economies (i.e. a total of 62 countries and economies). Data on students' environmental awareness is available for 30 OECD countries and 36 partner countries and economies (i.e. a total of 66 countries and economies). Data on students' self-efficacy in environmental understanding is available for 28 OECD countries and 36 partner countries and economies (i.e. a total of 64 countries and economies).

Because data is not available for 11 (in the case of environmental sense-of-purpose), eight (in the case of environmental awareness) or 10 (in the case of self-efficacy in environmental understanding) out of the 38 OECD countries that took part in PISA 2018, the OECD average is not a good measure of central trends in PISA-participating countries. The average across all countries and economies with available data (i.e. "overall average") will be used instead throughout this chapter.

Data on parents' environmental attitudes and behaviours is available for 15 countries and economies that took part in the optional PISA 2018 Parent Questionnaire.

ENVIRONMENTAL ATTITUDES ACROSS PISA-PARTICIPATING COUNTRIES

An environmental sense-of-purpose is the extent to which a young person feels meaningfully connected to and cares about the environment – how important the environment is "to me". The development of a sense-of-purpose during adolescence is part of a person's search for meaning and their desire to make a difference in the world (Damon, Menon and Cotton Bronk, 2003[2]). Environmental sense-of-purpose can motivate a young person to learn about the environment and how it is changing. It can also motivate a young person to take action to protect the environment. See Box 3.1 about the measurement of environmental sense-of-purpose in PISA.

Of the three attitudes measured in this report, which include environmental awareness and self-efficacy in environmental understanding, environmental sense-of-purpose shows the highest incidence among 15-year-old students[1]. Almost four out of five students reported having environmental sense-of-purpose (Figure 3.1) on average across countries and economies with available data in PISA 2018. In a few countries, nine out of ten students reported that looking after the global environment is important to them. In no country or economy was the share of students who displayed environmental sense-of-purpose lower than two-thirds of the student population.

Figure 3.1 **Environmental sense-of-purpose**

Percentage of students who reported that looking after the global environment is important to them

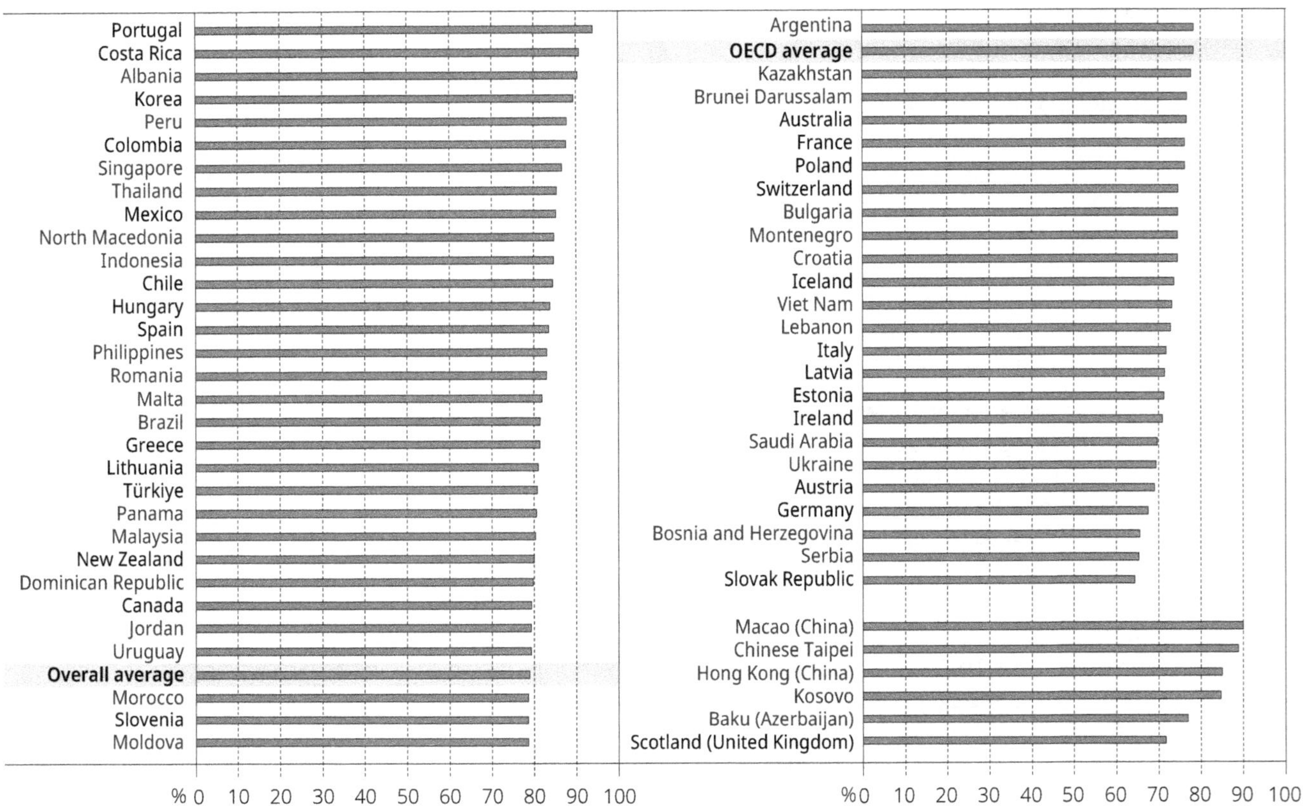

Countries and economies are ranked in descending order of the percentage of students.

Source: OECD, PISA 2018 Database, Table B.3.5.

StatLink https://stat.link/rwnyez

Whereas sense-of-purpose has to do with what is important "to me" – values and goals – environmental awareness and self-efficacy are about students' feelings about their knowledge of and skills regarding environmental issues. See Box 3.1 about the measurement of environmental awareness and self-efficacy in PISA.

On average across countries and economies with available data in PISA 2018, some three out of four students reported having environmental awareness (Figure 3.2). In some countries, more than 80% of students reported that they know something or are very familiar with climate change and global warming. In most countries and economies the share of environmentally aware students was no lower than 50%, and in no country or economy was it lower than 40%.

Self-efficacy is the extent to which individuals believe in their own ability to engage in certain activities and perform specific tasks, especially when facing adverse circumstances (Bandura, 1978[3]). PISA has traditionally asked students to judge their capabilities in specific content areas, such as mathematics or science. In 2018 PISA asked students about their ability to explain environmentally-related phenomena.

On average across countries and economies, some six out of ten students reported they were confident they understood climate change. In a few countries, seven or eight out of ten students reported that they could explain how carbon-dioxide emissions affect global climate change easily or with a bit of effort (Figure 3.3). In most countries and economies, the share of students who displayed this self-efficacy in environmental understanding was no lower than 40%, and in no country or economy was it lower than 30%.

Figure 3.2 **Environmental awareness**

Percentage of students who reported knowing about or being very familiar with climate change and global warming

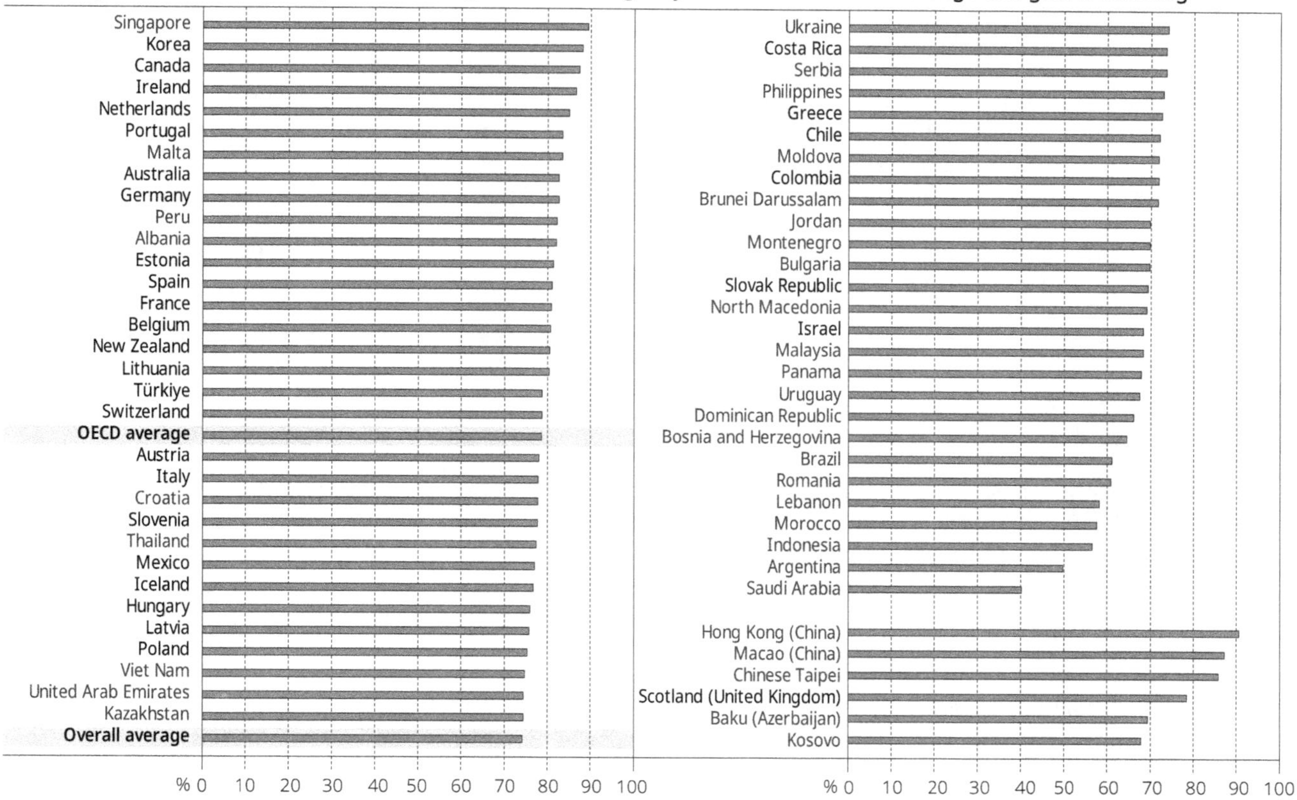

Countries and economies are ranked in descending order of the percentage of students.

Source: OECD, PISA 2018 Database, Table B.3.1.

StatLink https://stat.link/s4nqub

Figure 3.3 **Self-efficacy in environmental understanding**

Percentage of students who reported they could explain how carbon-dioxide emissions affect global climate change easily or with a bit of effort

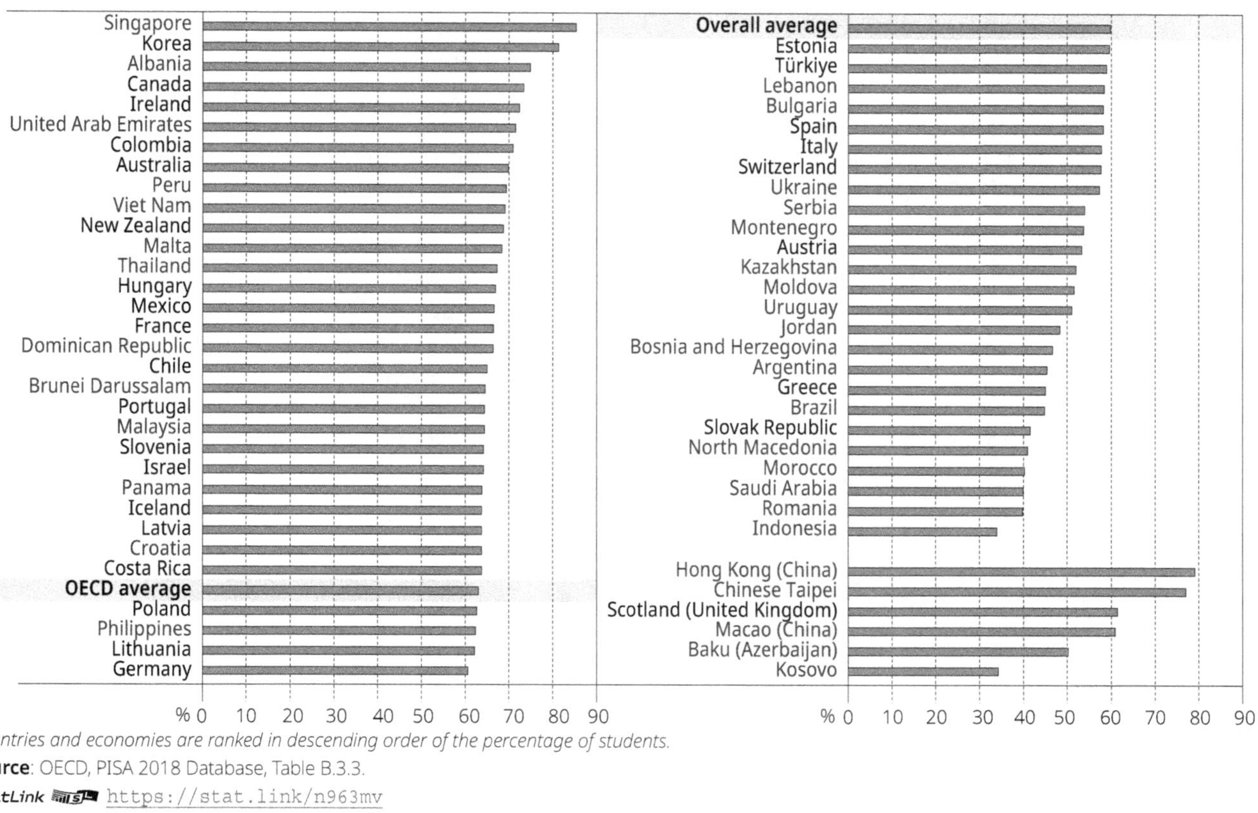

Countries and economies are ranked in descending order of the percentage of students.

Source: OECD, PISA 2018 Database, Table B.3.3.

StatLink https://stat.link/n963mv

OVERLAP OF ENVIRONMENTAL ATTITUDES

By design in this report, a student can have as many as three environmental attitudes and as few as none. Students who display three environmental attitudes (i.e. environmental awareness, self-efficacy in environmental understanding and environmental sense-of-purpose) are referred to here as "environmentally enthusiastic" students because they display all the environmental attitudes that would be expected of a student who is ready to act responsibly for the environment. In this definition, environmental enthusiasm refers to caring for the environment (sense-of-purpose) and students' sense not only of an awareness of environmental problems such as climate change but a scientific understanding of climate change that is proficient enough that they can explain it to others (self-efficacy).

Some 45% of students are environmentally enthusiastic (Figure 3.4) on average across countries and economies. In 19 out of 62 countries and economies, half or more of students are environmentally enthusiastic.

In other words, the average student population is split in two in terms of how they feel about the environment. Half of students are aware, confident about their knowledge of and care about environmental issues. The other half varies in all these measures. This includes students who are "environmentally indifferent" (see below) and those who have one or two environmental attitudes.

Students who do not display any of the environmental attitudes considered in this report are referred here as "environmentally indifferent" students. These students are unfamiliar with climate change, unable to explain its causes and reported that looking after the environment is not important to them. It would be alarming if this group was large but, on average across countries and economies, only about 6% of students are environmentally indifferent (Figure 3.4). In 21 countries and economies the share of environmentally indifferent students is 5% or lower, and in a large majority of countries and economies it is lower than 10%.

Some students display two environmental attitudes. On average across countries and economies, 17% of students have environmental awareness and sense-of-purpose but not self-efficacy in environmental understanding; 8% have environmental awareness and self-efficacy but no sense-of-purpose; and 6% display self-efficacy in environmental understanding and sense-of-purpose but no awareness (Figure 3.4). In sum, 31% of students display two out of the three environmental attitudes examined in this report.

Some students display only one environmental attitude. On average across countries and economies, 12% of students have environmental sense-of-purpose but no self-efficacy or awareness; 5% display environmental awareness but no self-efficacy or sense-of-purpose; and 2% believe they understand climate change but have no environmental awareness or sense-of-purpose (Figure 3.4). In sum, 18% of students display only one out of the three environmental attitudes examined in this report.

At the system level, the share of students displaying environmental awareness is strongly correlated with the share of students who have self-efficacy in environmental understanding (Figure 3.5). The system-level correlation between environmental sense-of-purpose and awareness is positive but weaker than the correlation between environmental awareness and self-efficacy in environmental understanding[2]. Similarly, the system-level correlation between environmental sense-of-purpose and self-efficacy in environmental understanding is positive but weaker[3].

Environmental awareness and self-efficacy in environmental understanding are more strongly correlated to each other than to sense-of-purpose because awareness and self-efficacy have to do with students' sense of their knowledge of environmental issues whereas sense-of-purpose has to do with their values, personal goals and what is important "to me". While this qualitative difference is clear, it does not mean environmental sense-of-purpose is opposed to or incompatible with environmental awareness and self-efficacy. On the contrary, awareness, self-efficacy and sense-of-purpose very often overlap (as shown in Figure 3.4). In addition, as seen in the next section, students who have a combination of these attitudes tend to have stronger knowledge and skills in science, as measured by the PISA science assessment.

Figure 3.4 **Overlap of environmental attitudes**

Percentage of students who display different combinations of environmental attitudes

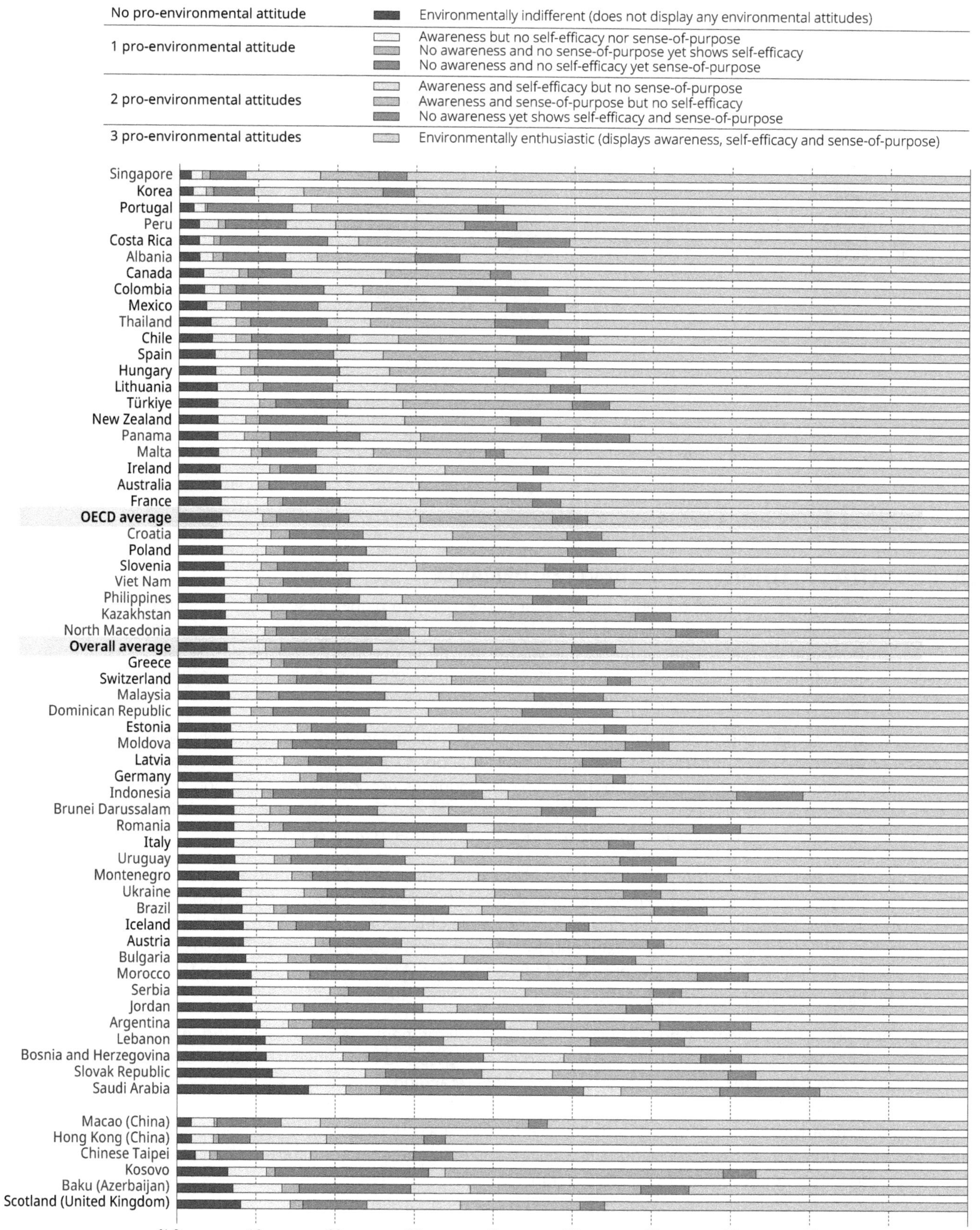

Countries and economies are ranked in ascending order of students who display environmentally indifferent attitudes.

Source: OECD, PISA 2018 Database, Table B.3.12.

StatLink https://stat.link/s4jimk

Figure 3.5 **Environmental awareness and self-efficacy in environmental understanding**

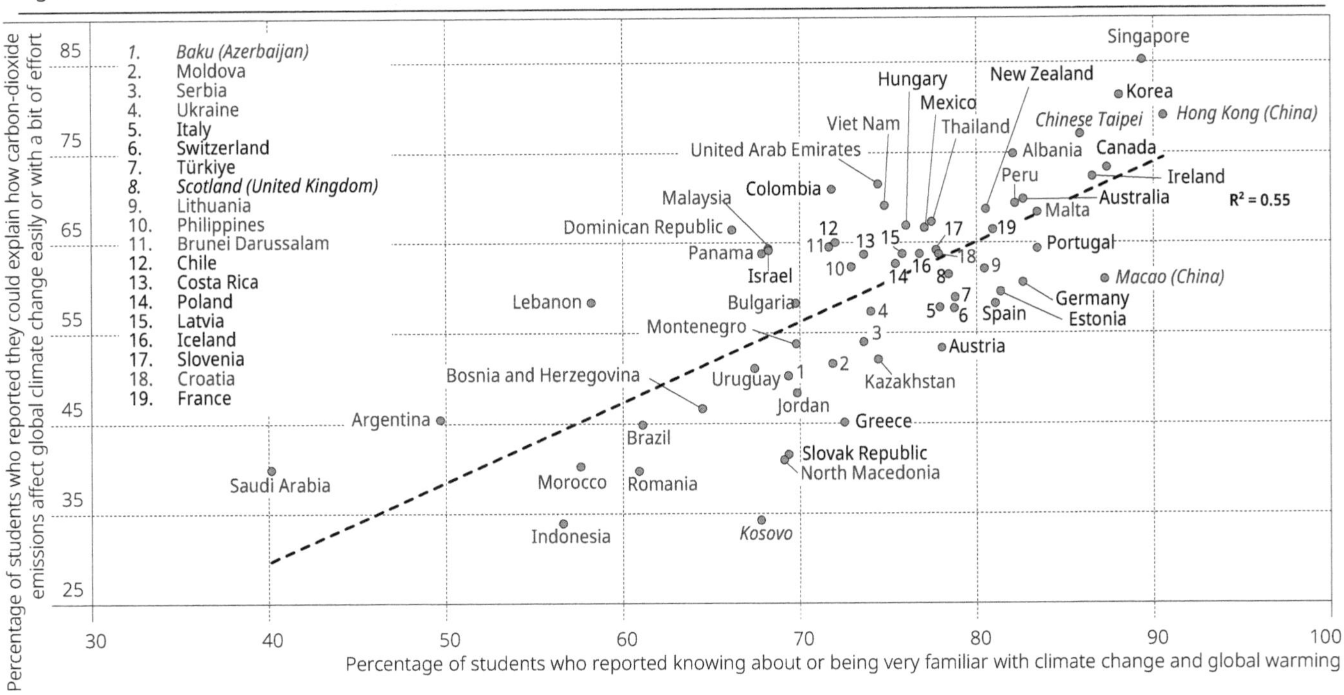

Source: OECD, PISA 2018 Database, Tables B.3.1 and B.3.3.

StatLink https://stat.link/mgsqle

ENVIRONMENTAL ATTITUDES AND STUDENT PERFORMANCE

Students who display one, two or three environmental attitudes perform higher in science than students who do not display any environmental attitude. As shown in Figure 3.6, on average across participating countries and economies in PISA 2018, environmentally enthusiastic students (i.e. who displayed environmental awareness, sense-of-purpose and self-efficacy in environmental understanding) scored almost 100 points higher in science than environmentally indifferent students (i.e. who did not display environmental attitudes).

After accounting for student socio-economic status, the difference in the mean score in science between environmentally enthusiastic students and environmentally indifferent students is about 82 score points, on average across countries and economies. This difference is 100 score points or higher in nine countries/economies (Austria, Hong Kong [China], Korea, Lebanon, Malta, North Macedonia, Portugal, Singapore and Slovenia), and 55 points or lower in only four countries and economies (Baku [Azerbaijan], Dominican Republic, Indonesia and Uruguay) (Table B.3.20).

Students who displayed two environmental attitudes also performed much higher than environmentally indifferent students, especially if environmental awareness was one of those attitudes. On average across countries and economies, students who displayed awareness and self-efficacy (but no sense-of-purpose) scored 63 points higher in science than environmentally indifferent students after accounting for student socio-economic status (Table B.3.20). Students who displayed awareness and sense-of-purpose (but no self-efficacy) scored 47 points higher in science than environmentally indifferent students after accounting for student socio-economic status (Table B.3.20).

The difference between students who displayed only one environmental attitude and students who display no environmental attitude is smaller in size. On average across countries and economies, the gap in science achievement between students who have self-efficacy in environmental understanding only (i.e. not awareness or sense-of-purpose) and environmentally indifferent students is 13 score points after accounting for student socio-economic status (Table B.3.20). Similarly, the size of the gap in science performance between students who display environmental sense-of-purpose only (i.e. not awareness nor self-efficacy) and environmentally indifferent students is 12 score points after accounting for student socio-economic status (Table B.3.20).

Interestingly, the gap in science performance between students who display environmental awareness only (i.e. not self-efficacy nor sense-of-purpose) and environmentally indifferent students is 32 points on average after accounting for student socio-economic status (Table B.3.20).

Figure 3.6 **Mean score in science, by overlap of environmental attitudes**

Overall average

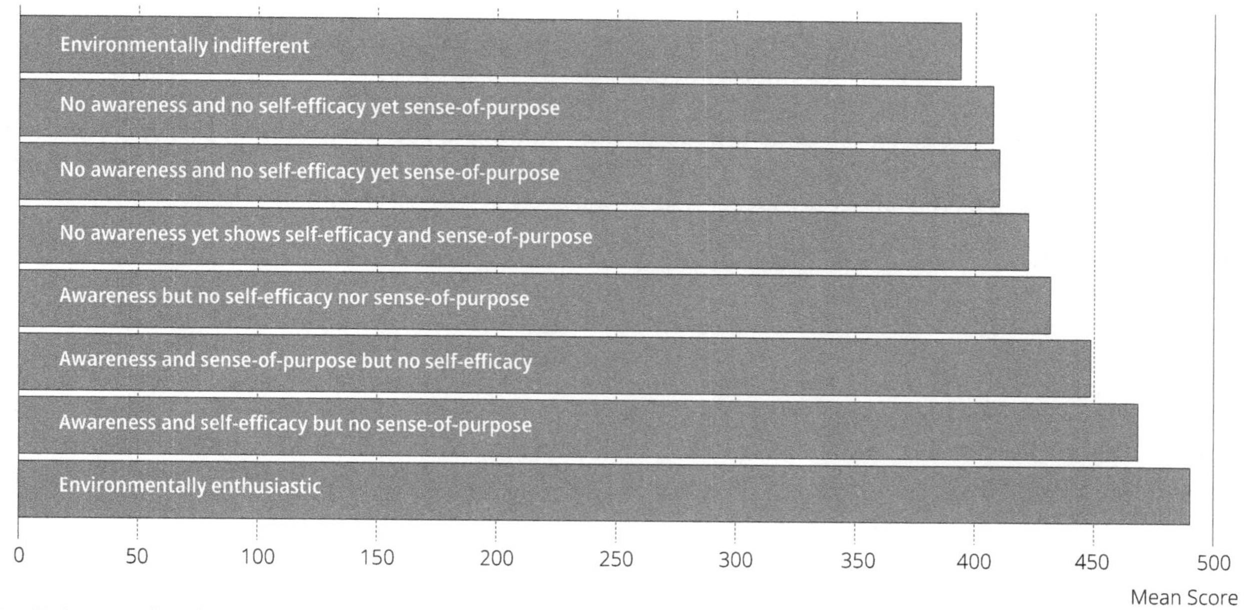

Notes: Environmentally enthusiastic students are those who display three environmental attitudes (i.e. environmental awareness, self-efficacy in environmental understanding and environmental sense-of-purpose).

Environmentally indifferent students are those who do not display any environmental attitudes.

Source: OECD, PISA 2018 Database, Table B.3.17.

StatLink https://stat.link/g7cq4z

Further to the above, reaching at least a baseline level of proficiency Level 2 in science is associated with environmental attitudes. As shown in Figure 3.7, on average across countries and economies, the share of environmentally aware students is about 26 percentage points higher among students who perform at Level 2 or above in science than among students who perform below Level 2 in science; the share of students who display self-efficacy in environmental understanding is about 23 percentage points higher among students who perform in science at Level 2 or above; and the share of students who display environmental sense-of-purpose is about 11 percentage points higher among students who perform in science at Level 2 or above.

In all countries and economies with available data, with few exceptions, environmental attitudes are more prevalent among students who performed at or above baseline proficiency Level 2 in science than those who did not (Tables B.3.2, B.3.4 and B.3.6).

Figure 3.7 **Environmental attitudes, by proficiency level in science**

Percentage of students who display environmental awareness, sense-of-purpose or self-efficacy in environmental understanding; Overall average

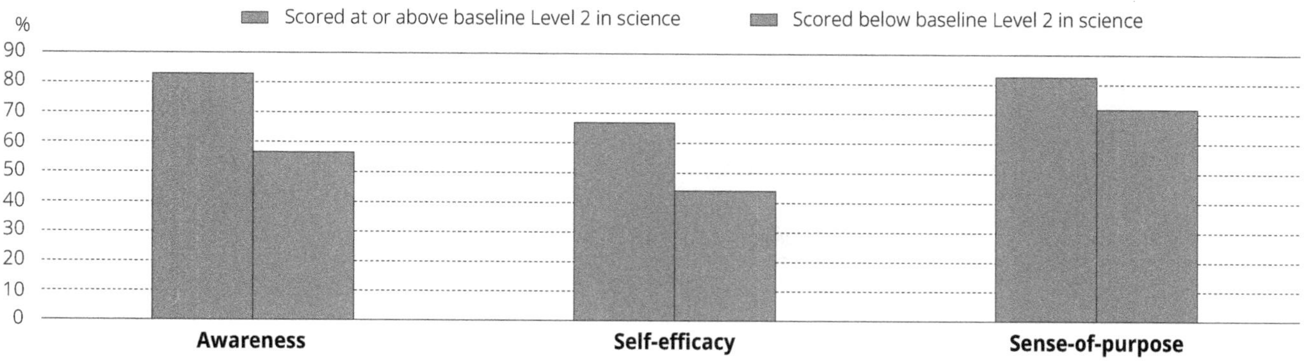

Note: differences between students who scored in science at or above baseline Level 2 in science and students who scored below baseline proficiency Level 2 are all statistically significant.

Source: OECD, PISA 2018 Database, Tables B.3.2, B.3.4 and B.3.6.

StatLink https://stat.link/fexg5y

WHAT DO WE KNOW ABOUT STUDENTS WHO ARE ENVIRONMENTALLY ENTHUSIASTIC OR INDIFFERENT?

Environmentally enthusiastic students – those who show environmental sense-of-purpose, awareness and self-efficacy in environmental understanding – come from diverse backgrounds and schools, and hold diverse personal beliefs.

As shown in Figure 3.8, the share of environmentally enthusiastic students is much greater among students who are proficient in science than among low-performing students (27 percentage points differences) and among socio-economically advantaged status than among disadvantaged students (23 percentage points difference), on average across countries and economies. In all countries and economies, the share of environmentally enthusiastic students is higher among students who are proficient in science and among socio-economically advantaged students (Table B.3.22).

Parental environmental attitudes and behaviours make it more likely that students are environmentally enthusiastic. Parental environmental awareness was measured in PISA 2018 using the Parent Questionnaire, which asked parents how informed they were about climate change and global warming and offered four response categories: parents who reported that they know something about or are very familiar with climate change and global warming are considered as displaying environmental awareness. The difference in the share of environmentally enthusiastic students between students who have parents who are environmentally aware and students whose parent are not environmentally aware is 16 percentage points difference, on average across countries and economies. Furthermore, the Parent Questionnaire asked parents if they were involved in two environmental actions: reducing energy use at home to protect the environment and boycotting products or companies for political, ethical or environmental reasons. The share of environmentally enthusiastic students is greater among students whose parents carry out environmentally conscious actions such as saving energy at home or boycotting products or companies for environmental or other reasons.

Environmental enthusiasm is also greater among students who hold a growth mindset[4] (the belief that intelligence is something they can change) rather than a fixed mindset, and who attend schools where climate change is included in the formal curriculum (rather than not included), on average across countries and economies. In the case of school curriculum, the share of environmentally enthusiastic students is not different among students who are enrolled in schools that cover or do not climate change in the school curriculum in 41 out of 52 countries/economies with available data (Table B.3.22).

Figure 3.8 **Environmentally enthusiastic students, by student, school and parent characteristics**

Percentage-point difference in the share of "enthusiastic" students (those who display environmental awareness, sense-of-purpose and self-efficacy in environmental understanding), by student, school and parent characteristics; overall average

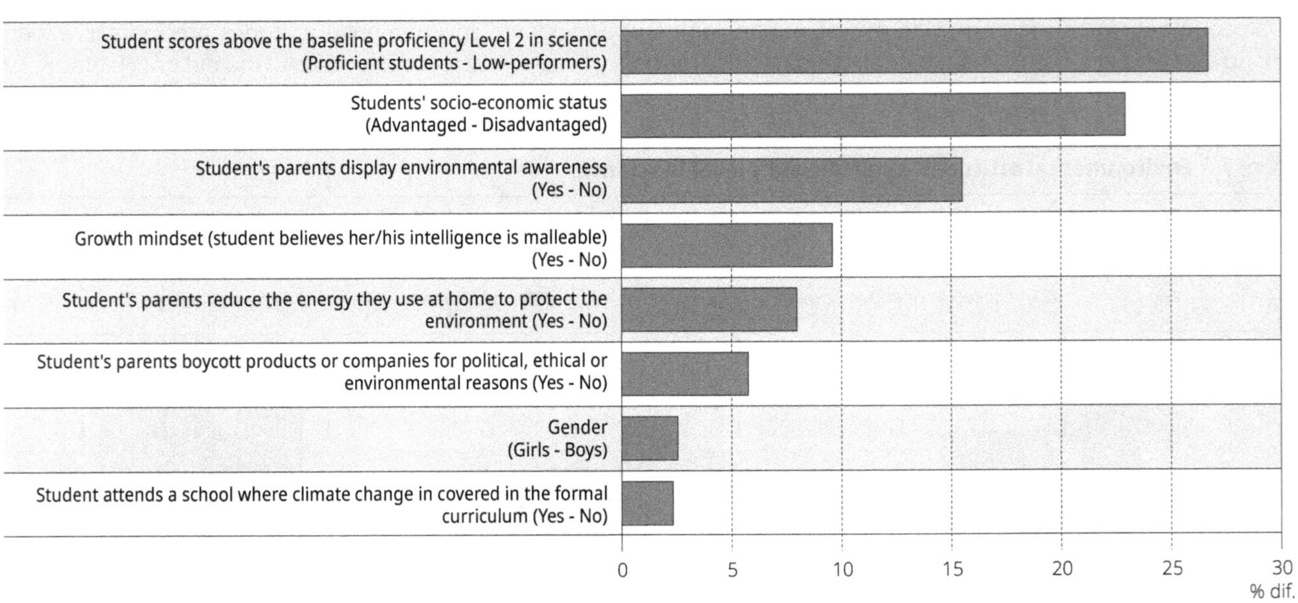

Note: Differences for all variables are all statistically significant.

Student, school and parental characteristics are ranked in descending order of the percentage-point difference.

Source: OECD, PISA 2018 Database, Table B.3.22.

StatLink https://stat.link/io9ler

Finally, the share of environmentally enthusiastic students is somewhat greater among girls than boys, on average across countries and economies and in 26 countries/economies. However, in 31 out of 62 countries/economies with available data the difference is not statistically significant, and in five countries (Austria, France, Romania, Spain and Switzerland) the share of environmentally enthusiastic students is greater among boys (Table B.3.22).

These result hold even after accounting for these student characteristics in the same statistical model (Figure 3.9).

Figure 3.9 **Likelihood of being an environmentally enthusiastic student**

Increased likelihood of being an environmentally enthusiastic student, by student characteristics, before and after accounting for other variables; overall average

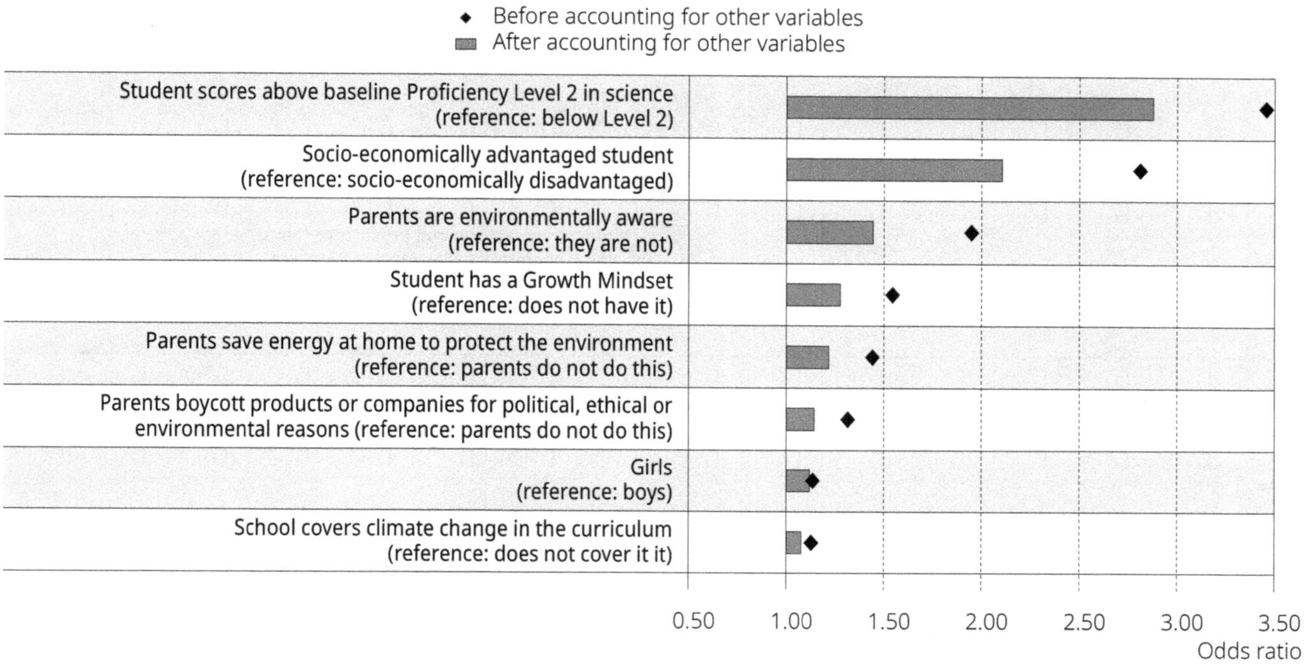

Notes: All odds ratio are statistically significant.
Odds ratios "after accounting for other variables" come from a logistic regression that includes as predictors all variables shown in the figure.
Student, school and parental characteristics are ranked in descending order of the odds ratio after accounting for other variables.
Source: OECD, PISA 2018 Database, Table B.3.24.
StatLink https://stat.link/ve8xdn

The profile of environmentally indifferent students – those who do not show sense-of-purpose, awareness or self-efficacy in environmental understanding– is the exact opposite of enthusiastic students.

As shown in Figure 3.10, among environmentally indifferent students, a greater share performs below the baseline proficiency Level 2 in science, comes from socio-economically disadvantaged families, and has parents who are unfamiliar or do not know much about climate change and global change (i.e. environmentally unaware parents), on average across countries and economies. Furthermore, a greater proportion of environmentally indifferent students, on average, endorses a fixed mindset (i.e. they do not believe that intelligence is something they can change), and have parents who do not carry out environmentally conscious actions such as saving energy at home or boycotting products or companies. There are proportionately more boys than girls among environmentally indifferent students and students who attend schools where climate change is not included in the formal curriculum.

These results hold even after accounting for these student characteristics in the same statistical model (Table B.3.25). The exception is that the inclusion of climate change in the curriculum is not a significant predictor of environmental indifference after accounting for other student characteristics.

Figure 3.10 **Environmentally indifferent students, by student, school and parent characteristics**

Percentage-point difference in the share of "indifferent" students (those who do not display environmental awareness, sense-of-purpose nor self-efficacy in environmental understanding), by student, school and parent characteristics; overall average

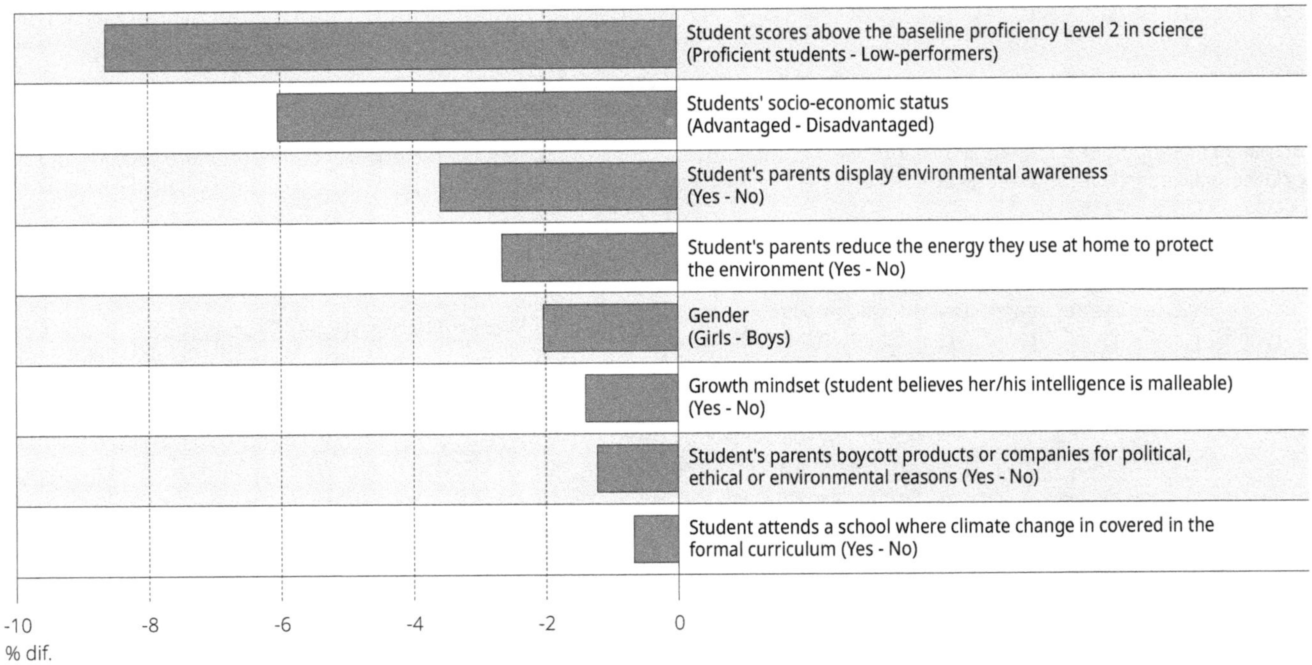

Note: Differences for all variables are all statistically significant.
Student, school and parental characteristics are ranked in ascending order of the percentage-point difference.
Source: OECD, PISA 2018 Database, Table B.3.23.
StatLink https://stat.link/trhbfo

POLICY IMPLICATIONS FROM THE CHAPTER

The findings included in this chapter suggest that multiple factors have a role in shaping students' environmental attitudes. This is consistent with the conceptual framework of this report (Figure 1.1).

At the student level, it is clear that pro-environmental attitudes are positively related to students' environmental science knowledge and skills, as measured by their performance in the PISA science test. Pro-environmental attitudes may foster curiosity and motivation for learning science, and scientific understanding of the environment may lay the foundation for pro-environmental attitudes. In any case, pro-environmental attitudes and science proficiency tend to reinforce each other.

Also at the student level, it is significant that environmental enthusiasm is more prevalent among students with a growth mindset. It is possible that because these students feel greater agency in their lives than those who believe they have a fixed mindset, they believe they can effect change in the world and combat the climate crisis. Policies that encourage pro-environmental attitudes would do well to include elements from growth-mindset interventions.

In terms of families, the data show clearly that parents play a key role in shaping their children's environmental attitudes. Parents who talk to their children about the climate crisis and model environmentally conscious behaviour are likely to bring up more environmentally conscious children. School programmes that include parents in activities that inform them of climate change challenges and promote concrete actions to protect the environment are a promising policy. These school programmes can be reinforced by community efforts aimed at local environmental preservation.

For schools, the inclusion of climate change in the formal curriculum is important but not enough. While there are more environmentally enthusiastic and fewer environmentally indifferent students in schools that have climate change in the curriculum, the differences between schools that do and those that don't are not as large as could be expected. This is partly because coverage of climate change in the school curriculum is nearly universal in most countries (Figure 3.11). It is also likely that the implementation of the formal curriculum in the classroom is heterogeneous across classrooms and schools. Almost one in four students across the OECD do not reach the baseline proficiency Level 2 in science; these are students who, on average, have weaker pro-environmental attitudes. More efforts should be made to improve the quality of environmental and science education.

At the education system level, supporting the needs of socio-economically disadvantaged students is vital. These students are more likely to be affected by environmental degradation such as exposure to contaminated water and air but are less likely to have the resources to address these problems. Taking steps to meet their concrete environmental needs while implementing educational programmes about the environment could be beneficial in two ways: students would better understand how environmental crises impact their own local communities when they experience real improvements in their quality of life and would become better informed and feel more agency over their lives and the environment.

Figure 3.11 **Coverage of climate change in the school curriculum**

Percentage of students in schools whose principal reported that climate change and global warming are covered in the school curriculum

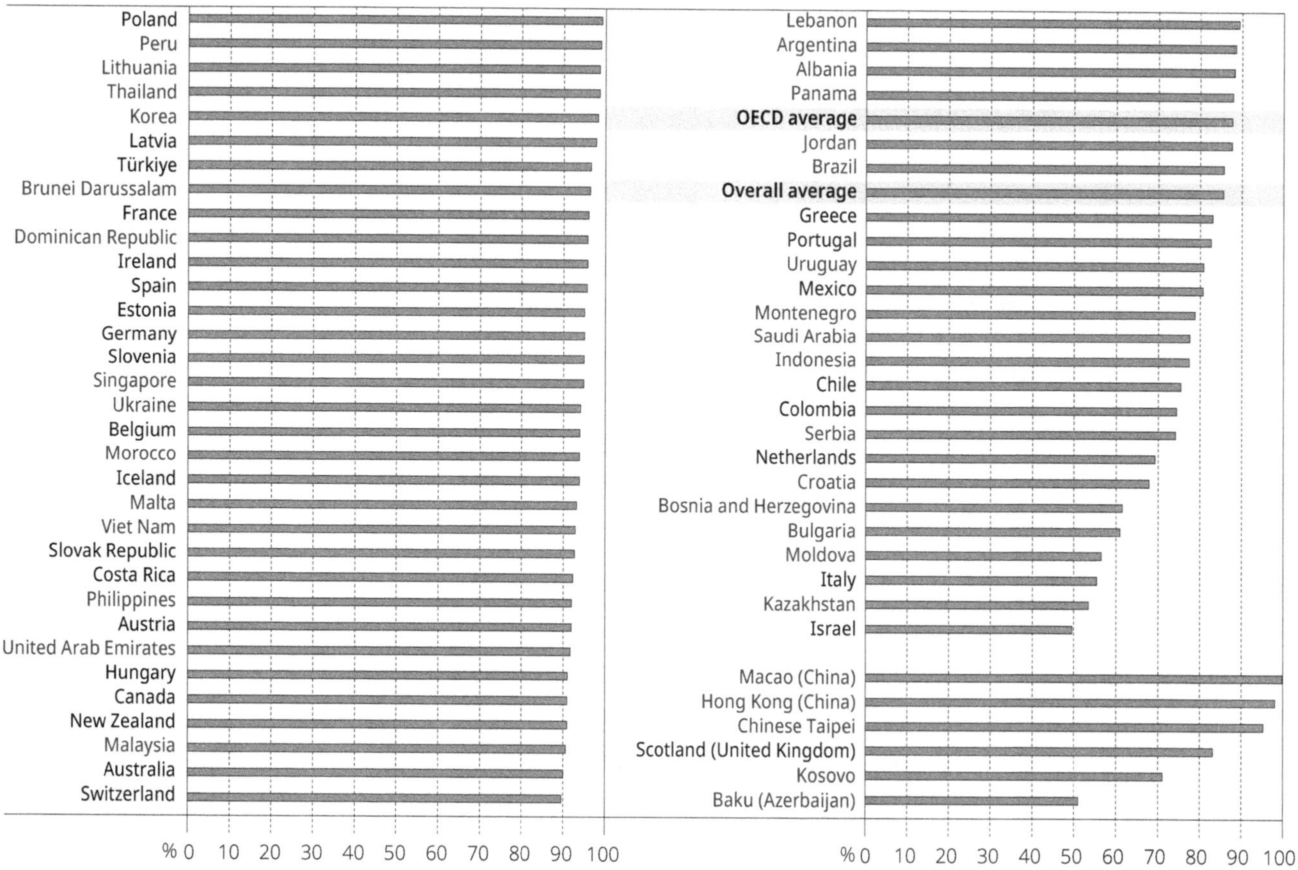

Countries and economies are ranked in descending order of percentage of students.

Source: OECD, PISA 2018 Database, Table B.3.27.

StatLink https://stat.link/i4j1d2

Notes

1. A statistical test was computed to test if the difference between the average percentage of students who display environmental sense-of-purpose across all countries and economies was greater than the average percentage of students who display environmental awareness across all countries and economies. In addition, a statistical test was computed to test if the difference between the average percentage of students who display environmental sense-of-purpose across all countries and economies was greater than the average percentage of students who display self-efficacy in environmental understanding across all countries and economies. In both cases, results show that the difference is statistically significant.

2. The Pearson correlation between the share of students who display environmental sense-of-purpose and share of students who display environmental awareness is 0.23.

3. The Pearson correlation between the share of students who display environmental sense-of-purpose and the share of students who display self-efficacy in environmental understanding is 0.29.

4. A growth mindset is the belief in the malleability of ability and intelligence (Dweck, 2006[4]). PISA 2018 asked students whether they agreed ("strongly disagree", "disagree, "agree", or "strongly agree") with the statement: "Your intelligence is something about you that you can't change much". Students who agreed are considered to have a fixed mindset and the students who disagreed with the statement are considered to have a growth mindset.

References

Bandura, A. (1978), "Self-efficacy: Toward a unifying theory of behavioral change", *Advances in Behaviour Research and Therapy*, Vol. 1/4, pp. 139-161, https://doi.org/10.1016/0146-6402(78)90002-4. [3]

Damon, W., J. Menon and K. Cotton Bronk (2003), "The Development of Purpose During Adolescence", *Applied Developmental Science*, Vol. 7/3, pp. 119-128, https://doi.org/10.1207/s1532480xads0703_2. [2]

Dweck, C. (2006), *Mindset*, Random House, New York, NY. [4]

OECD (2020), *PISA 2024 Strategic Vision and Direction for Science*, https://www.oecd.org/pisa/publications/PISA-2024-Science-Strategic-Vision-Proposal.pdf. [1]

4

Student involvement in environmental actions

What the data tell us

- On average across countries/economies, some two-thirds of students reported that they reduce energy consumption at home to protect the environment; a little less than half of students choose certain products for environmental or ethical reasons even if they are more expensive; some 44% of students participate in activities in favour of environmental protection; a bit more than a quarter of students boycott products or companies for environmental or other reasons; and a similar share sign environmental or social petitions online.
- About a fifth of students were "actively involved" in environmental actions (i.e. participated in four or five environmental actions) on average across countries/economies. A similar share of students was "entirely uninvolved" (i.e. did not participate in any environmental action considered in this report).
- Students are, on average across countries/economies, more likely to take action for the environment when they have pro-environmental attitudes such as an environmental sense-of-purpose, and awareness and self-efficacy in environmental understanding. Environmental sense-of-purpose is particularly strongly related to the environmental actions examined in this report.
- The relationship between science achievement and environmental action varies markedly depending on the type of environmental action. A positive relationship exists between science proficiency and saving energy at home. By contrast, science proficiency is negatively related on average to the other four environmental actions examined in this report.
- The share of students who are defined as "environmentally enthusiastic" (students who have an environmental sense-of-purpose, awareness and self-efficacy in environmental understanding) but who do not take part in environmental actions ranges from 22% (for those who do not save energy at home) to 70% (for those who do not boycott companies or products) on average across countries/economies. Some 8% of environmentally enthusiastic students do not take part in any of the five environmental actions examined in this chapter.
- Environmentally enthusiastic students are markedly more likely to take action to protect the environment when their circle of school peers and parents take part in environmental actions or have pro-environmental attitudes.

This chapter examines student involvement in actions regarding environmental issues. Students' participation in environmental actions at age 15 can be understood as the culmination of the knowledge, skills and pro-environmental attitudes they have acquired throughout their lives. According to the conceptual framework of this report, scientific knowledge and skills, pro-environmental attitudes and environmental actions are the key components of students' preparedness for environmental challenges. As such, it can be expected that better-performing students in science possess more pro-environmental attitudes and are more involved in environmental actions. The expectation that student performance in science is related to pro-environmental attitudes is clearly supported by PISA data, as shown in Chapter 3. Examining the relationship between science performance and environmental actions, and between pro-environmental attitudes and environmental actions using PISA data is the goal of this chapter.

According to PISA's Global Competence Framework, students who have knowledge of global and intercultural issues, who are able to understand the perspectives of others and who have an interest in other cultures are better able to translate such positive attributes into actions that benefit their local communities and the world in which they live (Milfont and Sibley, 2012[1]; OECD, 2018[2]). Similarly, it can be expected that students are more likely to take action for environmental issues if they have higher levels of proficiency in environmental science, greater awareness of environmental issues, stronger self-efficacy in environmental understanding and a stronger sense-of-purpose regarding environmental issues.

The first section of this chapter considers the incidence of environmental actions across countries and economies.

The second section examines how different types of environmental action are associated with students' attitudes towards environmental issues and students' performance in science.

The third and final section of this chapter examines misalignments between student involvement in environmental actions and students' attitudes towards environmental issues. Who are the students who, despite having pro-environmental attitudes, do not take part in environmental actions?

Box 4.1. How students' environmental actions are measured in PISA

Environmental actions in PISA

Data on student involvement in environmental actions comes from a question included in the PISA 2018 student questionnaire that was part of the Global Competence module. This question asked, *"Are you involved in the following activities?"* and listed eight statements requiring a yes-or-no answer. Five out of these eight statements are related to environmental issues and thus are defined here as environmental actions. These five statements are the following:

- I reduce the energy I use at home (e.g. by turning the heating down or turning the air conditioning down or by turning off the lights when leaving a room) to protect the environment (action 1).
- I choose certain products for ethical or environmental reasons, even if they are a bit more expensive (action 2).
- I sign environmental or social petitions online (action 3).
- I boycott products or companies for political, ethical or environmental reasons (action 4).
- I participate in activities in favour of environmental protection (action 5).

Students who answered "yes" to a particular statement are considered as taking part in that particular action. Students who answered "no", and students who had an opportunity to answer the question but did not respond (i.e. they were presented the question according to the survey design but left it blank), are considered as not taking part in the action. By design, a student can take part in as many as five different environmental actions and as few as none.

Data limitations and interpretation

The five environmental actions are diverse in nature and provide rich information on what students do or do not do for the environment. However, they do not cover the full range of possible environmental actions carried out by students. For example, practices such as recycling and composting waste are not measured nor organising or initiating environmental actions as opposed to joining in actions organised by others. This means that students can do more than what is being measured in PISA. Furthermore, some of the actions examined here are not exclusively "environmental" in their nature as they might also be motivated by ethical, social or political reasons. This is the case with three of the five environmental actions examined in this report (i.e. actions 2, 3 and 4). In addition, environmental actions may not be equally culturally appropriate in all countries and economies (see Box 4.2). PISA will improve its measurement of environmental actions in the context of the new PISA 2025 Science Framework, which has a stronger focus on student environmental agency (OECD, 2020[3]).

Data availability

Data for students' environmental actions is available for 27 OECD countries and 36 partner countries and economies (i.e. a total of 63 countries and economies). Because data is not available for 11 out of the 38 OECD countries that took part in PISA 2018, the OECD average is not a good measure of central trends in PISA-participating countries. The average across all countries and economies with available data (i.e. "overall average") is used instead throughout this chapter.

Sources: OECD (2020), *PISA 2024 Strategic Vision and Direction for Science*, https://www.oecd.org/pisa/publications/PISA-2024-Science-Strategic-Vision-Proposal.pdf.

STUDENTS TAKING ACTION ON ENVIRONMENTAL ISSUES

The environmental actions measured in PISA 2018 are diverse in nature, as described in Table 4.1. A key difference between environmental actions examined in this chapter is their *sphere of action,* meaning whether the action is carried out in private (i.e. at home or individually, without interacting with other people) or in public (i.e. in a public space or interacting with other people involved in a collective action).

Table 4.1 **Types of environmental actions**

	Environmental Actions	Action characteristics	
		Sphere of action	Barriers to action
Action 1	I reduce the energy I use at home (e.g. by turning the heating down or turning the air conditioning down or by turning off the lights when leaving a room) to protect the environment	Private sphere	None
Action 2	I choose certain products for ethical or environmental reasons, even if they are a bit more expensive.	Private sphere	Requires money and information
Action 3	I sign environmental or social petitions online	Public sphere	Requires an external organiser
Action 4	I boycott products or companies for political, ethical or environmental reasons	Public or private sphere	Requires an external organiser
Action 5	I participate in activities in favour of environmental protection	Public sphere	Requires time and an external organiser

Private environmental actions such as saving energy at home (action 1) or choosing environmentally-sustainable products (action 2) are ways in which young people reduce their carbon footprint and contribute – even if only a little – to mitigating climate change. These actions often have other benefits, as well: saving energy lowers energy bills, for example, and environmentally sustainable products may improve one's health or life satisfaction. Still, private individual actions are not the only avenue to tackling the climate crisis.

Young people also employ high-visibility collective environmental actions to challenge institutional inertia on climate (i.e. lack of action of political and economic authorities) and demand large-scale changes to environmental and economic policies (Munck af Rosenschöld, Rozema and Frye-Levine, 2014[4]; Snow A. and Soule, 2010[5]). These kinds of public actions typically attract media attention and range from signing online petitions (action 3); and boycotting products or companies (action 4); to, generally, participating in activities in favour of environmental protection (action 5).

Private actions can be perceived or experienced as easier to carry out and public actions as more demanding for several reasons. In the public sphere, ideas and claims about issues are exposed to criticism and debate (Habermas, 1991[6]). Students who are averse to possible conflict with those who are unsympathetic towards or sceptical of environmental actions may prefer not to publicly engage. Students might also choose not to take part in public environmental actions organised online for fear of online retaliation or harassment. Young people view incivility (e.g. personal attacks on those with opposing views) as a significant problem on social media platforms; as a result, they tend to avoid potentially divisive topics on social media in favour of "happy" interactions (Kruse, Norris and Flinchum, 2017[7]). Online harassment is an issue for today's 15-year-olds and particularly for girls; survey data from the United States shows that young people and women suffer more often from online harassment than older adults and men (Pew Research Center, 2021[8]).

The criticism and online harassment that young people can experience when they take part in public climate change actions are often fuelled by "environmental countermovements"; that is, organised efforts to resist action on climate change (Brulle and Aronczyk, 2019[9]). Research on environmental countermovements shows that these groups use a variety of tactics to influence cultural perceptions of climate change, including the promulgation of climate misinformation and the use of advertising campaigns to promote positive perceptions of fossil fuel corporations (Freudenburg, Gramling and Davidson, 2008[10]; Greenberg, Knight and Westersund, 2011[11]).

Another reason students may find public environmental actions more demanding is that they typically include confrontational tactics like strikes, protests, sit-ins, and site occupations. Generally, contemporary environmental activism is peaceful and non-violent (Rootes, 2004[12]). In democratic societies protests have become an increasingly accepted and institutionalised form of collective action with venues and times negotiated between authorities and protesters ahead of time (e.g. protest permits) (McCarthy and McPhail, 1998[13]; Elliott et al., 2022[14]). At times, however, law enforcement agents intervene, exposing demonstrators to arrest or physical harm (Scheidel et al., 2020[15]; Porta and Reiter, 1998[16]).

Another set of differences between environmental actions are certain barriers to action over which students have little or no control. Acting for the environment might require the use of resources (McCarthy and Zald, 1977[17]). One of these resources is money: some environmental actions require using financial resources that some students might not have – for example, choosing environmentally-sustainable products can be more expensive than regular products. Another resource required for engaging in action is time: while some actions can be a one-off event, others require more time commitment, which some students might not be able to fulfil due to school or family responsibilities. The additional effort it takes to make an informed decision and the transportation cost required to participate in activities that take place in distant locations is another cost that can shape student involvement in environmental actions (Snow A. and Soule, 2010[5]). Actions that are not costly in terms of money, time or effort are easier to carry out; in contrast, when there are these barriers to action, it is more difficult for students to participate even if they have pro-environmental attitudes. Turning off the lights when leaving a room or signing an online environmental petition are examples of actions that do not take too much time or effort.

A different kind of barrier to action is that many types of environmental actions require a match between a student and an external agent or organiser. In order to sign an environmental petition, boycott products or companies, or participate in an environmental activity, somebody has to write or organise those petitions, boycotts and activities. As social movement researchers put it, external agents and environmental activist organisers need to give students opportunities to mobilise (Klandermans, 2007[18]). At school, friends and peers can serve as social networks that connect individual students with opportunities for participation (Diani, 2007[19]).

Incidence of environmental actions

Reducing energy use at home to protect the environment is the most frequent environmental action among students participating in PISA 2018. As shown in Figure 4.1, some two-thirds of students on average across countries and economies reported that they reduce energy consumption at home to protect the environment. More students engage in this over other environmental actions included in PISA 2018. A possible explanation is that it is relatively easy to carry out: it does not require too much time and does not demand public exposure. It also has immediate - even if, small - environment benefits (e.g. lower carbon-footprint) as well as private benefits (e.g. lower energy bills for the student's family).

The cross-national distribution of this variable is shown in Figure 4.2. In 17 countries and economies, some 75% or more of students reported that they reduce energy use at home to protect the environment; in a few countries/economies, about half of students reduce energy use at home. This shows that reducing energy use at home to protect the environment is a very common environmental action worldwide.

Some 70% of socio-economically advantaged students save energy at home and 64% of disadvantaged students do it (6 percentage points difference) on average across countries and economies (Table B.4.1). In terms of gender, the incidence of reducing energy consumption at home is greater among girls (70%) than boys (65%) on average across countries and economies (Table B.4.1).

Figure 4.1 **Student involvement in environmental actions**

Overall average

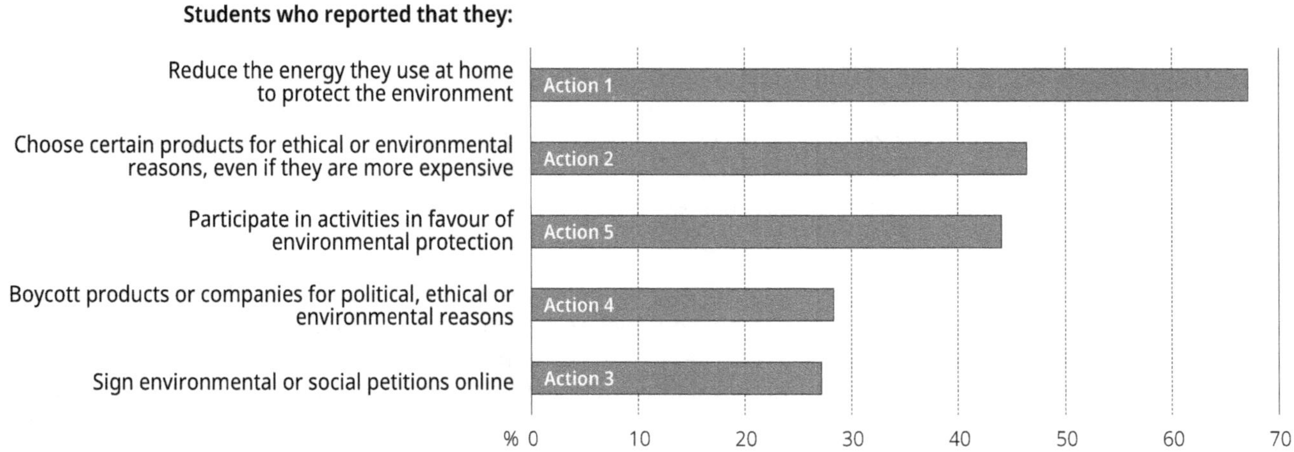

Actions are ranked in descending order of the percentage of students.

Source: OECD, PISA 2018 Database, Tables B.4.1 to B.4.5

StatLink https://stat.link/cqxuhm

Figure 4.2 **Percentage of students who reduce the energy they use at home to protect the environment (action 1)**

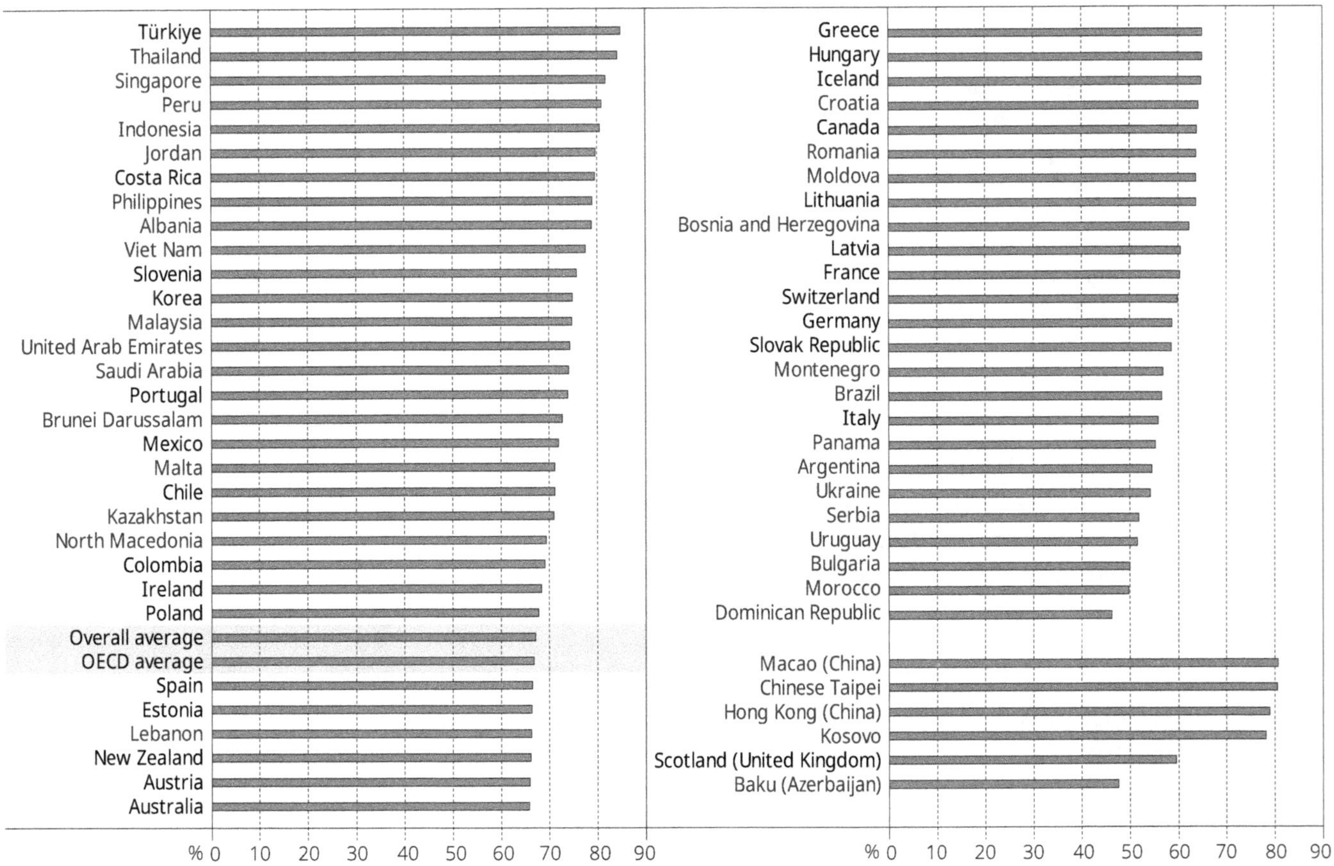

Countries and economies are ranked in descending order of the percentage of students.

Source: OECD, PISA 2018 Database, Table B.4.1.

StatLink https://stat.link/dcr7sk

A little less than half of students reported that they choose certain products for environmental or ethical reasons even if they are more expensive, on average across countries and economies (Figure 4.3). Compared to saving energy at home, this action may be less popular because choosing environmentally sustainable products can require more effort if clear and reliable information on products is not available. In addition, some students (e.g. socio-economically disadvantaged) might not have the freedom to choose products that are more expensive even if they care about the environment.

As opposed to reducing energy use at home, the percentage of students who choose certain products for ethical or environmental reasons did not climb higher than 70% in any country or economy (Figure 4.3). In the nine countries and economies with the greatest percentage of students who choose certain products for ethical or environmental reasons, the share was 60% of students or greater. In another 7 countries, the share was about 35% or lower. In most countries, more than a third but less than two-thirds of students reported that they choose products for ethical or environmental reasons even if they are more expensive.

The socio-economic disparity in choosing products for environmental reasons even if they are "a bit more expensive" is large compared with other actions. On average across countries and economies, 52% of advantaged students reported that they choose products for environmental reasons even if they are more expensive but only 41% of disadvantaged students did (11 percentage points difference). Advantaged students are more likely than disadvantaged students to take part in this environmental action in 61 out of the 63 countries and economies involved in this analysis (Table B.4.2). This finding shows that environmental actions that require financial commitment are particularly difficult for disadvantaged students. In terms of public policy, it poses the question of how to enhance access to environmentally sustainable products for socio-economically disadvantaged families.

Figure 4.3 **Percentage of students who choose products for ethical or environmental reasons even if they are more expensive (action 2)**

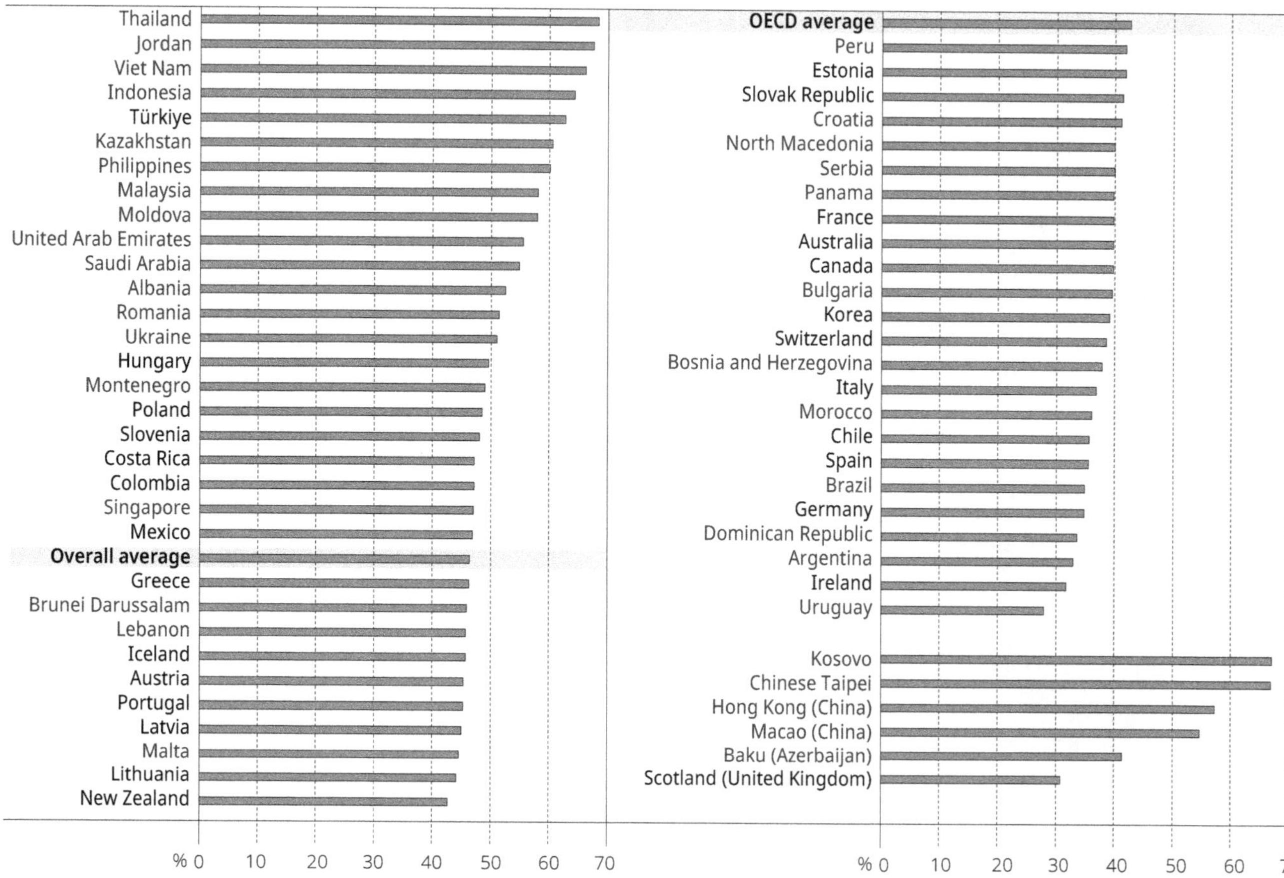

Countries and economies are ranked in descending order of the percentage of students.

Source: OECD, PISA 2018 Database, Table B.4.2.

StatLink https://stat.link/198t6j

On average across countries/economies, some 44% of students reported that they participate in activities in favour of environmental protection (Figure 4.4). Environmental protection activities can be varied, including some that students perceive as demanding more commitment, such as protests, sit-ins, strikes, etc. The time commitment required to participate in these activities (i.e. not a one-off event) might be another reason why more students do not take part in this kind of action. And transportation costs are another possible factor.

The share of students who participate in environmental protection actions ranges between 20% and 50% in most countries/economies that participated in PISA 2018. Remarkably, 60% or more of students reported that they participate in activities to protect the environment in 10 countries/economies; in Vietnam, this was the case for almost nine in ten students (Figure 4.4).

On the other hand, less than 30% of students reported taking part in actions for the environment in 10 countries and economies. In Italy, France, Germany and Scotland (United Kingdom), less than one in four students reported that they participate in activities to protect the environment (Figure 4.4).

A greater share of socio-economically advantaged (46%) than disadvantaged (42%) students participate in activities in favour of environmental protection on average across countries/economies (Table B.4.5).

A greater share of girls (45%) than boys (43%) students participate in activities in favour of environmental protection on average across countries/economies (Table B.4.5).

Figure 4.4 **Percentage of students who participate in activities in favour of environmental protection (action 5)**

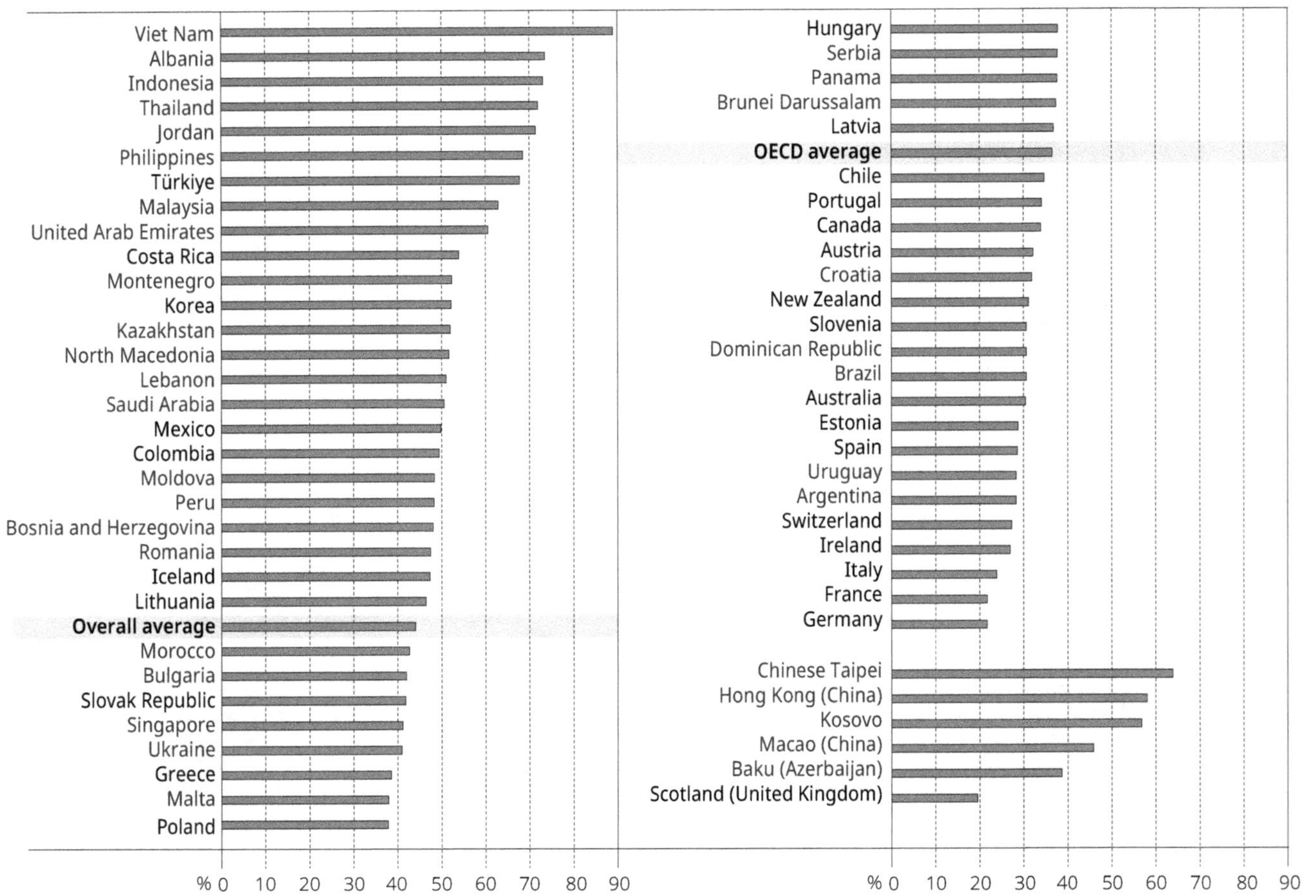

Countries and economies are ranked in descending order of the percentage of students.

Source: OECD, PISA 2018 Database, Table B.4.5.

StatLink https://stat.link/bjznh2

Finally, only a bit more than a quarter of students boycott products or companies for environmental or other reasons (Figure 4.6), and a similar share sign environmental or social petitions online (Figure 4.5). That the percentages are so low may have to do with potential exposure to criticism and online harassment in signing online environmental petitions[1]. In the case of boycotts, students might consider the personal cost of not consuming the products or services in question greater than the possible environmental benefit the boycott brings about (Nguyen et al., 2018[20]). It is possible, as well, that students think boycotts and petitions are ineffective or inappropriate (see Box 4.2). Lastly, there is also the "noise" factor of climate change boycott and petition campaigns competing for young people's attention with a growing abundance of information on social media.

In most countries/economies that participated in PISA 2018, the share of students who reported signing environmental or social petitions online ranged between 20% and 40% (Figure 4.5). In three countries (Jordan, Thailand and Türkiye), about half of students reported signing environmental or social petitions online. In 10 countries/economies, less than a fifth of students reported signing environmental or social petitions online.

A slightly greater share of socio-economically advantaged (28%) than disadvantaged (26%) students sign environmental or social petitions online on average across countries/economies (Table B.4.3). Advantaged students sign environmental or social petitions online more often than disadvantaged students in 27 out of the 63 countries and economies.

A smaller share of girls (25%) than boys (29%) sign environmental or social petitions online, on average across countries and economies (Table B.4.3).

In most countries/economies that participated in PISA 2018, the share of students who boycott products or companies for political, ethical or environmental reasons ranges between 20% and 40%. In two countries (Jordan and Saudi Arabia) about half or more of students reported that they boycott products or companies for political, ethical or environmental reasons. In eight countries/economies, less than a fifth of students did (Figure 4.6).

A greater share of socio-economically advantaged (31%) than disadvantaged (26%) students boycott products or companies on average across countries/economies (Table B.4.4).

A greater share of boys (32%) than girls (25%) students boycott products or companies on average across countries and economies (Table B.4.4).

Figure 4.5 **Percentage of students who sign environmental or social petitions online (action 3)**

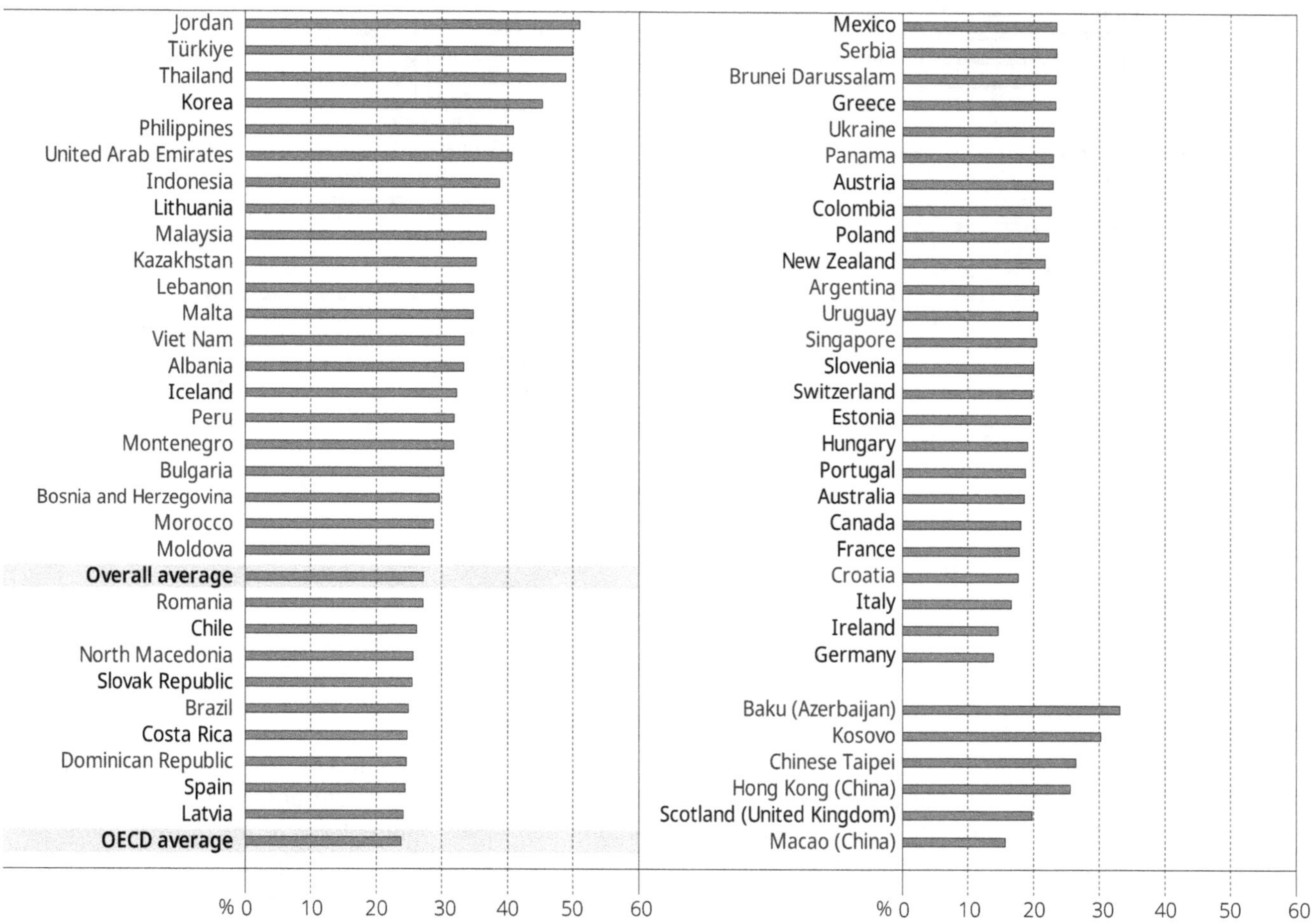

Countries and economies are ranked in descending order of the percentage of students.

Source: OECD, PISA 2018 Database, Table B.4.3.

StatLink https://stat.link/59qpe6

Figure 4.6 **Percentage of students who boycott products for political, ethical or environmental reasons (action 4)**

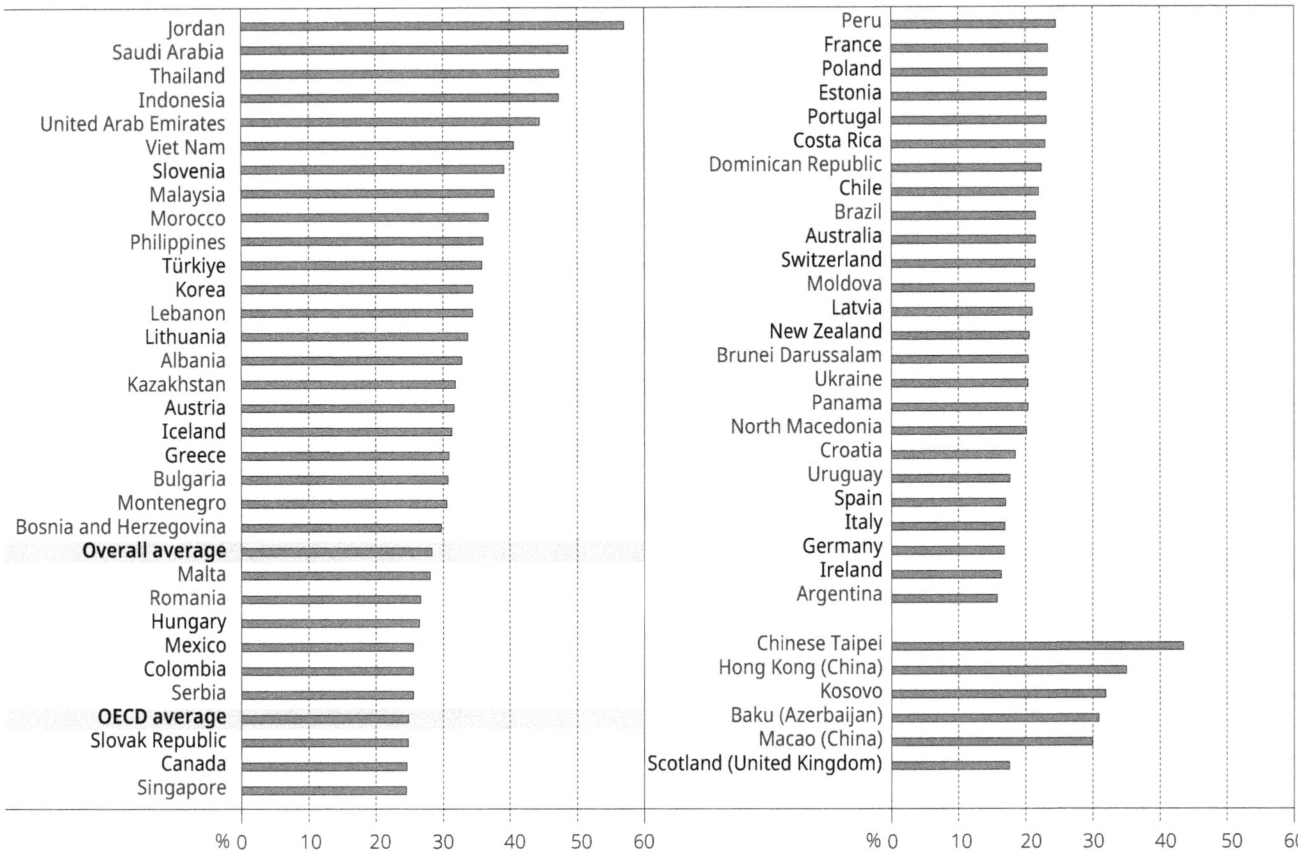

Countries and economies are ranked in descending order of the percentage of students.

Source: OECD, PISA 2018 Database, Table B.4.4.

StatLink https://stat.link/bj4ytf

Box 4.2. **Student perceptions of boycotts**

Student involvement in environmental actions can be influenced by the values and norms of countries and communities. Some research suggests that in the spectrum between *collectivism* and *individualism*, for example, societies in East Asia and Western Europe situate themselves differently in terms of their value orientations: this can influence students' environmental attitudes and behaviours (Berglund et al., 2019[21]; Hoffmann, 2014[22]). One study found that environmental ways of thinking and acting conform well to traditional Asian values and norms whereas in Western European countries environmental values are linked to altruistic values that are perceived as contrary to traditional ones (Aoyagi-Usui, Vinken and Kuribayashi, 2003[23]).

PISA 2018 illustrates this with regards to student perceptions of boycotts. In PISA 2018, students were asked if they agreed or disagreed with the statement: *"It is right to boycott companies that are known to provide poor workplace conditions for their employees"*. Although this is not a question about environmental boycotts, it provides information about students' perception about boycotts as a legitimate method of collective action. As shown in Figure 4.7, there are noticeable cross-national differences in students' perceptions of whether boycotts are a legitimate form of collective action.

Some 66% of students agreed that it is right to boycott companies that provide poor workplace conditions, on average across countries and economies. In several Latin-American countries (e.g. Argentina, Brazil, the Dominican Republic, Panama, Peru and Uruguay) and in some Eastern European countries (e.g. Moldova,

Romania and Ukraine), less than 60% of students agreed with the statement. By contrast, more than 70% of students agreed with the statement in some Asian countries and economies participating in PISA 2018 (e.g. Hong Kong [China], Korea, Macao [China], Singapore Chinese Taipei and Viet Nam). Some Western European countries/economies (e.g. France, Portugal, Spain, and Scotland [United Kingdom]) are closer to the overall average of 66%. These patterns suggest that some regional differences do exist, but they are far from deterministic as divergent cases are found in each region.

Across countries and economies, there is a positive correlation between the share of students who think that it is right to boycott companies that provide poor workplace conditions and the share of students who take part in boycotts of products or companies for environmental or other reasons (Figure 4.7).

Figure 4.7 **Student perception of boycotts and student participation in boycotts for social or environmental reasons**

Percentage of students who reported the following

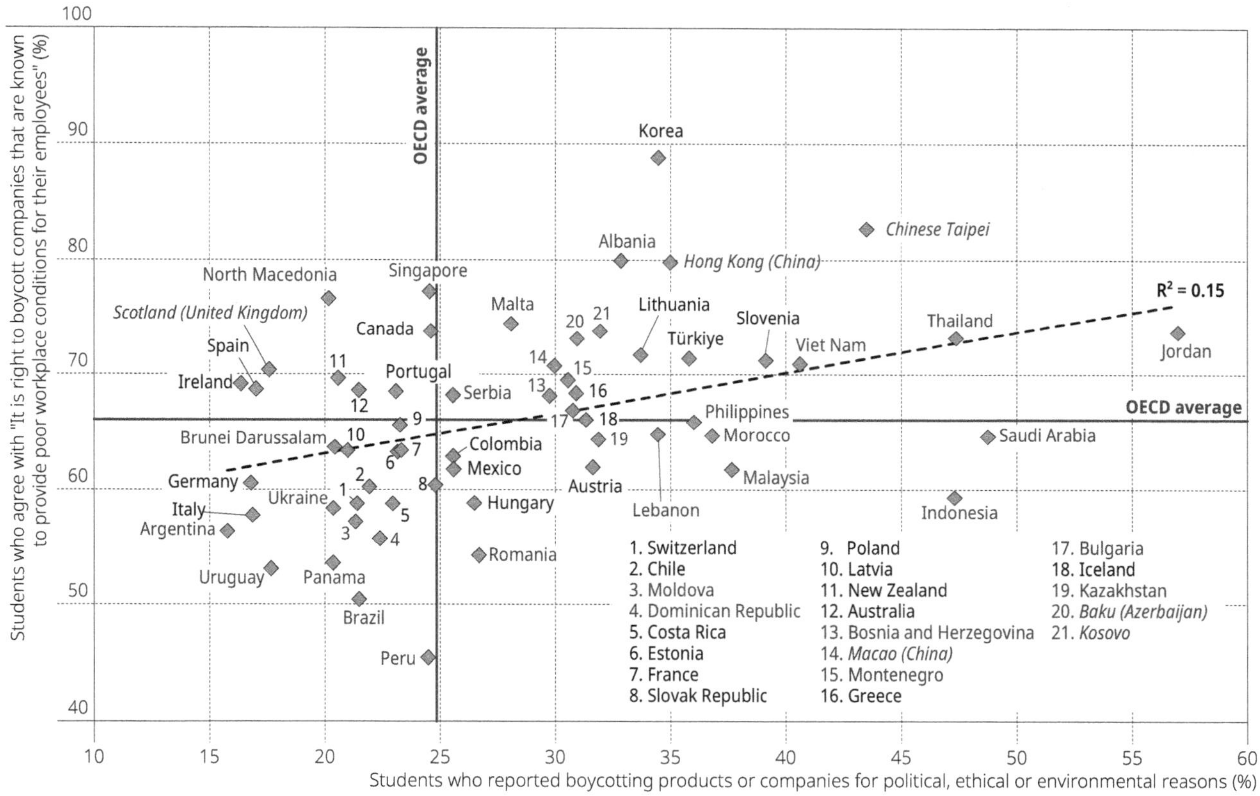

Source: OECD, PISA 2018 Database, Tables B.4.4 and B.4.29.
StatLink https://stat.link/cir3xm

At the student level, students who think that boycotts are a legitimate method of action are more likely to participate in environmentally motivated boycotts even after accounting for student science performance, socio-economic status, gender and environmental attitudes (Table B.4.43). Furthermore, after restricting the analysis only to students who are enthusiastic about environmental issues (i.e. those who have an environmental sense-of-purpose, awareness and self-efficacy in environmental understanding), students who perceive boycotts as a legitimate method of action are less likely *not* to boycott products or companies for environmental or other reasons even after accounting for student science performance, socio-economic status and other student characteristics (Table B.4.44).

Overlap of environmental actions

The number of environmental actions that students reported themselves to have taken part in is a measure of their degree of involvement in environmental actions. The PISA 2018 student questionnaire was designed in such a way that students could respond that they participated in as few as zero or one environmental action and as many as five environmental actions.

On average across countries and economies, about a fifth of students were entirely uninvolved in environmental actions (i.e. did not participate in any action measured in PISA 2018) and a similar share of students were actively involved (i.e. participated in four or five environmental actions) (Figure 4.8).

The share of students who are entirely uninvolved in environmental actions varied widely across countries. In 14 countries, the percentage of students who did not participate in any environmental action was 25% or more; among this group are large OECD countries/economies such as France, Germany, Italy and Scotland (United Kingdom) (Figure 4.8).

By contrast, in 18 countries and economies the share of students actively involved in environmental actions was 25% or more. Around 40% or more of students participated in four or five environmental actions in Indonesia, Jordan, Thailand and Türkiye.

On average across countries and economies, most students are what we might call moderately involved in environmental actions, meaning that they take part in either one (20%), two (22%) or three environmental actions (19%).

ENVIRONMENTAL ACTIONS, PRO-ENVIRONMENTAL ATTITUDES AND PERFORMANCE IN SCIENCE

Environmental actions and pro-environmental attitudes

Students are more likely to act for the environment when they have pro-environmental attitudes such as environmental sense-of-purpose, awareness and self-efficacy in environmental understanding (see Box 3.1 in Chapter 3 on how these attitudes are measured in PISA). An environmental sense-of-purpose is especially strongly related to the environmental actions examined in this report, as shown in Figure 4.9.

Students who have an environmental sense-of-purpose are almost twice as likely to reduce energy consumption at home and participate in activities in favour of environmental protection relative to those who do not have environmental sense-of-purpose. This is so even after accounting for other environmental attitudes and student characteristics such as science performance, socio-economic status and gender, on average across countries and economies (Figure 4.9). This is also observed in a great majority of PISA-participating countries and economies, as shown in Figure 4.10.

Similarly, the relationship between self-efficacy in environmental understanding and environmental actions is positive for all actions examined in this report. When it comes, for example, to choosing "green" products and participating in activities in favour of environmental protection, students with self-efficacy in environmental understanding are 1.3 times more likely to take part in these actions than students without it even after accounting for other student attitudes and characteristics, on average across countries and economies (Tables B.4.12 and B.4.15).

Environmental awareness is a good predictor of some environmental actions but not others. In particular, awareness is weakly related to actions that are more difficult or demanding such as signing petitions online or boycotting products or companies. This indicates that awareness, on its own, is not enough to motivate students to action – among environmentally aware students, 18% say that taking care of the environment is not important to them (Table B.3.6).

Figure 4.8 **Number of environmental actions students are involved in**

Percentage of students who participate in 0, 1, 2, 3, 4 or 5 environmental actions

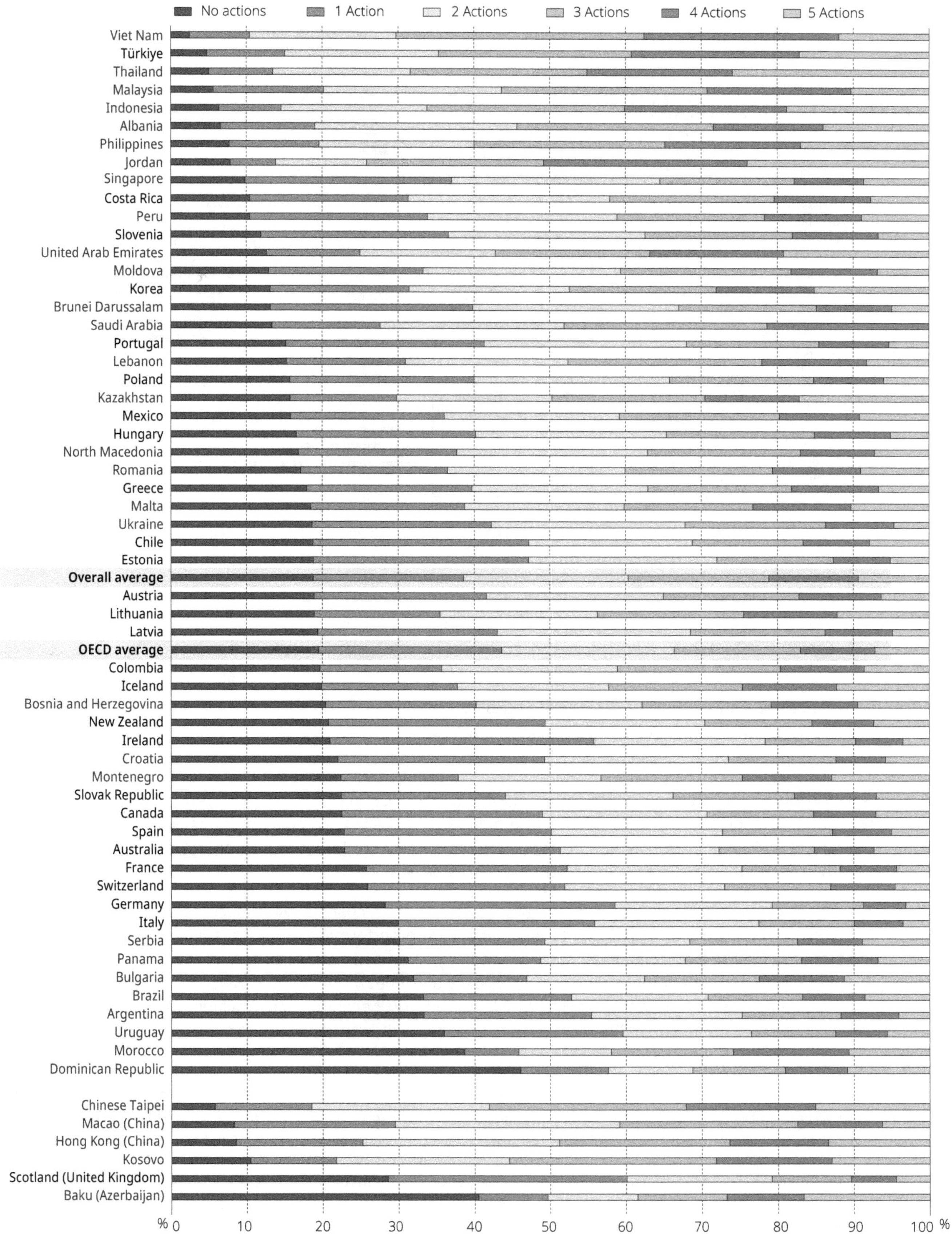

Countries and economies are ranked in ascending order of the percentage of students who reported to participate in any environmental actions.

Source: OECD, PISA 2018 Database, Table B.4.16.

StatLink https://stat.link/bx4prh

Figure 4.9 **Student involvement in environmental actions, environmental attitudes and proficiency in science**

Increased likelihood of students' involvement in environmental actions, by student pro-environmental attitudes proficiency in science, before and after accounting for socio-economic status and gender; overall average

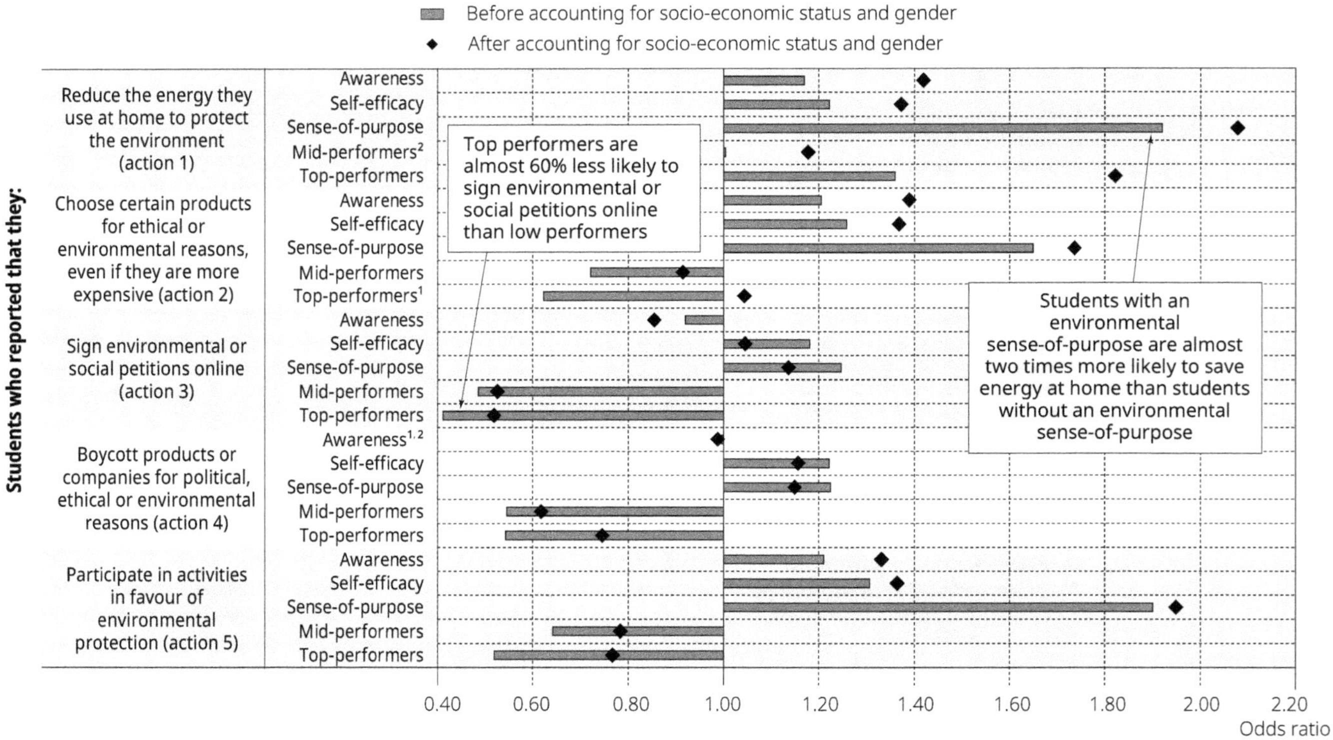

Note: The results shown in the figure account for students' socio-economic status and gender.

1. Odds ratio for before accounting for socio-economic status and gender is not statistically significant.
2. Odds ratio for after accounting for socio-economic status and gender is not statistically significant.

Source: OECD, PISA 2018 Database, Tables B.4.11 to B.4.15.

StatLink https://stat.link/zvhayw

Environmental actions and student proficiency in science

The relationship between science achievement and environmental action varies markedly depending on the type of environmental action.

A positive relationship exists between science proficiency and the first action examined in this report, i.e. reducing energy consumption at home to protect the environment. The mean score in science among students who reduce the energy they use at home is 458 points, and it is 438 points among students who do not reduce energy at home (difference is 20 score points) on average across countries and economies (Table B.4.30).

Furthermore, after accounting for environmental attitudes and student characteristics such as socio-economic status and gender, students who score at proficiency Levels 5 and 6 ("top performers") in science are 1.36 times more likely to reduce the energy they use at home than students who score at proficiency Levels 1 or below ("low performers") (Figure 4.9). In France and Slovenia, top performers in science are two times more likely to save energy than low performers, after accounting for attitudes and student characteristics. In no country or economy with available data are top performers less likely to save energy at home but in 39 countries or economies with available data the odds of saving energy are not different for top and low performers (Table B.4.11).

Saving energy at home – for example, by turning the heating or air conditioning down or turning off the lights when leaving a room– is easy and takes little time. It may be a good compromise for better-performing students who want to do something for the environment but have little time because they study a great deal (OECD, 2014$_{[24]}$).

With the exception of saving energy at home, science proficiency is negatively related on average to all the other (four) environmental actions examined in this report[2]. This is the most pronounced for actions that students perceive as more difficult or demanding: signing petitions online and boycotting products or companies. On average across all countries and economies, the mean score in science among students who sign environmental or social petitions online is 437, and it is 458 among students who do not sign petitions (difference is -21 score points). Similarly, the mean score in science among students who boycott products or companies for political, ethical or environmental reasons is 442 points, and it is 454 among students who do not (difference is -12 score points) (Table B.4.30).

Even after accounting for environmental attitudes and student characteristics, top-performing students are less likely to sign online petitions and boycott products or companies than low-performing students, on average across all countries and economies (Figure 4.9). In no country or economy with available data are top performers more likely to sign online petitions, and only in 10 countries or economies are the odds of signing online petitions no different for top and low performers (Table B.4.13).

Better-performing students tend to spend more time than low-performing students studying and completing schoolwork (OECD, 2014[24]). It is possible that better-performing students (both top-performers and mid-performers) are less likely to sign online petitions or boycott products and companies than low-performing students because they perceive these actions as more difficult and demanding in terms of the time and effort they would normally allocate to studying and homework. Additional factors might also play a role. For example, the effects of petitions and boycotts might not be as immediate as other environmental actions. This adds uncertainty to the decision of joining an environmental action. Cultural and normative considerations, such as the social legitimacy of boycotts as a form of collective action (see Box 4.2), might play a role.

When interpreting these results, it is important to consider that better performers have, on average, more pro-environmental attitudes than lower-performing students (as seen in Chapter 3 of this report), and that students with pro-environmental attitudes are more likely to act for the environment. The relationship between performance and environmental actions might be mediated by environmental attitudes.

Nevertheless, a plausible conclusion from this analysis is that scientific knowledge and skills are not enough on their own to activate students' environmental agency. Rather, it is the combination of science proficiency and pro-environmental attitudes that is conducive to action. Additional data and further research are needed to fully understand the complex interactions between performance, environmental attitudes and actions.

Box 4.3. **Youth taking action for the environment: #FridaysForFuture and Extinction Rebellion**

One of the environmental actions PISA asked 15-year-olds about in 2018 was whether they participated in activities in favour of environmental protection (Action 5). This could include everything from volunteering for plastic clean-up campaigns of public spaces to something that ignited into a global, generational movement the year students sat the PISA test: peaceful climate strikes and mass environmental protests. On 20 August 2018, the then-15-year-old Swedish activist Greta Thunberg skipped Friday classes to do a lone sit-in in front of the Swedish parliament. Her "school strike for climate" set in motion an unprecedented wave of protests around the world among her fellow Generation Z students (born after 1995). Since November 2018, #FridaysForFuture (FFF) has mobilised about 18 million young climate strikers in over 200 countries, according to data collected by FFF from reports of local organisers. FFF calls for global adherence to the Paris Agreement and warming to be kept under 1.5°C.

Young people have been active in another climate movement, Extinction Rebellion (XR), as well. In February 2019, they formed an influential wing of XR – XR Youth – aimed at activists under 26 who are often as young as 10. They frame the climate-change problematic as one that requires systemic change and solidarity between the Global North and Global South: debt forgiveness for countries on the front line of climate upheaval is one of their concerns. At the core of their demands is zero carbon emissions by 2025.

Where FFF strikers sacrifice classtime to demonstrate against governments they feel are not moving fast enough on climate change issues, XR Youth favours non-violent civil disobedience tactics. Temporary obstructions like stopping traffic and blockading oil depots, and door-knocking campaigns to invite people to local talks on climate change are part of the XR Youth repertory. Both movements combine social media organising and decentralised local-global structuring with creative on-the-ground climate change action. As PISA 2018 data was collected before these and other youth climate activist movements hit their stride, little or none of these activities are reflected in Action 5. If these campaigns continue, however, they will be captured in PISA 2025 data.

Sources: https://fridaysforfuture.org, https://extinctionrebellion.uk/

Figure 4.10 **Environmental sense-of-purpose and student participation in activities in favour of environmental protection**

Increased likelihood of participating in activities in favour of environmental protection for students with environmental sense-of-purpose, relative to students without it, after accounting for other environmental attitudes and student characteristics

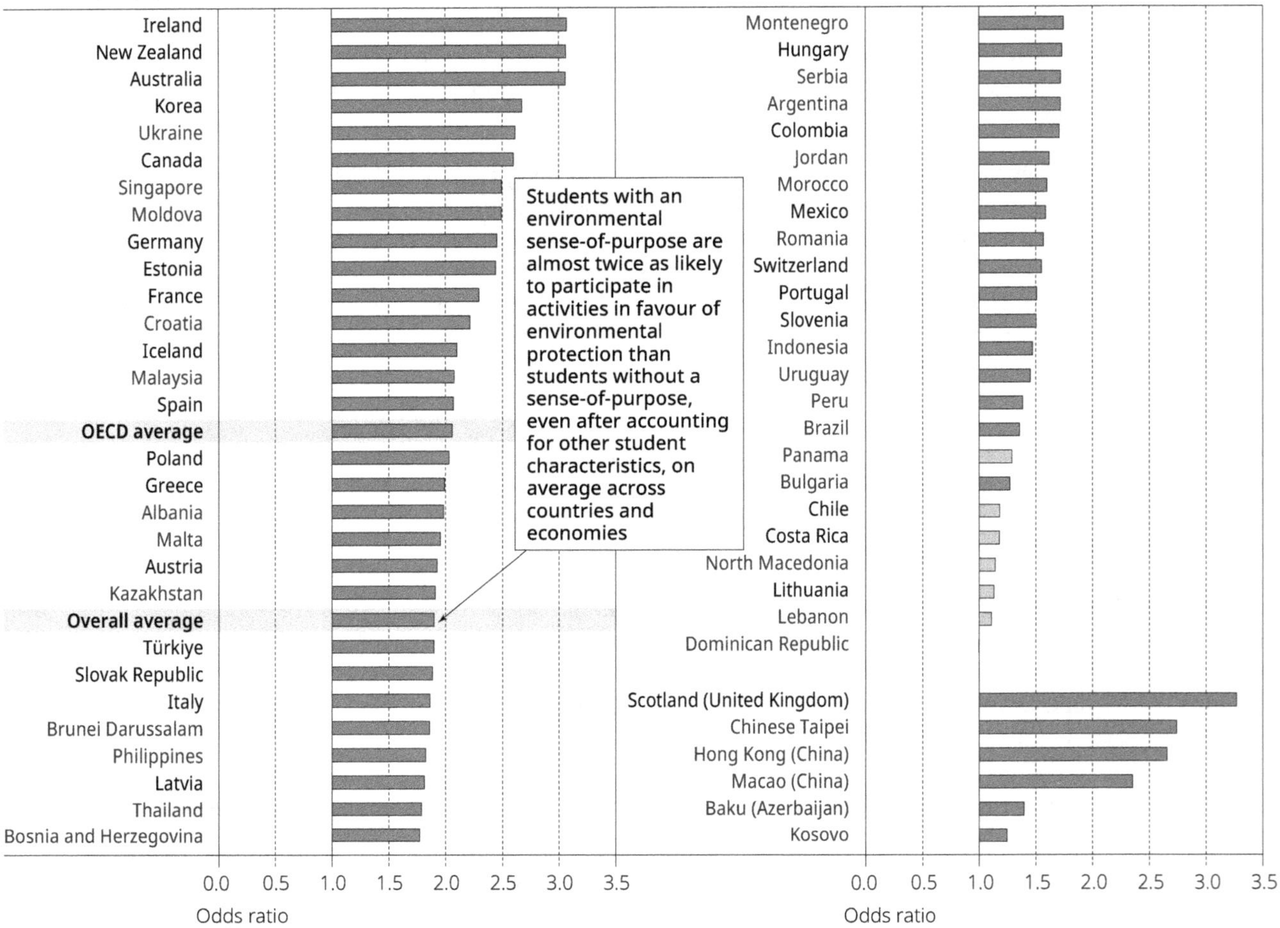

Note: Results come from a logistic regression predicting whether a student responded Yes or No to the statement "I participate in activities in favour of environmental protection". As predictors, the model includes the following variables: environmental sense-of-purpose, environmental awareness, self-efficacy in environmental understanding, science proficiency, socio-economic status and gender.

Countries and economies are ranked in descending order of the likelihood of students participating in favour of environmental protection.

Source: OECD, PISA 2018 Database, Table B.4.15.

StatLink https://stat.link/h37ufk

MISALIGNMENTS BETWEEN ENVIRONMENTAL ATTITUDES AND ACTIONS

Pro-environmental attitudes are correlated with acting for the environment. Still, not all students who sympathise with environmental issues take action. This section explores misalignments between environmental attitudes and environmental actions; that is, when students who possess pro-environmental attitudes do not take part in environmental actions (hereafter, environmental misalignment). How much environmental misalignment is there across PISA-participating countries/economies? Which students show sense-of-purpose, awareness, and self-efficacy regarding climate change but do not take part in environmental actions? And what can students, schools and parents do to help young people turn their environmental convictions into action on climate change?

If one considers environmental attitudes and environmental actions separately, 15 types of environmental misalignment can be examined, as shown in Table 4.2. The most common types of misalignment on average across countries and economies are the following: students who are environmentally aware but do not sign environmental or social petitions online (54%) or do not boycott products or companies for political, ethical or environmental reasons (52%); students who show self-efficacy in environmental understanding but do not sign environmental or social petitions online (43%) or do not boycott products or companies for political, ethical or environmental reasons (41%).

The least common types of misalignment on average across countries and economies are related to environmental sense-of-purpose. The shares of misalignment for students who show environmental sense-of-purpose are no higher than 15% in any of the environmental actions examined in PISA 2018.

Table 4.2 also shows that signing environmental or social petitions online and boycotting products or companies for political, ethical or environmental reasons show more misalignment than other actions. This may be because both are perceived as more difficult and demanding than other actions; there are also more obstacles as students need to find boycotts and petitions organised by others. Lastly, boycotts and petitions may be characterised by greater misalignment because these actions, as measured in PISA, are motivated not just by environmental reasons but social, ethical and political ones as well.

Table 4.2 **Types of misalignment between student environmental attitudes and environmental actions**

Percentage of students who endorse a pro-environmental attitude but do not take part in an environmental action (Overall average)

	Students who show environmental...		
	...awareness but do not...	...self-efficacy but do not...	...sense-of-purpose but do not...
...reduce the energy they use at home to protect the environment	20%	16%	8%
...choose certain products for ethical or environmental reasons, even if they are a bit more expensive	36%	29%	13%
...sign environmental or social petitions online	54%	43%	15%
...boycott products or companies for political, ethical or environmental reasons	52%	41%	15%
...participate in activities in favour of environmental protection	39%	30%	13%

Source: OECD, PISA 2018 Database, Tables B.4.17, B.4.21 and B.4.25.

Enthusiastic but uninvolved students

An additional type of misalignment – arguably the most important in terms of policy – is that of students who are environmentally enthusiastic but nevertheless do not take environmental action. "Environmentally enthusiastic" students are defined in Chapter 3 as students who have environmental sense-of-purpose and awareness, and self-efficacy in environmental understanding; that is, the three environmental attitudes measured in PISA 2018.

The share of environmentally enthusiastic students who does not act varies depending on the environmental action, as shown in Figure 4.11. Some 22% of environmentally enthusiastic students do not save energy at home to protect the environment; a little less than 50% do not choose products for ethical or environmental reasons or do not participate in activities in favour of environmental protection; and more than 65% do not boycott companies or products or do not sign online petitions.

Strikingly, around 8% of environmentally enthusiastic students are entirely uninvolved in environmental action – though they have a robust set of pro-environmental attitudes they do not do anything for the environment as far as PISA 2018 can measure (Figure 4.11).

Environmental misalignment and significant others: peers at school and parents

Understanding why a student is environmentally enthusiastic but does not act on climate change is important from a policy perspective for two reasons. If some of the factors associated are considered malleable by policy makers and educators, it would be possible to make changes that encourage student participation in environmental actions. Secondly, understanding the background of environmentally misaligned students can better target policy efforts on groups and schools where the probability of misalignment is greatest.

When it comes to malleable factors associated with individual environmental misalignment, the most consistent factor across environmental actions is the extent to which other students in the school are involved in environmental actions. The probability of misalignment among environmentally enthusiastic students is lower for students enrolled in schools where students are involved in more environmental actions.

To measure the incidence of environmental participation at school, the average number of environmental actions that students in a school take part in was computed. This was 1.7 actions on average across countries and economies. In some countries it was as low as 1.1 actions (France, Germany, Ireland, Italy, Scotland (United Kingdom) and Uruguay). In others it was as high as 2.5 or more (Indonesia, Jordan, Thailand, Türkiye and Viet Nam) (Table B.4.31).

Figure 4.11 **Misalignment between environmentally enthusiastic students and environmental actions**

Percentage of students who report having environmental sense-of-purpose, awareness and self-efficacy in environmental understanding but do not take part in environmental actions; overall average

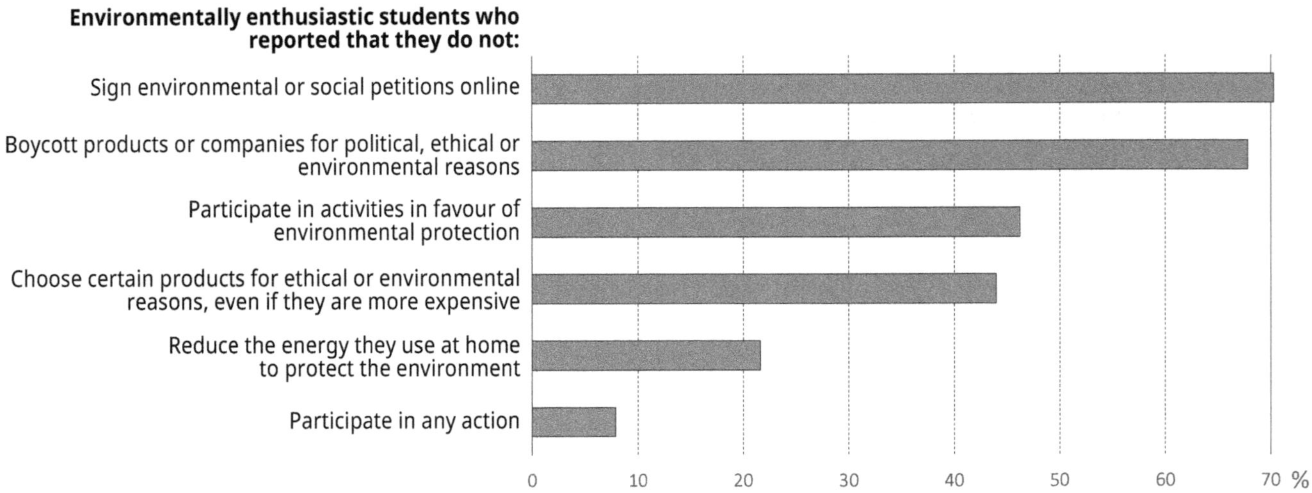

Actions are ranked in descending order of the percentage of students.

Source: OECD, PISA 2018 Database, Tables B.4.32 and B.4.38.

StatLink https://stat.link/q21cpo

As shown in Figure 4.12, students in schools where the average number of environmental actions that students take part in is three or more are about 60% less likely to *not* take part in each environmental action, after accounting for student characteristics such as proficiency level in science, socio-economic status, gender and other characteristics on average across countries and economies. Students in schools where the average number of environmental actions that students take part in is two are about 30% less likely to *not* take part in each environmental action after accounting for student characteristics, on average across countries and economies.

These results suggest that friends and peers at school are an important social network for 15-year-old students. They share information on environmental issues, encouragement, and concrete opportunities to become active participants. Research shows that social networks are good predictors of individual participation in social movements because they can create an initial disposition to participate, be a source of information and motivation for taking action, and also shaping a prospective participant decision to become involved (Diani, 2007[19]; Passy and Giugni, 2001[25]). Furthermore, social networks determine whether someone becomes the target of mobilisation attempts; in other words, whether a student has the opportunity to participate in actions organised by external agents (Klandermans, 2007[18]).

Parents' pro-environmental attitudes and actions is another factor that works against environmental misalignment. As shown in Figure 4.13, for each environmental action there is at least one parental environmental attitude or action that makes environmental misalignment less likely. Environmentally enthusiastic students whose parents save energy at home are about 55% less likely to *not* save energy at home themselves, and about 20% less likely to *not* participate in activities in favour of environmental protection after accounting for student characteristics on average across countries and economies. Similarly, environmentally enthusiastic students whose parents take part in boycotts are about 30% less likely *not* to sign environmental petitions online and about 42% less likely *not* take part in boycotts themselves after accounting for student characteristics on average across countries and economies.

The intergenerational transmission of pro-environmental values from parents to children can explain these results. Research on political participation has found that growing up in families with a given set of political attitudes and behaviours can nourish their children's attitudes and behaviours (Snow A. and Soule, 2010[5]). In particular, conversations about politics in the family, as well as joint participation (e.g. parent taking children to collective actions when they were younger), have been identified as mechanisms for intergenerational transmission of participation in collective actions (Cornejo et al., 2020[26]). Similarly, parents' ideas and experiences regarding environmental issues can be resonating socialisation experiences for their children. Similar to peers in school, parents are significant others whose values, expectations and behaviours can shape students' decisions about whether or not to act for the environment. They play an important role in whether environmentally enthusiastic students make the transition from "sympathiser" to "participant" (Klandermans, 2007[18]) or not.

Figure 4.12 **Environmentally enthusiastic students who do not take part in environmental actions, by average involvement in environmental actions among students in school**

Increased likelihood of students not taking part in each environmental action, for environmentally enthusiastic students in schools where the average number of environmental actions students are involved in is greater than one, after accounting for student characteristics[1]; overall average

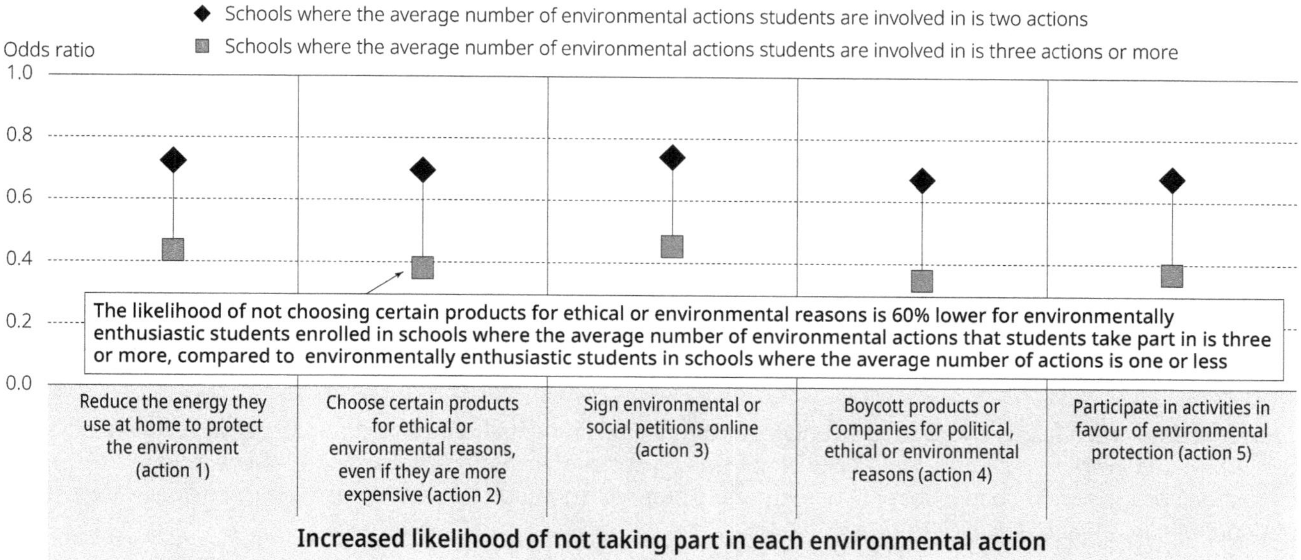

Note: Odds ratio are all statistically significant.

1. Student characteristics include the following variables: student socio-economic status, gender, growth mindset, fear of failure, and proficiency level in science.

Source: OECD, PISA 2018 Database, Table B.4.40.

StatLink https://stat.link/7m5bt2

Figure 4.13 **Environmentally enthusiastic students who do not take part in environmental actions, by parents' environmental attitudes and actions**

Increased likelihood of students' not taking part in each environmental action, for environmentally enthusiastic students with environmentally aware parents or parents who take environmental actions, after accounting for student characteristics[1]; overall average

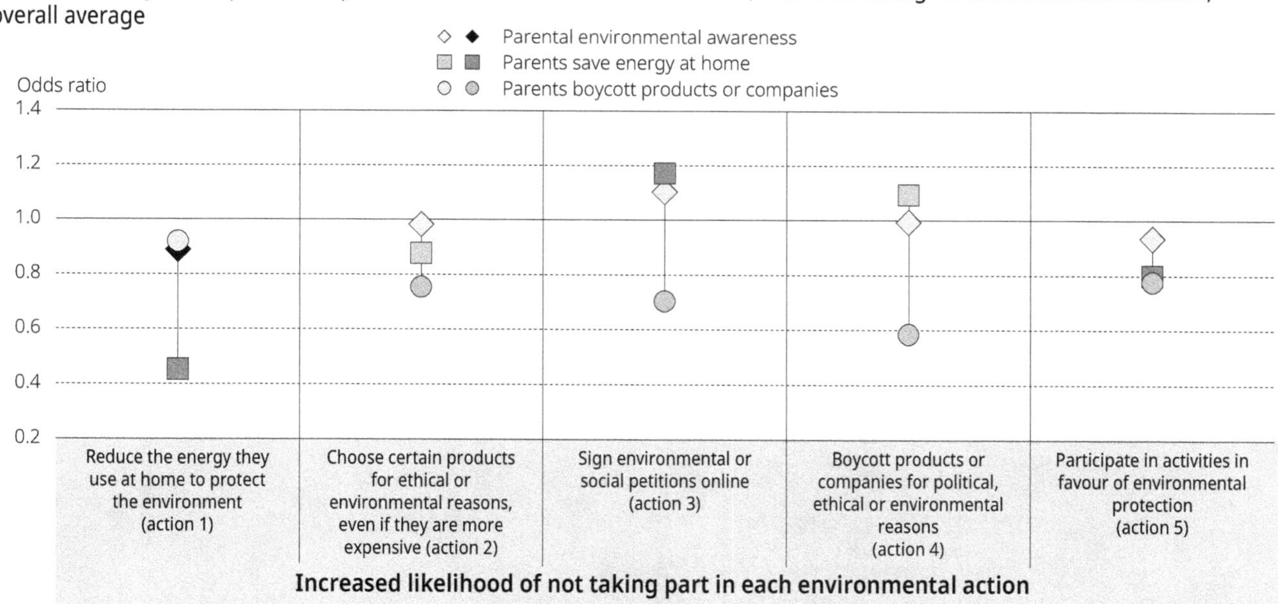

Note: Odds ratio that are statistically significant are shown in a darker colour.

1. Student characteristics include the following variables: student socio-economic status, gender, growth mindset, fear of failure, average number of environmental actions that students in the school take part in and proficiency level in science. The odds ratio for parental environmental awareness also account for parents saving energy at home and parents boycotting products or companies. The odds ratio for each parental environmental action also account for parental environmental awareness and for the other parental environmental action.

Source: OECD, PISA 2018 Database, Table B.4.41.

StatLink https://stat.link/2y79el

Environmental misalignment and fear of failure /growth mindset

PISA 2018 collected data on fear of failure and growth mindset that are potentially related to whether students' environmental enthusiasm translates into action.

Fear of failure[3] is the tendency to avoid mistakes that may be regarded as shameful or could signal a lack of innate ability and an uncertain future (Atkinson, 1957[27]; Conroy, Willow and Metzler, 2002[28]). The level of fear is determined by the perceived risk of failure in a given activity or task, but also by the perceived negative consequences associated with failing (Warr, 2000[29]). A moderate sense of fear may urge students to expend greater effort on academic tasks; however, students who are overly concerned about failing often avoid challenging situations that are essential for their personal growth (Kaye, Conroy and Fifer, 2008[30]). Given these characteristics, students with greater fear of failure may be more inclined to avoid acting for the environment than students with less fear of failure.

PISA data support this expectation for three out of the five environmental actions examined in this report. As shown in Figure 4.14, environmentally enthusiastic students with the most fear of failure are about 20% more likely than those with the least fear of failure to *not* save energy at home. They are about 7% more likely than students with the lowest fear of failure not to choose certain products for environmental reasons and *not* to participate in activities in favour of environmental protection after accounting for student characteristics on average across countries and economies.

Additional data and analysis are needed to understand why environmentally enthusiastic students with a greater fear of failure have, on average, a smaller probability of not signing social or environmental petitions online (odd ratio=-0.79) or boycotting products or companies for environmental and other reasons (odd ratio=0.79) than environmentally enthusiastic students with less fear of failure.

A growth mindset[4], as opposed to a fixed mindset, is the belief in the malleability of ability and intelligence. It is one possible explanation why some people fulfil their potential while others do not (Dweck, 2006[31]). Holding a growth mindset is associated with a number of positive attributes in the learning context, such as setting more challenging learning goals; appreciating effort as an inherent part of the process; and more perseverance in the face of setbacks. PISA 2018 data also showed a positive relationship between students' growth mindsets and performance as well as with motivational measures (OECD, 2021[32]). Because of these features, students with a growth mindset might be expected to be more inclined to act for the environment than students without a growth mindset.

Figure 4.14 **Environmentally enthusiastic students who do not take part in environmental actions, by students' fear of failure and growth mindset**

Increased likelihood of students not taking part in each environmental action, for environmentally enthusiastic students who hold a growth mindset or have high fear of failure, after accounting for student characteristics[1]; overall average

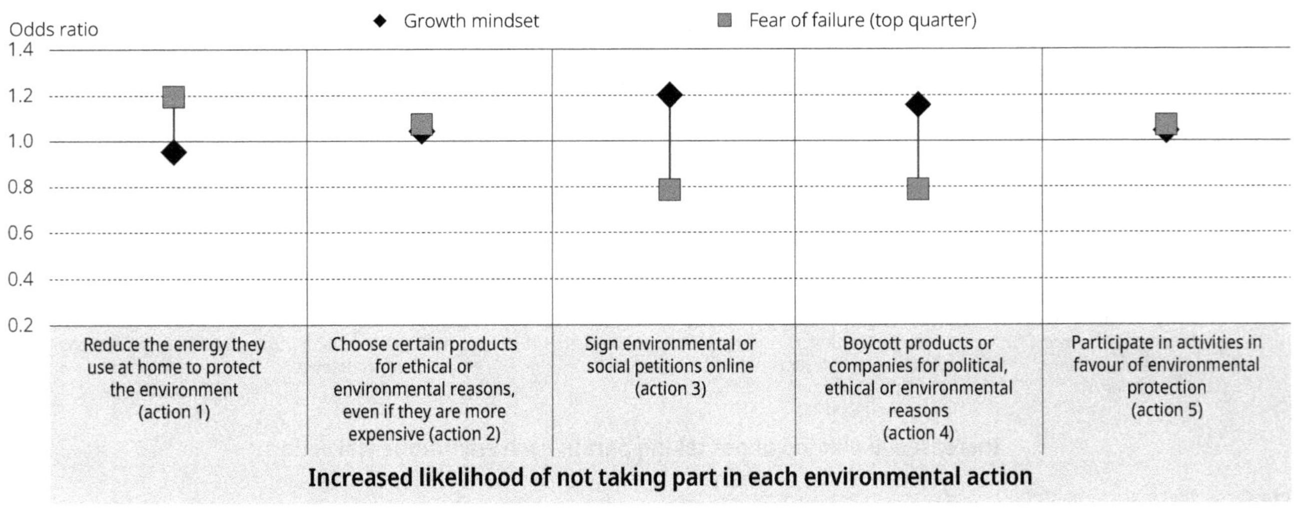

Note: Odds ratio are all statistically significant.

1. Student characteristics include the following variables: student socio-economic status, gender, average number of environmental actions that students in the school take part in (3 categories: less than 2 actions, 2 actions, 3 or more actions) and proficiency level in science. The odds ratio for fear of failure also account for growth mindset. The odds ratio for growth mindset also account for fear of failure.

Source: OECD, PISA 2018 Database, Table B.4.40.

StatLink https://stat.link/6iakrx

PISA data support this expectation for only one of the five environmental actions examined in this report. As shown in Figure 4.14, environmentally enthusiastic students with a growth mindset are 5% less likely than environmentally enthusiastic students without a growth mindset *not* to reduce the energy they us at home to protect the environment after accounting for student characteristics on average across countries and economies. For the remaining 4 actions, growth mindset is related with a greater probability of environmental misalignment. More data and analysis are needed to understand these patterns.

Environmental misalignment, proficiency in science and student background

Figure 4.15 shows that the odds of not saving energy among environmentally enthusiastic students who score in science at proficiency Levels 5 and 6 (i.e. top performers) are smaller than the odds of misalignment for environmentally enthusiastic students who do not reach the baseline proficiency Level 2 in science (i.e. low performers) (odds ratio=0.72). This finding suggests that higher levels of knowledge and skills in science have the potential to reduce environmental misalignment. However, this doesn't happen often.

In four out of the five environmental actions examined in this report, the opposite relationship is found, i.e. the odds of misalignment are higher among top performers than low performers. For example, environmentally enthusiastic top-performing students are about 2.7 times more likely to *not* sign environmental or social petitions online, and nearly 2 times more likely *not* to boycott products and companies than environmentally enthusiastic low-performing students after accounting for student characteristics on average across countries and economies.

Environmentally enthusiastic students who are socio-economically disadvantaged are more likely *not* to act for the environment than environmentally enthusiastic advantaged students. This holds for four out of the five actions examined in this report. For example, advantaged students are about 34% less likely than disadvantaged students *not* to choose certain products for ethical or environmental reasons even if they are more expensive (Figure 4.15 and Table B.4.40). Only when it comes to saving energy at home is the probability of environmental misalignment the same for both socio-economic groups.

No clear pattern of association across actions is found in terms of gender. For actions 1, 2 and 5 girls are less likely to show environmental misalignment. However, when it comes to boycotting companies or products and signing petitions online environmentally enthusiastic girls are more likely *not* to act than environmentally enthusiastic boys (Figure 4.15).

In sum, there is a high level of heterogeneity in the academic and demographic profile of environmentally enthusiastic students who do not perform different types of action.

Environmental misalignment and school curriculum

The likelihood of environmental misalignment does not vary between students enrolled in schools that have a formal curriculum on climate change and global warming, and students in schools that don't have a formal curriculum on these topics, on average across countries and economies and in almost all countries and economies (Table B.4.42). In other words, for each of the environmental actions measured in this report, the odds of environmentally enthusiastic students *not* taking action for the environment are, on average, the same regardless of whether they are enrolled in a school that has or doesn't have a formal curriculum on climate change.

These results must be interpreted with caution. They do not necessarily mean that climate change curriculum at school is unrelated to environmental actions. In fact, climate change curriculum at school is related (even if not strongly) to student pro-environmental attitudes, which, in turn, are related to action. An important limitation of this analysis is that PISA data only measures if climate change and global warming are covered in the school curriculum based on school principals' reports; it does not measure what this school curriculum looks like and, more importantly, how it is carried out in the classroom. Research suggests that implementation of environmental education varies dramatically at the local level and is shaped by domestic forces (Pizmony-Levy, 2011[33]). Better data is needed to understand the true relationship between environmental curriculum at school and students' environmental actions.

Figure 4.15 **Environmentally enthusiastic students who do not take part in environmental actions, by proficiency in science, socio-economic status and gender**

Increased likelihood of students not taking part in each environmental action, for environmentally enthusiastic students who score at middle and top levels of proficiency in science, socio-economically advantaged students and girls, after accounting for student characteristics[1]; overall average

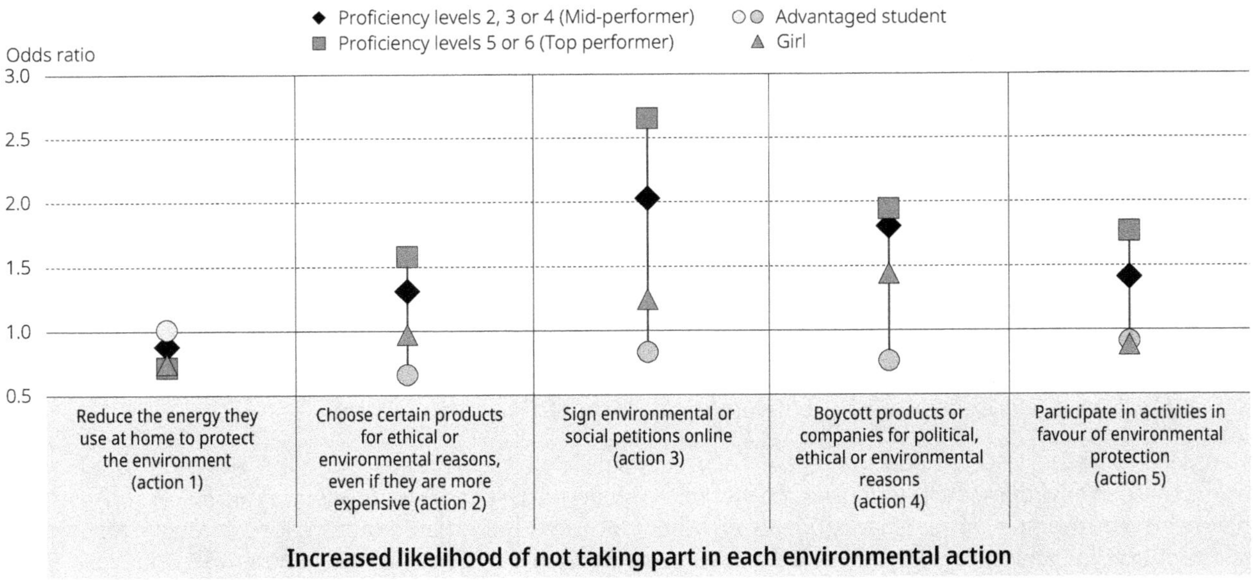

Note: Odds ratio that are statistically significant are shown in a darker colour.

1. Student characteristics include the following variables: growth mindset, fear of failure, and average number of environmental actions that students in the school take part in (3 categories: less than 2 actions, 2 actions, 3 or more actions). Odds ratio for science proficiency also account for student socio-economic status and gender. Odds ratio for socio-economic status also account for student science proficiency and gender. Odds ratio for girls also account for student science proficiency and socio-economic status.

Source: OECD, PISA 2018 Database, Table B.4.40.

StatLink https://stat.link/1h5rjf

POLICY IMPLICATIONS FROM THIS CHAPTER

Being prepared for today's environmental challenges requires young people to have solid scientific skills and knowledge. It requires confidence in one's environmental understanding, awareness of the issues and a sense of stewardship of the planet. But all of this is not enough if they do not translate into students responsibly acting on climate change. What the findings in this chapter reveal is that scientific knowledge and skills do not always lead to action; the share of students who perform well in science but do not act for the environment is considerable. Still, better performers have, on average, more pro-environmental attitudes than lower-performing students, and students with pro-environmental attitudes are more likely to act for the environment. It is the combination of science proficiency and pro-environmental attitudes that galvanises action. If schools help students find an environmental sense-of-purpose, this can mobilise their knowledge and propel them into action.

A clear finding of this chapter is that pro-environmental attitudes are a good predictor of student involvement in environmental actions. Students with an environmental sense-of-purpose, in particular, are more likely to carry out different types of environmental actions. This is good news because, on average, some 8 out of 10 students reported that they care about the environment. But this sense-of-purpose is unevenly distributed in terms of socio-economics and gender: students who are girls and/or socio-economically advantaged are more likely to have an environmental sense-of-purpose than those who are boys and/or socio-economically disadvantaged. More efforts are needed to target these groups.

Though an environmental sense-of-purpose on its own is a powerful motivator for action, it is students with a combination of different pro-environmental attitudes, values and beliefs who are more likely to act. This report shows that environmental awareness and self-efficacy in environmental understanding also nudge students toward acting on climate change.

The report also points out a worrying phenomenon called environmental misalignment. This occurs when students are enthusiastic about environmental issues but do not take action to protect the environment. By identifying the factors associated with misalignment, this report highlights what educators and policy makers can do.

Significantly, environmental misalignment is less likely to occur when students are in close contact with school peers or parents involved in environmental actions. This suggests that environmental education initiatives that target school communities as a whole and not just individuals are promising.

There are important differences between types of environmental actions. When acting for the environment is easy, such as reducing energy use at home, students who are proficient at science and have pro-environmental attitudes are more likely to do so. This is why saving energy is popular and the misalignment between attitudes and energy saving is comparatively rare. When there are more obstacles and demands in an environmental action – such as signing environmental or social petitions online – it is harder to transform science skills and pro-environmental attitudes into action. This is why signing environmental or social petitions online and boycotting products or companies for environmental or other reasons are less popular and why the misalignment between attitudes and actions is greater.

The likelihood of student misalignment in terms of socio-economic status, gender, science performance, growth mindset or fear of failure depends on which type of environmental action is being looked at. Put another way, to better align students' pro-environmental attitudes with actual environmental action requires targeting a specific sub-group and using a specific intervention, both of which depend on which action is desired. For example, when it comes to saving energy at home, environmentally enthusiastic girls are less likely *not* to do this than environmentally enthusiastic boys, but the opposite is true of boycotting companies or products and signing petitions online. Similarly, socio-economically disadvantaged students are more likely *not* to choose certain products even if they are more expensive than environmentally enthusiastic advantaged students but no differences in socio-economic background are observed when the action is reducing energy at home. Further research is needed to better understand the mechanism behind these observed differences. The bottom line is that a "universal" intervention for all kinds of environmental action will not work well. Understanding these differences is important to foster responsible student participation in climate and environmental action.

Notes

1. Some online petitions allow people who sign them to choose between making their name public or not. PISA 2018 data does not allow distinguishing between the two. The exposure to criticism or online harassment would certainly be minimal for students who choose not to make their name public in the petition.

2. Consistent with these findings, a separate analysis of PISA data that used a slightly different model specification than the one used in this report found an average negative relationship between student performance in science and engagement in environmental actions (Borgonovi et al., 2022[34]).

3. To measure fear of failure, PISA 2018 asked students whether they agreed ("strongly disagree", "disagree", "agree", "strongly agree") with the following statements about themselves: "When I am failing, I worry about what others think of me"; "When I am failing, I am afraid that I might not have enough talent"; and "When I am failing, this makes me doubt my plans for the future". These statements were combined to create the index of fear of failure whose average is 0 and standard deviation is 1 across OECD countries. Positive values in this index mean that the student reported a greater fear of failure than the average student in OECD countries.

4. To measure growth mindset, PISA 2018 asked students whether they agreed ("strongly disagree", "disagree", "agree", "strongly agree") with the following statement: "Your intelligence is something about you that you can't change very much". Students who disagreed with the statement are considered to have a stronger growth mindset than students who agreed with the statement.

References

Aoyagi-Usui, M., H. Vinken and A. Kuribayashi (2003), "Pro-environmental attitudes and behaviors: An international comparison", *Human Ecology Review*, Vol. 10/1, pp. 23–31. [23]

Atkinson, J. (1957), "Motivational determinants of risk-taking behavior.", *Psychological Review*, Vol. 64/6, Pt.1, pp. 359-372, https://doi.org/10.1037/h0043445. [27]

Berglund, T. et al. (2019), "A cross-cultural comparative study of sustainability consciousness between students in Taiwan and Sweden", *Environment, Development and Sustainability*, Vol. 22/7, pp. 6287-6313, https://doi.org/10.1007/s10668-019-00478-2. [21]

Borgonovi, F. et al. (2022), "The environmental sustainability competence toolbox: From leaving a better planet for our children to leaving better children for our planet", *OECD Social, Employment and Migration Working Papers*, No. 275, OECD Publishing, Paris, https://doi.org/10.1787/27991ec0-en. [34]

Brulle, R. and M. Aronczyk (2019), *Environmental countermovements. Organised opposition to climate change action in the United States,* Routledge. [9]

Conroy, D., J. Willow and J. Metzler (2002), "Multidimensional Fear of Failure Measurement: The Performance Failure Appraisal Inventory", *Journal of Applied Sport Psychology*, Vol. 14/2, pp. 76-90, https://doi.org/10.1080/10413200252907752. [28]

Cornejo, M. et al. (2020), "The intergenerational transmission of participation in collective action: The role of conversation and political practices in the family", *British Journal of Social Psychology*, Vol. 60/1, pp. 29-49, https://doi.org/10.1111/bjso.12420. [26]

Diani, M. (2007), "Networks and Participation", in *The Blackwell Companion to Social Movements*, Blackwell Publishing Ltd, Oxford, UK, https://doi.org/10.1002/9780470999103.ch15. [19]

Dweck, C. (2006), Mindset: The new psychology of success, Random House. [31]

Elliott, T. et al. (2022), "Softer Policing or the Institutionalization of Protest? Decomposing Changes in Observed Protest Policing over Time", *American Journal of Sociology*, Vol. 127/4, pp. 1311-1365, https://doi.org/10.1086/719001. [14]

Freudenburg, W., R. Gramling and D. Davidson (2008), "Scientific Certainty Argumentation Methods (SCAMs): Science and the Politics of Doubt*", *Sociological Inquiry*, Vol. 78/1, pp. 2-38, https://doi.org/10.1111/j.1475-682x.2008.00219.x. [10]

Greenberg, J., G. Knight and E. Westersund (2011), "Spinning climate change: Corporate and NGO public relations strategies in Canada and the United States", *International Communication Gazette*, Vol. 73/1-2, pp. 65-82, https://doi.org/10.1177/1748048510386742. [11]

Habermas, J. (1991), *The structural transformation of the public sphere: An inquiry into a category of bourgeois society*, MIT press. [6]

Hoffmann, S. (2014), "Does national culture impact consumer boycott prevalence? A multi-country study", *European J. of International Management*, Vol. 8/2, p. 141, https://doi.org/10.1504/ejim.2014.059580. [22]

Kaye, M., D. Conroy and A. Fifer (2008), "Individual Differences in Incompetence Avoidance", *Journal of Sport and Exercise Psychology*, Vol. 30/1, pp. 110-132, https://doi.org/10.1123/jsep.30.1.110. [30]

Klandermans, B. (2007), "The Demand and Supply of Participation: Social-Psychological Correlates of Participation in Social Movements", in *The Blackwell Companion to Social Movements*, Blackwell Publishing Ltd, Oxford, UK, https://doi.org/10.1002/9780470999103.ch16. [18]

Kruse, L., D. Norris and J. Flinchum (2017), "Social Media as a Public Sphere? Politics on Social Media", *The Sociological Quarterly*, Vol. 59/1, pp. 62-84, https://doi.org/10.1080/00380253.2017.1383143. [7]

McCarthy, J. and C. McPhail (1998), "The Instituitionalization of Protest in the United States", *The Social Movement Society: Contentious Politics for the New Centuy*, [13]

McCarthy, J. and M. Zald (1977), "Resource Mobilization and Social Movements: A Partial Theory", *American Journal of Sociology*, Vol. 82/6, pp. 1212–41. [17]

Milfont, T. and C. Sibley (2012), "The big five personality traits and environmental engagement: Associations at the individual and societal level", *Journal of Environmental Psychology*, Vol. 32/2, pp. 187-195, https://doi.org/10.1016/j.jenvp.2011.12.006. [1]

Munck af Rosenschöld, J., J. Rozema and L. Frye-Levine (2014), "Institutional inertia and climate change: a review of the new institutionalist literature", *Wiley Interdisciplinary Reviews: Climate Change*, Vol. 5/5, pp. 639-648, https://doi.org/10.1002/wcc.292. [4]

Nguyen, T. et al. (2018), "Understanding the Motivations Influencing Ecological Boycott Participation: An Exploratory Study in Viet Nam", *Sustainability*, Vol. 10/12, p. 4786, https://doi.org/10.3390/su10124786. [20]

OECD (2021), *Sky's the limit: Growth mindset, students, and schools in PISA,* OECD Publishing. [32]

OECD (2020), *PISA 2024 Strategic Vision and Direction for Science,* https://www.oecd.org/pisa/publications/PISA-2024-Science-Strategic-Vision-Proposal.pdf. [3]

OECD (2018), *Preparing our youth for an inclusive and sustainable world: The OECD PISA global competence framework.*, OECD Publising, https://www.oecd.org/pisa/Handbook-PISA-2018-Global-Competence.pdf. [2]

OECD (2014), "Does Homework Perpetuate Inequities in Education?", *PISA in Focus,* No. 46, OECD Publishing, Paris, https://doi.org/10.1787/5jxrhqhtx2xt-en. [24]

Passy, F. and M. Giugni (2001), "Social Networks and Individual Perceptions: Explaining Differential Participation in Social Movements", *Sociological Forum*, Vol. 16/1, pp. 123-153, https://doi.org/10.1023/a:1007613403970. [25]

Pew Research Center (2021), *The State of Online Harassment.* [8]

Pizmony-Levy, O. (2011), "Bridging the Global and Local in Understanding Curricula Scripts: The Case of Environmental Education", *Comparative Education Review*, Vol. 55/4, pp. 600-633, https://doi.org/10.1086/661632. [33]

Porta, D. and H. Reiter (1998), "Introduction: The Policing of Protest in Western Democracies", in della Porta, D. and H. Reiter (eds.), *Policing Protest: The Control of Mass Demonstrations in Western Democracies,* University of Minnesota Press, https://doi.org/10.5749/j.ctttv1tv.3. [16]

Rootes, C. (2016), *Environmental Movements.*, John Wiley & Sons, Ltd, Oxfod, UK, https://doi.org/10.1002/9781405165518.wbeose054.pub2. [12]

Scheidel, A. et al. (2020), "Environmental conflicts and defenders: A global overview", *Global Environmental Change*, Vol. 63, p. 102104, https://doi.org/10.1016/j.gloenvcha.2020.102104. [15]

Snow A., D. and S. Soule (2010), *A Primer on Social Movements*, W.W. Norton. [5]

Warr, M. (2000), "Fear of crime in the United States: Avenues for research and policy", *Criminal Justice*, Vol. 4, pp. 451-489. [29]

5

Preparing students to build a sustainable future: Implications for policy, practices and research

Results from PISA 2018 show that countries and economies vary in how prepared their students are for the urgent environmental challenges that humanity is facing. Young people will experience the consequences of climate and environmental change more directly during their lifetime than any previous generation in recent history (Thiery et al., $2021_{[1]}$). Schools need to keep pace by preparing students with more robust, complex scientific knowledge and skills; and strengthening their pro-environmental attitudes and capacity to act.

This chapter summarises key results discussed in this report and identifies the types of education policy and practices that can help prepare students to build an environmentally sustainable future. Everybody has an important role to play: policy makers, teachers and educators, parents, and students themselves.

When reading these recommendations, bear in mind that PISA results do not establish causality. Rather, PISA identifies correlations between variables that show consistent patterns across countries and economies. By combining this correlational evidence with previous research it is possible to draw some implications for policy and practices. Note also that the data were collected in 2018 and that the percentage of students involved in environmental actions may have changed in recent years. However, the correlational results still shed light on how educators, parents and students themselves can enhance student readiness to take on environmental challenges.

STRENGTHEN STUDENT PROFICIENCY IN ENVIRONMENTAL SCIENCE

Students need stronger scientific knowledge of and skills in environmental issues than they currently have, especially in countries/economies where student performance in science tends to be lower. Whereas in some countries/economies (Canada, Hong Kong [China], Scotland [United Kingdom], Singapore, Spain and Chinese Taipei) half or more of students were able to respond correctly to a variety of PISA questions on environmental sustainability, in others only a minority of students were able to do so (Albania, Indonesia, Kazakhstan, Morocco, Panama and the Philippines). Low performance is more pronounced among lower-income countries/economies[1], some of which are also the most vulnerable to disruptions caused by climate change (IPCC, $2022_{[2]}$). Furthermore, analysis of student performance evolution in environmental science items shows no improvement between 2006 and 2015 in most countries/economies with available data.

One area educators could focus on is students' understanding of different responses to climate change. As shown in Chapter 2 of this report, many students could not adequately distinguish between short-term and long-term responses to the rise in sea levels caused by climate change[2]. While it is common knowledge to 15-year-old students that reducing greenhouse gases is a long-term solution to global warming, students misidentifying building sea defences as a long-term solution reveals a need for more complex and nuanced differentiation between combatting climate change and adaptation to its effects.

FOSTER PRO-ENVIRONMENTAL ATTITUDES AT SCHOOL

Pro-environmental attitudes are prevalent across countries and economies. Almost half of students in PISA 2018 are "environmentally enthusiastic", meaning that they reported having a sense of stewardship of the planet, awareness of climate change and confidence in their environmental understanding on average across countries and economies. However, there are still many students who reported that looking after the global environment is not important for them (more than 30% of students in Austria, Bosnia and Herzegovina, Germany, Serbia, Slovak Republic and Ukraine) and who report they know little or have never heard of climate change and global warming (more than 40% of students in Argentina, Indonesia, Lebanon, Morocco and Saudi Arabia). This shows that there is still room to boost adolescents' environmental attitudes and values.

Pro-environmental attitudes and science proficiency tend to reinforce each other: students' environmental science knowledge and skills, as measured by their performance in the PISA science test, are positively related to pro-environmental attitudes. Pro-environmental attitudes can foster curiosity and motivation for learning science; at the same time, scientific understanding of the environment lays the foundation for pro-environmental attitudes. In either case, basic science education for all students has the potential of improving the overall level of student proficiency in environmental science and student endorsement of pro-environmental attitudes.

At the national level, communicating information to the public on how climate policies work increases policy support (Dechezleprêtre et al., $2022_{[3]}$). Governments can use information campaigns to explain to students, and citizens in general, how climate policies reduce emissions and who can benefit from them.

FOSTER RESPONSIBLE ACTING FOR THE ENVIRONMENT AT AND OUTSIDE OF SCHOOL

As important as proficiency in environmental science and pro-environmental attitudes are, being prepared for today's environmental challenges also requires students to responsibly act on climate change. This report analysed five types of environmental actions that range from private individual actions that are relatively easy to carry out to public actions that are more challenging and require more effort (see Chapter 4). Results shows that, on average, about a fifth of students were "actively involved" in environmental actions (i.e. participated in four or five environmental actions) and a similar share of students were "entirely uninvolved" (i.e. did not participate in any environmental action considered in this report).

Many more students carry out easier actions such as reducing energy consumption at home to protect the environment than more demanding collective actions such as boycotting products or companies for environmental or other reasons and participating in activities in favour of environmental protection.

Findings in this report reveal that scientific knowledge and skills do not automatically lead to action; the share of students who perform well in science but who report not to act for the environment is considerable. Still, better performers have, on average, more pro-environmental attitudes than lower-performing students, and students with pro-environmental attitudes are more likely to act for the environment. It is the combination of science proficiency and pro-environmental attitudes that galvanises action.

If schools help students develop pro-environmental attitudes, this can mobilise their knowledge and propel them into action. Students with an environmental sense-of-purpose are more likely to carry out environmental actions. This is good news because, on average, some 8 out of 10 students reported that they care about the environment. A sense of purpose is a stable desire or intention to accomplish something that is meaningful to the self and has a beneficial impact on the world (Damon, Menon and Cotton Bronk, 2003[4]; Malin, Liauw and Damon, 2017[5]). Adolescents with a greater sense of purpose are more likely to engage in goal-directed activities, hopeful thinking and to report greater agency (Burrow, O'Dell and Hill, 2009[6]). Teachers can foster environmental sense-of-purpose with classroom opportunities for students to reflect on how taking care of the environment is meaningful to them and how their current actions for the environment are related to or aligned with their life goals and environmental concerns (Tirri, Moran and Menon Mariano, 2016[7])[3].

Furthermore, this report shows that environmental awareness and self-efficacy in environmental understanding also nudge students to act on climate change.

Schools can empower students to take environmental action by having them learn about climate action (e.g. the history of efforts to stop and mitigate climate change) and also by learning through and from action (UNESCO, 2016[8]). For example, students can be invited to carry out climate action projects at school, either in the classroom or after regular school hours in extracurricular activities, to make their school more "climate-friendly". Planting trees or bee forage plants in outdoors school facilities; recycling and composting garbage; and encouraging everybody in the school community to buy local products and use sustainable transport are examples of actions through which a school can model climate action.

ADDRESS THE MISALIGNMENT BETWEEN ENVIRONMENTAL ATTITUDES AND ACTIONS

The report points out a worrying phenomenon called environmental misalignment. This occurs when students are enthusiastic about environmental issues (as defined above) but report that they do not take action to protect the environment[4]. By identifying the factors associated with misalignment, this report highlights what educators and policy makers can do.

Significantly, environmental misalignment is less likely to occur when students are in close contact with school peers or parents involved in environmental actions. This suggests that environmental education initiatives that target school communities as a whole and not just individuals are promising.

There are important differences between types of environmental actions. When acting for the environment is relatively easy, such as reducing energy use at home, students who are proficient at science and have pro-environmental attitudes are more likely to do so. This is why saving energy is popular and the misalignment between attitudes and energy saving is comparatively rare.

When there are more obstacles and demands in an environmental action – such as signing environmental or social petitions online – it is harder to transform science skills and pro-environmental attitudes into action. This is why signing environmental or social petitions online and boycotting products or companies for environmental or other reasons are less popular and why the misalignment between attitudes and actions is greater.

The likelihood of student misalignment in terms of socio-economic status, gender, science performance, growth mindset or fear of failure depends on which type of environmental action is being looked at. Put another way, to better align students' pro-environmental attitudes with actual environmental action requires targeting a specific sub-group and using a specific intervention, both of which depend on which action is desired. For example, when it comes to saving energy at home, environmentally enthusiastic girls are less likely *not* to do this than environmentally enthusiastic boys but the opposite is true of boycotting companies or products and signing petitions online. Similarly, socio-economically disadvantaged students are more likely *not* to choose certain products even if they are more expensive than environmentally enthusiastic advantaged students but no differences in socio-economic background are observed when the action is reducing energy at home. Further research is needed to better understand the mechanism behind these observed differences.

Understanding these differences is important to fostering responsible student participation in climate and environmental action.

TEACHING AND LEARNING ENVIRONMENTAL ISSUES: CURRICULUM DESIGN AND IMPLEMENTATION

PISA 2018 data show that coverage of climate change in the formal or intended school curriculum is nearly universal in most countries and economies. The worldwide spread of environmental education in secondary education textbooks occurred between 1970 and the end of the 2000s (Bromley, Meyer and Ramirez, 2011[9]). A similar process occurred at the higher education level, where the prevalence of environmental education degree programmes in universities has increased markedly in the last decades (John Frank, Jeong Robinson and Olesen, 2011[10]).

The inclusion of climate change in the formal curriculum is important but not enough. While there are more environmentally enthusiastic students in schools that have climate change in the curriculum, the differences between schools that do and those that don't are not as large as could be expected. Greater attention should be paid to the implementation of the environmental curriculum in the classroom. For example, school principals and teachers, together with members of the school community, can develop concrete plans on how to implement the climate change curriculum in ways that are relevant to their local community. They can ensure that the learning environment at school is respectful and supportive of students and student organisations that are interested in environmental issues.

Furthermore, initiatives like UNESCO's Whole-School approach to climate change provide tools and examples of how students' classroom learning about climate change can be reinforced by the formal and informal messages promoted by the school's values and actions (UNESCO, 2016[8]). Such an approach consists of involving all internal and external school stakeholders, including students, teachers, principals, school staff as well as the wider school community of families and community members in reflecting and acting on climate change.

ENGAGING THE SCHOOL COMMUNITY: THE ROLE OF STUDENTS AS ENVIRONMENTAL PEERS

PISA 2018 results show that students are more likely to take part in environmental actions if they are enrolled in schools where other students are also involved in environmental actions. The extent to which other students in the school are involved in environmental actions is one the most consistent factors in preventing environmental misalignment. The probability of misalignment among environmentally enthusiastic students is lower for students enrolled in schools where students are involved in more environmental actions.

At school, friends and peers serve as social networks that share information on environmental issues, and provide encouragement and concrete opportunities for students to actively participate. Environmental activities at school that motivate not only individual engagement but the participation of groups of students and the entire student community are promising.

ENGAGING THE SCHOOL COMMUNITY: THE ROLE OF PARENTS AS ENVIRONMENTAL MENTORS

Parents play a key role in shaping their children's environmental attitudes and actions. PISA 2018 results show that students whose parents are environmentally aware, and students whose parents carry out environmentally conscious actions such as saving energy at home or boycotting products or companies for environmental or other reasons are more likely to be environmentally enthusiastic than students whose parents do not. Furthermore, the probability of environmental misalignment is lower among environmentally enthusiastic students whose parents take part in environmental actions.

Parents who talk to their children about the climate crisis and model environmentally conscious behaviour are likely to bring up more environmentally conscious children. School programmes that include parents in activities that inform them of climate change challenges and promote concrete actions to protect the environment are a promising policy. These school programmes can be reinforced by community efforts aimed at local environmental preservation.

Box 5.1. **Teaching for Climate Action**

From July 2021 to December 2021, the OECD, UNESCO and Education International ran the Teaching for Climate Action initiative to gather teacher expertise on what helps promote student agency and encourages students to act and lead on climate matters (OECD, 2022[11]).

Teachers from across the globe were invited to share their initiatives and projects through short video explainers in the Global Teaching InSights site, a digital platform with classroom videos that facilitates a unique dialogue on teaching and learning across borders. They participated in five global dialogues together with peers, teacher educators, school leaders, organisations, and climate experts. Overall, about 850 teachers actively contributed to this initiative, with engagement from more than 6 500 visitors across 157 countries. This box provides a summary of the main insights from this initiative.

Transforming climate education

Teachers and experts emphasised the importance of cultivating climate literacy as a foundational and critical requirement of climate education. This includes students' capacity to understand the causes and consequences of climate change, assess scientifically credible information about climate change, communicate about climate issues in a meaningful way to peers, teachers and parents, and make informed and responsible decisions with regards to actions that are related to climate.

There was common agreement among teachers, however, that knowledge alone is not enough and thus on the need to go beyond climate literacy to foster student awareness, agency and empowerment for climate action. To teachers teaching for climate action, student empowerment signified taking action, fostering hope, building knowledge and fighting for justice.

When teachers were asked about pedagogies they believed may be most effective for empowering students for action, they agreed that traditional teaching methods were not enough and recommended active and student-centred approaches such as project-based and experiential learning. In addition, teachers felt that climate education could be taught in different grades and subject areas through an interdisciplinary approach to help students develop a more comprehensive and nuanced understanding of climate change.

Source: OECD (2022), "Teaching for climate action", *Teaching in Focus*, No. 44, OECD Publishing, Paris, https://doi.org/10.1787/d3a72e77-en; https://www.globalteachinginsights.org/.

DEVELOP (GENERAL) SOCIAL AND EMOTIONAL SKILLS: FOSTERING A GROWTH MINDSET

PISA 2018 results show that environmental enthusiasm is greater among students who hold a growth mindset (the belief that intelligence is something they can change) rather than a fixed mindset. Students with a growth mindset are also more likely to save energy at home to protect the environment than students without a growth mindset.

Holding a growth mindset is associated with a number of positive attributes in the learning context, such as setting more challenging learning goals; appreciating effort as an inherent part of the process; and more perseverance in the face of setbacks. It is possible that because these students feel greater agency in their lives than those who believe they have a fixed mindset, they believe they can effect change in the world and combat the climate crisis. Policies that encourage pro-environmental attitudes would do well to include elements from growth-mindset interventions.

ENSURE THAT VULNERABLE GROUPS HAVE THE SUPPORT THEY NEED

The socio-economic gap in environmental science performance is pervasive across countries and economies, and persistent over time. Pro-environmental attitudes are also unevenly distributed: socio-economically advantaged students are more likely to have an environmental sense-of-purpose, environmental awareness, and self-efficacy in their environmental understanding than disadvantaged students. Furthermore, environmentally enthusiastic students who are socio-economically disadvantaged are more likely *not* to act for the environment than environmentally enthusiastic advantaged students.

Supporting the needs of socio-economically disadvantaged students is vital. These students are more likely to be affected by environmental degradation such as exposure to contaminated water and air but are less likely to have the resources to address these problems (Shepard and Corbin-Mark, 2009[12]). Taking steps to meet their concrete environmental needs while implementing educational programmes about the environment could be beneficial in two ways. Students would better understand how environmental crises impact their own local communities when they experience real improvements in their quality of life. Students would become better informed and feel more agency over their lives and the environment.

In terms of gender, environmental science performance is, on average, slightly higher among boys than girls but in many countries/economies boys and girls perform at similar levels. Special attention needs to be paid to girls in countries and economies that show a significant gender gap in favour of boys such as Chile, Denmark, the Slovak Republic and the United Kingdom, and to boys in countries such as Jordan and Qatar whose gap is in favour of girls.

Gender gaps also exist when it comes to pro-environmental attitudes. Girls are more likely on average to be environmentally enthusiastic than boys but in some countries/economies the opposite is true. More efforts are needed to target these groups and foster the participation of both girls and boys in environmental education and activities.

IMPROVE DATA ON STUDENTS' ENVIRONMENTAL COMPETENCES AND FOSTER PARTNERSHIP BETWEEN RESEARCH AND PRACTICE

The results presented in this report are part of an on-going effort by the OECD to provide high-quality information about student environmental skills, attitudes, and actions. PISA has collected data on student performance in environmental science since 2000. Building on what has been learned from analyses of past PISA data, PISA continues its efforts to collect relevant data that will contribute to students' preparedness for environmental challenges. PISA 2025 will feature an updated Science Framework, making student performance on environmental issues and environmental agency a central focus. In addition, further test items will be publicly released after 2025 to concretely describe what PISA is measuring and what students know and are able to do about climate change and the environment.

At the local level, a partnership between policy makers and researchers in the field of environmental and sustainability education can help develop evidence-based sustainability initiatives that improve school engagement (Pizmony-Levy, McDermott and Copeland, 2021[13]).

Notes

1. A recent PISA 2018 report analysed the relationship between national income, as measured by per capita GDP, and students' average reading performance (OECD, 2019[17]). Results suggest that 44% of the variation in countries'/economies' mean scores is related to per capita GDP (33% in OECD countries). Countries with higher national incomes thus tend to score higher in PISA, yet the relationship is non-linear, i.e. the correlation is stronger among countries /economies under a certain threshold after which the correlation weakens. Correlational data provides no indications about the causal nature of the relationship.

2. As a recent OECD report puts it: "Sea-level rise is one of the major challenges identified in the recent Intergovernmental Panel on Climate Change's Special Report "Global Warming of 1.5°C". It is almost certain that we will experience at least one metre of sea-level rise, with some models estimating this will happen within the next 80 years. This will have serious implications for damage to infrastructure, loss of land and displacement of communities. Even if we succeed in limiting the temperature increase to 1.5 degrees, sea levels will continue to rise for centuries to come, due to emissions we have already locked in. While living on the coast has always come with a certain level of flooding and erosion risks, climate change will alter our coastlines and we must prepare for this new reality." (OECD, 2019[14]).

3. The following paper compiles key research references related to "sense of purpose": OECD (forthcoming). OECD Future of Education and Skills 2030. *Construct Analysis for the OECD Learning Compass.*

4. A similar phenomenon of weak correlations between environmental attitudes and behaviour is referred to as the "attitude-action gap" in the environmental psychology literature (Lane and Potter, 2007[15]; Hines, Hungerford and Tomera, 1987[16]).

References

Bromley, P., J. Meyer and F. Ramirez (2011), "The Worldwide Spread of Environmental Discourse in Social Studies, History, and Civics Textbooks, 1970–2008", *Comparative Education Review*, Vol. 55/4, pp. 517-545, https://doi.org/10.1086/660797. [9]

Burrow, A., A. O'Dell and P. Hill (2009), "Profiles of a Developmental Asset: Youth Purpose as a Context for Hope and Well-Being", *Journal of Youth and Adolescence*, Vol. 39/11, pp. 1265-1273, https://doi.org/10.1007/s10964-009-9481-1. [6]

Damon, W., J. Menon and K. Cotton Bronk (2003), "The Development of Purpose During Adolescence", *Applied Developmental Science*, Vol. 7/3, pp. 119-128, https://doi.org/10.1207/s1532480xads0703_2. [4]

Dechezleprêtre, A. et al. (2022), "Fighting climate change: International attitudes toward climate policies", *OECD Economics Department Working Papers*, No. 1714, OECD Publishing, Paris, https://doi.org/10.1787/3406f29a-en. [3]

Hines, J., H. Hungerford and A. Tomera (1987), "Analysis and Synthesis of Research on Responsible Environmental Behavior: A Meta-Analysis", *The Journal of Environmental Education*, Vol. 18/2, pp. 1-8, https://doi.org/10.1080/00958964.1987.9943482. [16]

IPCC (2022), *Climate Change 2022: Impacts, Adaptation, and Vulnerability. Contribution of Working Group II to the Sixth Assessment Report of the Intergovernmental Panel on Climate Change.* [2]

John Frank, D., K. Jeong Robinson and J. Olesen (2011), "The Global Expansion of Environmental Education in Universities", *Comparative Education Review*, Vol. 55/4, pp. 546-573, https://doi.org/10.1086/661253. [10]

Lane, B. and S. Potter (2007), "The adoption of cleaner vehicles in the UK: exploring the consumer attitude–action gap", *Journal of Cleaner Production*, Vol. 15/11-12, pp. 1085-1092, https://doi.org/10.1016/j.jclepro.2006.05.026. [15]

Malin, H., I. Liauw and W. Damon (2017), "Purpose and Character Development in Early Adolescence", *Journal of Youth and Adolescence*, Vol. 46/6, pp. 1200-1215, https://doi.org/10.1007/s10964-017-0642-3. [5]

OECD (2022), "Teaching for climate action", *Teaching in Focus*, No. 44, OECD Publishing, Paris, https://doi.org/10.1787/d3a72e77-en. [11]

OECD (2019), *PISA 2018 Results (Volume I): What Students Know and Can Do*, PISA, OECD Publishing, Paris, https://doi.org/10.1787/5f07c754-en. [17]

OECD (2019), *Responding to Rising Seas: OECD Country Approaches to Tackling Coastal Risks*, OECD Publishing, Paris, https://doi.org/10.1787/9789264312487-en. [14]

Pizmony-Levy, O., M. McDermott and T. Copeland (2021), "Improving ESE policy through research-practice partnerships: Reflections and analysis from New York City", *Environmental Education Research*, Vol. 27/4, pp. 595-613, https://doi.org/10.1080/13504622.2021.1890696. [13]

Shepard, P. and C. Corbin-Mark (2009), "Climate Justice", *Environmental Justice*, Vol. 2/4, pp. 163-166, https://doi.org/10.1089/env.2009.2402. [12]

Thiery, W. et al. (2021), "Intergenerational inequities in exposure to climate extremes", *Science*, Vol. 374/6564, pp. 158-160, https://doi.org/10.1126/science.abi7339. [1]

Tirri, K., S. Moran and J. Menon Mariano (2016), "Education for purposeful teaching around the world", *Journal of Education for Teaching*, Vol. 42/5, pp. 526-531, https://doi.org/10.1080/02607476.2016.1226551. [7]

UNESCO (2016), *Getting Climate-Ready: A Guide for Schools on Climate Action*, UNESCO. [8]

PISA

ANNEX A

PISA 2018 technical background

ANNEX A1
Construction of indices

EXPLANATION OF THE INDICES

This section explains the indices derived from the PISA 2018 student, school and parent questionnaires used in this report.

Several PISA measures reflect indices that summarise responses from students, their parents or school representatives (typically principals) to a series of related questions. The questions were selected from a larger pool on the basis of theoretical considerations and previous research. The *PISA 2018 Assessment and Analytical Framework* (OECD, 2019[1]) provides an in-depth description of this conceptual framework. Item response theory modelling was used to confirm the theoretically expected behaviour of the indices and to validate their comparability across countries. For this purpose a joint model across all countries was estimated. Item fit (RMSD) was evaluated separately for each item and each group (country by language). This procedure is in line with the PISA 2015 scaling approach. For a detailed description of other PISA indices and details on the methods, see the *PISA 2015 Technical Report* (OECD, 2017[2]) and the *PISA 2018 Technical Report* (OECD, 2020[3]).

There are three types of indices: simple indices, scale indices and trend scale indices. For this report no trend indices were included in the analysis.

Simple indices are the variables that are constructed through the arithmetic transformation or recoding of one or more items in exactly the same way across assessments. Here, item responses are used to calculate meaningful variables, such as the recoding of the four-digit ISCO-08 codes into "Highest parents' socio-economic index (HISEI)" (one of the 3 components of the PISA index of economic, social and cultural status [ESCS]).

Scale indices are the variables constructed through the scaling of multiple items. Unless otherwise indicated, the index was scaled using a two-parameter item-response model (a generalised partial credit model was used in the case of items with more than two categories) and values of the index correspond to Warm likelihood estimates (WLE) (Warm, 1989[4]). For details on how each scale index was constructed, see the *PISA 2018 Technical Report* (OECD, 2020[3]). In general, the scaling was done in two stages:

1. The item parameters were estimated based on all students from equally-weighted countries and economies; only cases with a minimum number of three valid responses to items that are part of the index were included.
2. For new scale indices, the Warm likelihood estimates were then standardised so that the mean of the index value for the OECD student population was zero and the standard deviation was one (countries were given equal weight in the standardisation process).

Sequential codes were assigned to the different response categories of the questions in the sequence in which the latter appeared in the student, school or parent questionnaires. Where indicated in this section, these codes were inverted for the purpose of constructing indices or scales. Negative values for an index do not necessarily imply that students responded negatively to the underlying questions. A negative value merely indicates that the respondents answered less positively than all respondents did on average across OECD countries. Likewise, a positive value on an index indicates that the respondents answered more favourably, or more positively, on average, than respondents in OECD countries did. Terms enclosed in brackets < > in the following descriptions were replaced in the national versions of the student, school and parent questionnaires by the appropriate national equivalent. For example, the term <qualification at ISCED level 5A> was translated in the United States into "Bachelor's degree, post-graduate certificate program, Master's degree program or first professional degree program". Similarly the term <classes in the language of assessment> in Luxembourg was translated into "German classes" or "French classes", depending on whether students received the German or French version of the assessment instruments.

In addition to simple and scaled indices described in this annex, there are a number of variables from the questionnaires that were used in this report and correspond to single items not used to construct indices. All the context questionnaires, and the PISA international database, including all variables, are available through www.oecd.org/pisa.

STUDENT-LEVEL SIMPLE INDICES

Immigrant background

Information on the country of birth of the students and their parents was collected. Included in the database are three country-specific variables relating to the country of birth of the student, mother and father (ST019). The variables are binary and indicate whether the student, mother and father were born in the country of assessment or elsewhere. The index on immigrant background (IMMIG) is calculated from these variables, and has the following categories: (1) native students (those students who had at least one parent born in the country); (2) second-generation students (those born in the country of assessment but whose parent[s] were born in another country); and (3) first-generation students (those students born outside the country of assessment and whose parents were also born in another country). Students with missing responses for either the student or for both parents were given missing values for this variable. In this report, "immigrant students" groups second- and first-generation students.

Growth mindset

A growth mindset is the belief in the malleability of ability and intelligence (Dweck, 2006[5]). PISA 2018 asked students whether they agreed ("strongly disagree", "disagree, "agree", or "strongly agree") with the statement: "Your intelligence is something about you that you can't change very much" (ST184Q01HA). Students who agreed are considered to have a fixed mindset and the students who disagreed with the statement are considered to have a growth mindset.

Environmental sense-of-purpose

PISA 2018 asked students the extent to which they agreed with the following statement: "Looking after the global environment is important to me" (ST219Q06HA). Four response categories were offered to them. Students who selected "strongly agree" or "agree" are considered to have environmental sense-of-purpose. Students who selected "strongly disagree" or "disagree" are considered as not displaying environmental sense-of-purpose. In other words, in this report, students with an environmental sense-of-purpose are students who reported that looking after the global environment is important to them.

Environmental awareness

PISA 2018 asked students how informed they were about "climate change and global warming" (ST197Q01HA) and offered four response categories. Students who selected the categories "I am familiar with this and I would be able to explain this well" or "I know something about this and could explain the general issue" are considered as displaying environmental awareness. Students who selected "I have never heard of this" or "I have heard about this but I would not be able to explain what it is really about" are considered as not displaying environmental awareness. In other words, in this report, environmentally aware students are students who reported that they know something about or are very familiar with climate change and global warming.

Self-efficacy in environmental understanding

PISA 2018 asked students how easy they thought it would be for them to perform the following task: "Explain how carbon-dioxide emissions affect global climate change" (ST196Q02HA). Four response categories were offered to them. Students who selected "I could do this easily" or "I could do this with a bit of effort" were considered to have self-efficacy in their knowledge and understanding of environmental issues. Students who selected "I would struggle to do this on my own" or "I could not do this" were considered as not displaying self-efficacy in environmental understanding. In other words, in this report, students displaying self-efficacy in environmental understanding are students who reported that they could explain how carbon-dioxide emissions affect global climate change easily or with a bit of effort.

Data limitations and interpretation of the three pro-environmental attitudes (Environmental sense-of-purpose, Environmental awareness and Self-efficacy in environmental understanding)

Each of the three pro-environmental attitudes considered in this report is measured using a single questionnaire item. This means they are proxy measures that capture part of each construct but do not cover every aspect of it. For example, environmental awareness and self-efficacy use questions asking about climate change, but more robust measures might want to include topics such as bio-diversity loss, pollution, invasive species, genetic modification, etc. The same is true for sense-of-purpose, which could ask about care for the local environment, not just the global environment as it currently stands. PISA will improve its measurement of pro-environmental attitudes in the new PISA 2025 Science Framework, which will include "scientific identity" as a new dimension of the assessment (OECD, 2020[6]).

In addition, environmental attitudes are not observed but are based on students' self-reports. Care must be taken when comparing these self-reported attitude results as they may be influenced by cultural norms. Also notice that in the text of the report students are sometimes described as "displaying" or "having" environmental attitudes. This is done for economy of language, with the understanding that these attitudes are self-reported and thus it is more precise to say that students reported having environmental attitudes.

STUDENT-LEVEL SCALE INDICES

Scaling of indices related to the PISA index of economic social and cultural status

The PISA index of economic, social and cultural status (ESCS) was derived, as in previous cycles, from three variables related to family background: parents' highest level of education (PARED), parents' highest occupational status (HISEI), and home possessions (HOMEPOS), including books in the home. PARED and HISEI are simple indices. HOMEPOS is a proxy measure for family wealth. These three indices are described in detail in the *PISA 2018 Technical Report* (OECD, 2020[3]).

Computation of ESCS

For the purpose of computing the PISA index of economic, social and cultural status (ESCS), values for students with missing PARED, HISEI or HOMEPOS were imputed with predicted values plus a random component based on a regression on the other two variables. If there were missing data on more than one of the three variables, ESCS was not computed and a missing value was assigned for ESCS.

In previous cycles, the PISA index of economic, social and cultural status was derived from a principal component analysis of standardised variables (each variable has an OECD mean of zero and a standard deviation of one), taking the factor scores for the first principal component as measures of the PISA index of economic, social and cultural status. In PISA 2018, ESCS is computed by attributing equal weight to the three standardised components. As in PISA 2015, the three components were standardised across all countries and economies (both OECD and partner countries/economies), with each country/economy contributing equally (in cycles prior to 2015, the standardisation and principal component analysis were based on OECD countries only). As in every previous cycle, the final ESCS variable was transformed, with 0 the score of an average OECD student and 1 the standard deviation across equally weighted OECD countries.

SCHOOL-LEVEL SIMPLE INDICES

Coverage of climate change and global warming in the school curriculum

PISA 2018 asked school principals to select which topics were part of the formal curriculum. School principals were asked to consider curriculum based on national, state, regional or school policies. Schools are considered as covering climate change and global warming in the formal curriculum when their principal select "yes" for the topic "Climate change and global warming" (SC158Q01HA).

PARENT-LEVEL SIMPLE INDICES

Parental environmental awareness

PISA 2018 asked parents how informed they were about climate change and global warming (PA170Q01HA) and offered four response categories. Parents who selected the categories "I am familiar with this and I would be able to explain this well" or "I know something about this and could explain the general issue" are considered as displaying environmental awareness. Parents who selected "I have never heard of this" or "I have heard about this but I would not be able to explain what it is really about" are considered as not displaying environmental awareness. In other words, in this report, environmentally aware parents are parents who reported that they know something about or are very familiar with climate change and global warming.

References

Dweck, C. (2006), *Mindset, Random House*, New York, NY. [5]

OECD (2020), *PISA 2018 Technical Report*, https://www.oecd.org/pisa/data/pisa2018technicalreport/. [3]

OECD (2020), *PISA 2024 Strategic Vision and Direction for Science*, https://www.oecd.org/pisa/publications/PISA-2024-Science-Strategic-Vision-Proposal.pdf. [6]

OECD (2019), *PISA 2018 Assessment and Analytical Framework*, OECD Publishing, Paris, https://dx.doi.org/10.1787/b25efab8-en. [1]

OECD (2017), *PISA 2015 Technical Report*, OECD Publishing, Paris, http://www.oecd.org/pisa/data/2015-technical-report/. [2]

Warm, T. (1989), "Weighted likelihood estimation of ability in item response theory", *Psychometrika*, Vol. 54/3, pp. 427-450, https://doi.org/10.1007/BF02294627. [4]

ANNEX A2
Technical notes on analyses in this report

STANDARD ERRORS, CONFIDENCE INTERVALS AND SIGNIFICANCE TESTS

The statistics in this report represent estimates based on samples of students, rather than values that could be calculated if every student in every country had answered every question. Consequently, it is important to measure the degree of uncertainty of the estimates. In PISA, each estimate has an associated degree of uncertainty, which is expressed through a standard error. The use of confidence intervals provides a way to make inferences about the population parameters (e.g. means and proportions) in a manner that reflects the uncertainty associated with the sample estimates. If numerous different samples were drawn from the same population, according to the same procedures as the original sample, then in 95 out of 100 samples the calculated confidence interval would encompass the true population parameter. For many parameters, sample estimators follow a normal distribution and the 95% confidence interval can be constructed as the estimated parameter, plus or minus 1.96 times the associated standard error.

In many cases, readers are primarily interested in whether a given value in a particular country is different from a second value in the same or another country, e.g. whether girls in a country perform better than boys in the same country. In the tables and figures used in this report, differences are labelled as statistically significant when a difference of that size or larger, in either direction, would be observed less than 5% of the time, if there were actually no difference in corresponding population values. Similarly, the risk of reporting an association as significant if there is, in fact, no correlation between two measures, is contained at 5%.

Throughout the report, significance tests were undertaken to assess the statistical significance of the comparisons made.

Statistical significance of gender differences and differences between subgroup means

Gender differences in student performance or other indices were tested for statistical significance. Positive differences indicate higher scores for girls while negative differences indicate higher scores for boys. Generally, differences marked in bold in the tables in this report are statistically significant at the 95% confidence level.

Similarly, differences between other groups of students (e.g. socio-economically advantaged and disadvantaged students) were tested for statistical significance. The definitions of the subgroups can, in general, be found in the tables and the text accompanying the analysis. All differences marked in bold in the tables presented in Annex B of this report are statistically significant at the 95% level.

Statistical significance of differences between subgroup means, after accounting for other variables

For many tables, subgroup comparisons were performed both on the observed difference ("before accounting for other variables") and after accounting for other variables, such as the PISA index of economic, social and cultural status of students. The adjusted differences were estimated using linear regression and tested for significance at the 95% confidence level. Significant differences are marked in bold.

Statistical significance of performance differences between the top and bottom quarters of PISA indices and scales

Differences in average performance between the top and bottom quarters of the PISA indices and scales were tested for statistical significance. Figures marked in bold indicate that performance between the top and bottom quarters of students on the respective index is statistically significantly different at the 95% confidence level.

ODDS RATIOS

The odds ratio is a measure of the relative likelihood of a particular outcome across two groups. The odds ratio for observing the outcome when an antecedent is present is simply

Equation 1

$$OR = {(p_{11}/p_{12})}\Big/{(p_{21}/p_{22})}$$

where p_{11}/p_{12} represents the "odds" of observing the outcome when the antecedent is present, and p_{21}/p_{22} represents the "odds" of observing the outcome when the antecedent is not present.

Logistic regression can be used to estimate the log ratio: the exponentiated logit coefficient for a binary variable is equivalent to the odds ratio. A "generalised" odds ratio, after accounting for other differences across groups, can be estimated by introducing control variables in the logistic regression.

Statistical significance of odds ratios

Figures in bold in the data tables presented in Annex B of this report indicate that the odds ratio is statistically significantly different from 1 at the 95% confidence level. To construct a 95% confidence interval for the odds ratio, the estimator is assumed to follow a log-normal distribution, rather than a normal distribution.

In many tables, odds ratios after accounting for other variables are also presented. These odds ratios were estimated using logistic regression and tested for significance against the null hypothesis of an odds ratio equal to 1 (i.e. equal likelihoods, after accounting for other variables).

USE OF STUDENT AND SCHOOL WEIGHTS

The target population in PISA is 15-year-old students, but a two-stage sampling procedure was used. After the population was defined, school samples were selected with a probability proportional to the expected number of eligible students in each school. Only in a second sampling stage were students drawn from among the eligible students in each selected school.

Although the student samples were drawn from within a sample of schools, the school sample was designed to optimise the resulting sample of students rather than to give an optimal sample of schools. It is therefore preferable to analyse the school-level variables as attributes of students (e.g. in terms of the share of 15-year-old students affected) rather than as elements in their own right.

Most analyses of student and school characteristics are therefore weighted by student final weights (or their sum, in the case of school characteristics), and use student replicate weights for estimating standard errors.

ANNEX A3

Distribution of No response for items related to environmental actions in question ST222

Table A3.1 [1/4] **Percentage of students who answered yes, no or did not respond items of question ST222 used in this report**
Based on students' reports

	Percentage of students who reported the following[1]:																	
	"I reduce the energy I use at home to protect the environment" (st222q01ha)						"I choose certain products for ethical or environmental reasons, even if they are a bit more expensive" (st222q03ha)						"I sign environmental or social petitions online" (st222q04ha)					
	Yes		No		No response (.m)		Yes		No		No response (.m)		Yes		No		No response (.m)	
	%	S.E.	%	S.E.	%	S.E.	%	S.E.	%	S.E.	%	S.E.	%	S.E.	%	S.E.	%	S.E.
OECD																		
Australia	65.9	(0.5)	30.0	(0.5)	4.2	(0.3)	39.8	(0.5)	55.8	(0.6)	4.4	(0.3)	18.6	(0.4)	76.9	(0.5)	4.5	(0.3)
Austria	66.0	(0.7)	28.7	(0.6)	5.3	(0.4)	45.3	(0.8)	48.7	(0.8)	5.9	(0.4)	22.9	(0.7)	70.9	(0.8)	6.2	(0.4)
Canada	63.9	(0.6)	31.6	(0.5)	4.6	(0.3)	39.7	(0.5)	55.5	(0.6)	4.7	(0.3)	18.0	(0.4)	77.2	(0.5)	4.8	(0.3)
Chile	71.2	(0.9)	20.4	(0.6)	8.4	(0.8)	35.7	(0.7)	55.6	(0.8)	8.8	(0.8)	26.2	(0.7)	64.6	(1.0)	9.2	(0.8)
Colombia	69.2	(1.5)	16.2	(0.6)	14.6	(1.5)	47.2	(1.2)	38.0	(1.0)	14.8	(1.5)	22.6	(0.7)	62.4	(1.5)	15.0	(1.5)
Costa Rica	79.6	(0.7)	16.8	(0.6)	3.6	(0.4)	47.2	(0.7)	48.6	(0.8)	4.2	(0.5)	24.7	(0.7)	71.0	(0.8)	4.3	(0.5)
Estonia	66.4	(0.7)	30.8	(0.6)	2.8	(0.3)	41.8	(0.8)	55.3	(0.8)	2.9	(0.3)	19.6	(0.6)	77.2	(0.6)	3.2	(0.3)
France	60.4	(0.8)	30.4	(0.7)	9.1	(0.7)	39.8	(0.8)	50.8	(0.8)	9.4	(0.7)	17.8	(0.6)	72.2	(0.9)	10.0	(0.7)
Germany	58.7	(1.1)	31.7	(1.0)	9.6	(0.8)	34.8	(1.2)	54.8	(1.1)	10.4	(0.8)	13.9	(0.6)	74.8	(0.9)	11.3	(0.8)
Greece	65.1	(0.8)	27.7	(0.7)	7.3	(0.7)	46.3	(0.7)	46.0	(0.8)	7.7	(0.8)	23.3	(0.8)	69.0	(1.1)	7.7	(0.7)
Hungary	65.1	(0.8)	30.9	(0.8)	4.0	(0.3)	49.5	(0.9)	45.6	(0.8)	4.8	(0.4)	19.0	(0.8)	75.8	(0.9)	5.1	(0.4)
Iceland	64.9	(0.8)	28.7	(0.8)	6.5	(0.5)	45.7	(0.8)	46.6	(1.0)	7.7	(0.5)	32.2	(0.8)	60.4	(0.8)	7.4	(0.5)
Ireland	68.5	(0.7)	28.4	(0.7)	3.1	(0.3)	31.8	(0.7)	64.5	(0.7)	3.7	(0.4)	14.6	(0.5)	81.4	(0.6)	3.9	(0.3)
Italy	55.9	(0.8)	32.9	(0.7)	11.1	(0.8)	36.9	(0.8)	51.4	(0.9)	11.7	(0.8)	16.6	(0.7)	71.6	(1.1)	11.8	(0.8)
Korea	74.9	(0.6)	24.3	(0.5)	0.8	(0.1)	39.1	(0.9)	59.9	(0.9)	0.9	(0.2)	45.3	(0.7)	53.6	(0.8)	1.2	(0.2)
Latvia	60.5	(0.8)	35.7	(0.7)	3.8	(0.3)	45.1	(0.7)	51.0	(0.7)	3.9	(0.3)	24.1	(0.6)	71.6	(0.7)	4.2	(0.4)
Lithuania	63.7	(0.8)	32.0	(0.7)	4.4	(0.4)	44.1	(0.8)	51.2	(0.7)	4.7	(0.4)	37.9	(0.6)	56.7	(0.7)	5.4	(0.4)
Mexico	72.0	(1.2)	19.9	(0.7)	8.1	(1.2)	46.9	(1.0)	44.7	(0.9)	8.4	(1.2)	23.5	(0.9)	67.9	(1.2)	8.7	(1.2)
New Zealand	66.2	(0.7)	30.8	(0.6)	3.0	(0.3)	42.7	(0.8)	54.0	(0.8)	3.3	(0.3)	21.7	(0.7)	74.7	(0.8)	3.6	(0.3)
Poland	67.8	(0.9)	28.3	(0.8)	3.9	(0.4)	48.5	(0.9)	47.3	(0.8)	4.3	(0.4)	22.2	(0.8)	73.6	(0.9)	4.2	(0.4)
Portugal	73.9	(0.8)	22.0	(0.7)	4.1	(0.5)	45.3	(0.7)	50.2	(0.8)	4.5	(0.5)	18.7	(0.6)	76.6	(0.7)	4.7	(0.5)
Scotland (United Kingdom)	59.5	(1.0)	33.1	(0.9)	7.4	(0.7)	30.7	(1.0)	61.7	(1.0)	7.6	(0.7)	19.8	(0.9)	72.1	(1.0)	8.1	(0.8)
Slovak Republic	58.6	(0.7)	33.7	(0.6)	7.7	(0.6)	41.4	(0.8)	50.1	(0.8)	8.5	(0.6)	25.5	(0.7)	65.6	(0.9)	8.9	(0.6)
Slovenia	75.8	(0.8)	21.3	(0.7)	2.9	(0.3)	48.0	(0.8)	48.9	(0.8)	3.1	(0.3)	20.0	(0.6)	76.5	(0.7)	3.5	(0.3)
Spain	66.5	(0.7)	23.0	(0.4)	10.5	(0.8)	35.5	(0.5)	53.5	(0.7)	10.9	(0.8)	24.5	(0.4)	64.3	(0.8)	11.2	(0.8)
Switzerland	59.8	(0.8)	32.4	(0.7)	7.8	(0.7)	38.6	(1.0)	52.7	(1.0)	8.8	(0.7)	19.8	(0.7)	70.6	(1.0)	9.6	(0.8)
Türkiye	84.9	(0.6)	13.2	(0.5)	1.9	(0.2)	62.7	(0.8)	35.1	(0.7)	2.2	(0.2)	50.0	(0.8)	47.6	(0.7)	2.4	(0.2)
OECD average	66.8	(0.2)	27.2	(0.1)	5.9	(0.1)	42.6	(0.2)	51.0	(0.2)	6.4	(0.1)	23.8	(0.1)	69.5	(0.2)	6.7	(0.1)

1. In PISA 2018, question ST222 in the student questionnaire asked the following: "Are you involved in the following activities?" For analysis included in this report, students who answered "yes" to a particular statement are considered as taking part in that particular action. Students who answered "no", and students who had an opportunity to answer the question but did not respond (i.e. they were presented the question according to the survey design but left it blank), are considered as not taking part in the action.

StatLink https://stat.link/2z1bet

Table A3.1 [2/4] **Percentage of students who answered yes, no or did not respond items of question ST222 used in this report**
Based on students' reports

		Percentage of students who reported the following[1]:																	
		"I reduce the energy I use at home to protect the environment" (st222q01ha)						"I choose certain products for ethical or environmental reasons, even if they are a bit more expensive" (st222q03ha)						"I sign environmental or social petitions online" (st222q04ha)					
		Yes		No		No response (.m)		Yes		No		No response (.m)		Yes		No		No response (.m)	
		%	S.E.	%	S.E.	%	S.E.	%	S.E.	%	S.E.	%	S.E.	%	S.E.	%	S.E.	%	S.E.
Partners	Albania	78.9	(0.6)	17.5	(0.6)	3.6	(0.3)	52.5	(0.7)	43.6	(0.7)	4.0	(0.4)	33.3	(0.8)	62.2	(0.8)	4.5	(0.3)
	Argentina	54.5	(1.0)	22.9	(0.6)	22.6	(1.3)	33.0	(0.8)	43.5	(0.9)	23.5	(1.3)	20.7	(0.6)	55.1	(1.1)	24.2	(1.3)
	Baku (Azerbaijan)	47.6	(1.0)	15.3	(0.7)	37.1	(1.3)	41.4	(1.0)	21.3	(0.7)	37.3	(1.3)	33.1	(0.8)	28.6	(0.9)	38.3	(1.3)
	Bosnia and Herzegovina	62.3	(0.7)	27.1	(0.7)	10.6	(0.6)	37.8	(0.6)	50.9	(0.7)	11.3	(0.6)	29.6	(0.7)	58.6	(0.9)	11.8	(0.6)
	Brazil	56.6	(0.9)	19.0	(0.6)	24.3	(1.1)	34.9	(0.7)	40.2	(0.8)	25.0	(1.1)	24.9	(0.6)	49.2	(0.9)	25.9	(1.1)
	Brunei Darussalam	72.7	(0.6)	22.6	(0.6)	4.6	(0.3)	45.9	(0.5)	48.6	(0.5)	5.4	(0.3)	23.4	(0.6)	70.7	(0.6)	5.9	(0.3)
	Bulgaria	50.0	(0.8)	30.0	(0.8)	20.1	(1.2)	39.6	(0.8)	39.3	(1.0)	21.1	(1.3)	30.3	(0.8)	48.3	(1.2)	21.3	(1.3)
	Croatia	64.3	(0.7)	30.2	(0.6)	5.6	(0.4)	41.1	(0.7)	52.9	(0.8)	6.0	(0.5)	17.7	(0.6)	75.8	(0.8)	6.6	(0.4)
	Cyprus	60.8	(0.7)	25.6	(0.6)	13.7	(0.4)	41.3	(0.7)	44.6	(0.7)	14.1	(0.4)	28.6	(0.6)	57.1	(0.7)	14.2	(0.4)
	Dominican Republic	46.2	(1.8)	11.0	(0.7)	42.8	(2.3)	33.6	(1.5)	20.9	(1.1)	45.5	(2.3)	24.6	(1.3)	28.8	(1.5)	46.6	(2.3)
	Hong Kong (China)	78.9	(0.6)	20.3	(0.6)	0.8	(0.1)	57.3	(0.8)	41.9	(0.7)	0.8	(0.1)	25.5	(0.7)	73.6	(0.7)	0.8	(0.1)
	Indonesia	80.6	(0.9)	15.7	(0.5)	3.7	(0.8)	64.3	(1.0)	31.5	(0.8)	4.1	(0.8)	38.7	(0.9)	56.7	(1.1)	4.6	(0.9)
	Jordan	79.7	(0.7)	14.8	(0.5)	5.5	(0.6)	67.6	(0.8)	26.3	(0.5)	6.1	(0.6)	51.0	(0.9)	42.9	(0.9)	6.2	(0.6)
	Kazakhstan	71.0	(0.5)	22.0	(0.4)	6.9	(0.4)	60.6	(0.6)	31.6	(0.5)	7.9	(0.4)	35.2	(0.5)	56.5	(0.6)	8.3	(0.4)
	Kosovo	78.2	(0.6)	13.3	(0.5)	8.6	(0.5)	67.1	(0.7)	23.0	(0.7)	9.9	(0.6)	30.3	(0.8)	59.3	(0.9)	10.5	(0.5)
	Lebanon	66.3	(1.1)	25.7	(1.0)	8.1	(0.6)	45.7	(1.1)	44.5	(1.2)	9.7	(0.7)	34.8	(1.0)	55.1	(1.0)	10.0	(0.7)
	Macao (China)	80.7	(0.6)	18.9	(0.6)	0.4	(0.1)	54.6	(0.8)	45.0	(0.8)	0.3	(0.1)	15.7	(0.6)	83.9	(0.6)	0.4	(0.1)
	Malaysia	74.8	(0.6)	23.8	(0.6)	1.4	(0.3)	58.1	(0.8)	40.6	(0.8)	1.3	(0.3)	36.7	(1.0)	61.6	(1.0)	1.7	(0.3)
	Malta	71.2	(0.7)	18.4	(0.7)	10.4	(0.4)	44.6	(0.9)	44.5	(0.9)	10.9	(0.5)	34.8	(0.7)	54.0	(0.8)	11.3	(0.5)
	Moldova	63.7	(0.7)	31.8	(0.6)	4.6	(0.4)	58.0	(0.7)	37.4	(0.7)	4.6	(0.4)	28.2	(0.7)	66.3	(0.8)	5.6	(0.4)
	Montenegro	56.9	(0.7)	31.0	(0.6)	12.2	(0.4)	49.0	(0.5)	37.7	(0.5)	13.3	(0.4)	31.8	(0.6)	54.1	(0.6)	14.1	(0.5)
	Morocco	49.7	(1.3)	13.7	(0.6)	36.6	(1.6)	36.1	(1.0)	26.0	(0.9)	37.9	(1.6)	28.8	(0.9)	32.9	(1.1)	38.4	(1.6)
	North Macedonia	69.4	(0.7)	27.5	(0.7)	3.1	(0.2)	39.9	(0.8)	55.7	(0.8)	4.3	(0.3)	25.6	(0.7)	70.0	(0.7)	4.4	(0.3)
	Panama	55.3	(1.0)	16.8	(0.8)	27.9	(1.3)	39.8	(1.0)	30.0	(1.1)	30.2	(1.3)	22.9	(0.8)	46.1	(1.3)	31.0	(1.3)
	Peru	80.9	(0.7)	13.4	(0.5)	5.7	(0.5)	41.8	(0.9)	51.8	(0.9)	6.4	(0.5)	31.9	(1.0)	61.0	(1.1)	7.1	(0.6)
	Philippines	79.0	(0.7)	16.7	(0.6)	4.3	(0.5)	60.1	(0.8)	35.1	(0.7)	4.9	(0.5)	40.9	(0.8)	54.0	(0.9)	5.1	(0.5)
	Romania	63.7	(0.9)	30.9	(0.9)	5.3	(0.6)	51.4	(0.9)	42.6	(1.0)	6.1	(0.6)	27.2	(0.9)	66.1	(1.1)	6.8	(0.6)
	Saudi Arabia	74.1	(0.9)	18.7	(0.5)	7.2	(0.8)	54.9	(0.9)	36.6	(0.7)	8.5	(0.9)	m	m	m	m	m	m
	Serbia	51.9	(0.9)	30.5	(0.7)	17.7	(1.2)	39.9	(0.8)	41.9	(1.0)	18.2	(1.2)	23.5	(0.7)	58.1	(1.4)	18.5	(1.3)
	Singapore	81.8	(0.5)	17.3	(0.5)	0.8	(0.1)	47.1	(0.7)	52.0	(0.7)	1.0	(0.1)	20.4	(0.6)	78.5	(0.6)	1.1	(0.1)
	Chinese Taipei	80.5	(0.6)	18.5	(0.6)	1.0	(0.2)	66.9	(0.6)	32.1	(0.6)	1.0	(0.2)	26.4	(0.6)	72.5	(0.7)	1.1	(0.2)
	Thailand	84.2	(0.6)	14.2	(0.5)	1.6	(0.3)	68.4	(0.7)	29.8	(0.7)	1.8	(0.3)	48.9	(1.0)	49.3	(1.1)	1.9	(0.3)
	Ukraine	54.2	(0.8)	39.6	(0.9)	6.2	(0.5)	51.0	(0.8)	42.6	(0.7)	6.5	(0.5)	23.0	(0.7)	69.9	(0.8)	7.1	(0.6)
	United Arab Emirates	74.3	(0.4)	18.2	(0.4)	7.4	(0.3)	55.5	(0.7)	36.7	(0.7)	7.8	(0.3)	40.6	(0.6)	51.6	(0.7)	7.8	(0.3)
	Uruguay	51.5	(1.1)	27.1	(0.8)	21.4	(1.2)	27.9	(0.8)	49.2	(1.2)	22.9	(1.2)	20.6	(0.7)	56.6	(1.2)	22.8	(1.2)
	Viet Nam	77.6	(0.8)	21.7	(0.8)	0.6	(0.2)	66.2	(0.9)	33.0	(0.9)	0.8	(0.2)	33.4	(1.1)	65.7	(1.2)	1.0	(0.2)

1. In PISA 2018, question ST222 in the student questionnaire asked the following: "Are you involved in the following activities?" For analysis included in this report, students who answered "yes" to a particular statement are considered as taking part in that particular action. Students who answered "no", and students who had an opportunity to answer the question but did not respond (i.e. they were presented the question according to the survey design but left it blank), are considered as not taking part in the action.

StatLink https://stat.link/2z1bet

Table A3.1 [3/4] **Percentage of students who answered yes, no or did not respond items of question ST222 used in this report**
Based on students' reports

		Percentage of students who reported the following[1]:											
		"I boycott products or companies for political, ethical or environmental reasons" (st222q06ha)						"I participate in activities in favour of environmental protection" (st222q09ha)					
		Yes		No		No response (.m)		Yes		No		No response (.m)	
		%	S.E.	%	S.E.	%	S.E.	%	S.E.	%	S.E.	%	S.E.
OECD	**Australia**	21.5	(0.4)	73.5	(0.5)	5.1	(0.3)	30.4	(0.4)	64.8	(0.5)	4.8	(0.3)
	Austria	31.6	(0.7)	61.6	(0.8)	6.8	(0.4)	32.2	(0.7)	60.9	(0.9)	6.9	(0.5)
	Canada	24.6	(0.5)	70.3	(0.5)	5.1	(0.3)	33.9	(0.5)	61.0	(0.5)	5.1	(0.3)
	Chile	21.9	(0.6)	68.1	(0.9)	9.9	(0.8)	34.7	(0.8)	55.4	(1.0)	9.8	(0.8)
	Colombia	25.6	(1.0)	59.0	(1.3)	15.5	(1.6)	49.4	(1.2)	35.3	(1.0)	15.3	(1.6)
	Costa Rica	22.9	(0.6)	72.2	(0.8)	4.8	(0.5)	54.0	(1.0)	41.5	(0.9)	4.5	(0.5)
	Estonia	23.2	(0.7)	73.2	(0.8)	3.6	(0.3)	28.8	(0.8)	67.9	(0.9)	3.4	(0.3)
	France	23.3	(0.7)	66.1	(0.9)	10.6	(0.7)	21.7	(0.6)	67.8	(0.9)	10.5	(0.7)
	Germany	16.8	(0.6)	70.5	(1.0)	12.7	(0.8)	21.6	(0.7)	66.1	(0.9)	12.3	(0.8)
	Greece	30.9	(0.7)	60.9	(1.0)	8.2	(0.7)	38.5	(0.8)	53.7	(0.9)	7.8	(0.7)
	Hungary	26.5	(0.8)	67.8	(0.9)	5.7	(0.4)	37.8	(0.8)	56.4	(0.8)	5.8	(0.4)
	Iceland	31.3	(0.8)	60.1	(0.8)	8.5	(0.5)	47.3	(0.9)	45.0	(0.9)	7.6	(0.5)
	Ireland	16.4	(0.6)	79.0	(0.7)	4.6	(0.4)	26.9	(0.6)	68.4	(0.7)	4.6	(0.4)
	Italy	16.9	(0.7)	70.9	(1.0)	12.2	(0.8)	23.9	(0.6)	64.1	(1.0)	12.0	(0.8)
	Korea	34.5	(0.8)	64.4	(0.8)	1.1	(0.2)	52.3	(0.8)	46.6	(0.8)	1.1	(0.2)
	Latvia	21.0	(0.7)	74.4	(0.6)	4.6	(0.3)	36.8	(0.8)	58.9	(0.8)	4.3	(0.3)
	Lithuania	33.7	(0.7)	60.9	(0.7)	5.4	(0.4)	46.5	(0.7)	48.4	(0.8)	5.2	(0.4)
	Mexico	25.6	(0.9)	65.5	(1.0)	9.0	(1.2)	49.9	(1.2)	41.0	(1.0)	9.2	(1.2)
	New Zealand	20.6	(0.6)	75.0	(0.7)	4.4	(0.3)	31.2	(0.8)	64.9	(0.9)	4.0	(0.3)
	Poland	23.3	(0.7)	72.3	(0.8)	4.5	(0.4)	37.8	(0.8)	57.8	(0.8)	4.4	(0.5)
	Portugal	23.1	(0.5)	71.7	(0.7)	5.2	(0.5)	34.1	(0.9)	61.2	(1.0)	4.7	(0.5)
	Scotland (United Kingdom)	17.6	(0.8)	73.8	(0.9)	8.6	(0.7)	19.5	(0.9)	71.7	(1.0)	8.7	(0.8)
	Slovak Republic	24.8	(0.7)	65.7	(0.8)	9.5	(0.6)	41.8	(0.8)	49.0	(0.9)	9.2	(0.6)
	Slovenia	39.1	(0.9)	57.3	(0.9)	3.6	(0.3)	30.6	(0.8)	65.6	(0.8)	3.7	(0.3)
	Spain	17.0	(0.4)	71.2	(0.8)	11.8	(0.8)	28.6	(0.4)	59.6	(0.7)	11.8	(0.8)
	Switzerland	21.4	(0.7)	67.7	(1.0)	10.9	(0.8)	27.3	(0.8)	62.1	(1.0)	10.6	(0.8)
	Türkiye	35.8	(0.9)	61.4	(0.9)	2.7	(0.2)	67.7	(0.8)	29.8	(0.7)	2.5	(0.2)
	OECD average	24.8	(0.1)	67.9	(0.2)	7.2	(0.1)	36.5	(0.2)	56.5	(0.2)	7.0	(0.1)

1. In PISA 2018, question ST222 in the student questionnaire asked the following: "Are you involved in the following activities?" For analysis included in this report, students who answered "yes" to a particular statement are considered as taking part in that particular action. Students who answered "no", and students who had an opportunity to answer the question but did not respond (i.e. they were presented the question according to the survey design but left it blank), are considered as not taking part in the action.

StatLink https://stat.link/2z1bet

Table A3.1 [4/4] **Percentage of students who answered yes, no or did not respond items of question ST222 used in this report**
Based on students' reports

	Percentage of students who reported the following[1]:											
	"I boycott products or companies for political, ethical or environmental reasons" (st222q06ha)						"I participate in activities in favour of environmental protection" (st222q09ha)					
	Yes		No		No response (.m)		Yes		No		No response (.m)	
	%	S.E.	%	S.E.	%	S.E.	%	S.E.	%	S.E.	%	S.E.
Partners												
Albania	32.8	(0.8)	62.4	(0.9)	4.7	(0.4)	73.6	(0.8)	22.0	(0.8)	4.5	(0.4)
Argentina	15.8	(0.6)	59.6	(1.1)	24.6	(1.3)	28.3	(0.7)	47.1	(1.0)	24.6	(1.3)
Baku (Azerbaijan)	30.9	(0.7)	30.7	(0.9)	38.3	(1.3)	38.6	(0.8)	22.7	(0.8)	38.7	(1.2)
Bosnia and Herzegovina	29.7	(0.7)	57.4	(0.8)	12.9	(0.6)	48.0	(0.7)	39.3	(0.7)	12.6	(0.6)
Brazil	21.5	(0.5)	52.5	(0.9)	26.0	(1.1)	30.6	(0.7)	43.4	(0.8)	26.0	(1.1)
Brunei Darussalam	20.4	(0.4)	73.1	(0.5)	6.4	(0.3)	37.3	(0.6)	56.0	(0.6)	6.7	(0.3)
Bulgaria	30.8	(0.9)	47.5	(1.2)	21.8	(1.2)	42.0	(0.8)	36.5	(0.9)	21.5	(1.3)
Croatia	18.5	(0.6)	74.5	(0.8)	7.0	(0.5)	31.8	(0.7)	61.4	(0.8)	6.7	(0.5)
Cyprus	29.5	(0.6)	55.0	(0.7)	15.4	(0.5)	39.2	(0.7)	45.6	(0.7)	15.2	(0.5)
Dominican Republic	22.4	(1.1)	30.3	(1.6)	47.3	(2.3)	30.6	(1.5)	22.2	(1.1)	47.2	(2.2)
Hong Kong (China)	35.0	(0.7)	63.9	(0.7)	1.1	(0.1)	58.0	(0.8)	41.0	(0.8)	1.0	(0.1)
Indonesia	47.3	(1.0)	48.1	(1.0)	4.5	(0.9)	73.1	(1.0)	22.0	(0.7)	4.9	(0.9)
Jordan	57.0	(1.0)	36.4	(0.8)	6.6	(0.6)	71.4	(0.8)	22.4	(0.7)	6.2	(0.6)
Kazakhstan	31.9	(0.5)	59.6	(0.7)	8.6	(0.4)	52.0	(0.6)	39.2	(0.5)	8.8	(0.4)
Kosovo	31.9	(0.6)	57.3	(0.8)	10.8	(0.5)	56.8	(0.9)	32.7	(0.8)	10.5	(0.6)
Lebanon	34.4	(0.9)	54.5	(1.1)	11.1	(0.7)	51.0	(0.9)	39.4	(0.9)	9.6	(0.7)
Macao (China)	30.0	(0.8)	69.4	(0.8)	0.6	(0.1)	45.9	(0.7)	53.6	(0.7)	0.5	(0.1)
Malaysia	37.6	(1.0)	60.7	(1.0)	1.7	(0.3)	62.9	(0.8)	35.4	(0.8)	1.7	(0.3)
Malta	28.1	(0.8)	60.4	(0.8)	11.5	(0.5)	37.9	(0.8)	50.7	(0.9)	11.5	(0.5)
Moldova	21.3	(0.6)	72.5	(0.8)	6.2	(0.4)	48.3	(0.9)	46.0	(0.9)	5.7	(0.4)
Montenegro	30.6	(0.6)	54.7	(0.7)	14.7	(0.5)	52.4	(0.6)	33.8	(0.6)	13.8	(0.5)
Morocco	36.8	(1.2)	24.3	(0.9)	38.9	(1.6)	42.7	(1.3)	17.9	(0.6)	39.4	(1.6)
North Macedonia	20.2	(0.5)	75.3	(0.5)	4.6	(0.3)	51.7	(0.7)	43.8	(0.7)	4.5	(0.3)
Panama	20.4	(0.8)	47.1	(1.1)	32.6	(1.4)	37.7	(1.1)	30.0	(0.9)	32.3	(1.3)
Peru	24.5	(0.8)	68.0	(0.9)	7.5	(0.6)	48.3	(0.9)	44.2	(0.8)	7.5	(0.6)
Philippines	36.0	(0.9)	58.5	(0.9)	5.5	(0.5)	68.4	(0.8)	26.3	(0.7)	5.2	(0.5)
Romania	26.7	(0.9)	67.2	(1.2)	6.1	(0.6)	47.5	(0.9)	46.3	(0.9)	6.3	(0.6)
Saudi Arabia	48.8	(1.0)	42.5	(0.9)	8.7	(0.9)	50.7	(0.9)	41.0	(0.8)	8.3	(0.9)
Serbia	25.6	(0.7)	55.6	(1.3)	18.9	(1.2)	37.7	(0.7)	43.3	(1.0)	18.9	(1.3)
Singapore	24.5	(0.6)	74.1	(0.6)	1.3	(0.1)	41.2	(0.7)	57.7	(0.7)	1.1	(0.1)
Chinese Taipei	43.5	(0.8)	55.4	(0.8)	1.1	(0.2)	63.8	(0.7)	35.1	(0.7)	1.1	(0.2)
Thailand	47.4	(0.9)	50.6	(1.0)	2.0	(0.3)	71.9	(0.6)	26.1	(0.6)	2.0	(0.3)
Ukraine	20.4	(0.7)	72.6	(0.9)	7.1	(0.5)	40.9	(0.8)	52.1	(0.9)	7.0	(0.5)
United Arab Emirates	44.4	(0.5)	47.6	(0.6)	8.0	(0.3)	60.5	(0.5)	31.5	(0.5)	8.0	(0.3)
Uruguay	17.7	(0.6)	58.7	(1.2)	23.6	(1.2)	28.3	(0.8)	47.9	(1.3)	23.8	(1.2)
Viet Nam	40.6	(1.0)	58.6	(1.0)	0.8	(0.2)	88.9	(0.6)	10.1	(0.5)	0.9	(0.2)

1. In PISA 2018, question ST222 in the student questionnaire asked the following: "Are you involved in the following activities?" For analysis included in this report, students who answered "yes" to a particular statement are considered as taking part in that particular action. Students who answered "no", and students who had an opportunity to answer the question but did not respond (i.e. they were presented the question according to the survey design but left it blank), are considered as not taking part in the action.

StatLink https://stat.link/2z1bet

ANNEX A4

PISA data available for analysis of trends in environmental science performance

As shown in Table A4.1, 18 environmental science items were included in the PISA science assessment in 2006 and 2015. Of these, 11 have been found to remain comparable irrespective of their mode of administration (computer- or paper-based), and can therefore be used to compare student performance over time.

In PISA 2006, the science framework did not identify an independent conceptual basis for analysing environmental science with PISA data. However, a performance measure in environmental science (i.e. the environmental science performance index) was established post-hoc through additional analyses of the PISA data. Out of the 108 science cognitive items used in the PISA 2006 science assessment (OECD, 2009[1]), twenty-four PISA 2006 science items were included in the environmental science performance index. The thematic report *Green At Fifteen?* explored student performance in PISA 2006 using this environmental science performance index (OECD, 2009[2]).

PISA 2015 and PISA 2018 kept 18 out of the 24 science items included in PISA 2006's environmental science performance index but seven items were subsequently found to exhibit mode effects, meaning that their level of difficulty was affected by the change from paper- to computer-based administration. For these reasons, the index cannot be replicated, and trends analysis was conducted at the item level.

In PISA 2015, the 11 trend environmental science items were administered in all countries and economies. Thus, trend data are available for all countries and economies that participated in both PISA 2006 and 2015. In PISA 2015, a total of 184 science cognitive items used in the science assessment (OECD, 2017[3]).

In PISA 2018, however, only six out of the 11 trend items were administered in all countries and economies that took part in the test; the remaining five trend items were administered only in the eight countries that used paper-based (PB) administration in PISA 2018 (Argentina, Jordan, Lebanon, Moldova, North Macedonia, Romania, Saudi Arabia and Ukraine). For this reason, trend analyses are carried out in Chapter 2 using data from PISA 2015 rather than PISA 2018.

Table A4.1 **Items included in PISA 2006's environmental science performance index and availability of comparable data in PISA 2015 and 2018**

PISA 2006		PISA 2015		PISA 2018		Comparable across CB and PB?
Science item	Science item name	CB	PB	CB	PB	
1	Wild Oat Grass (Q04)	Yes	Yes	Yes	Yes	Yes
2	Solar Power Generation (Q02)	Yes	Yes	Yes	Yes	Yes
3	Penguin Island (Q02)	Yes	Yes	Yes	Yes	Yes
4	Penguin Island (Q03)	Yes	Yes	Yes	Yes	Yes
5	Penguin Island (Q04)	Yes	Yes	Yes	Yes	Yes
6	Development and Disaster (Q03)	Yes	Yes	Yes	Yes	No
7	Extinction of the Dinosaurs (Q04)	Yes	Yes	Yes	Yes	Yes
8	Algae (Q02)	Yes	Yes	No	Yes	Yes
9	Algae (Q06)	Yes	Yes	No	Yes	No
10	Earth Temperature (Q01)	Yes	Yes	No	Yes	No
11	Earth Temperature (Q03)	Yes	Yes	No	Yes	Yes
12	Earth Temperature (Q04)	Yes	Yes	No	Yes	Yes
13	Water (Q03a)	Yes	Yes	No	Yes	Yes
14	The Ice Mummy (Q01)	Yes	Yes	No	Yes	No
15	The Ice Mummy (Q02)	Yes	Yes	No	Yes	No
16	Different Climates (Q01)	Yes	Yes	No	Yes	No
17	Different Climates (Q04)	Yes	Yes	No	Yes	Yes
18	Forest Fires (Q05)	Yes	Yes	No	Yes	No
19	Greenhouse (Q03)	No	No	No	No	Unknown
20	Greenhouse (Q04)	No	No	No	No	Unknown
21	Greenhouse (Q05)	No	No	No	No	Unknown
22	Acid Rain (Q02)	No	No	No	No	Unknown
23	The Grand Canyon (Q03)	No	No	No	No	Unknown
24	The Grand Canyon (Q05)	No	No	No	No	Unknown

Note: PB means paper-based administration of the PISA test. CB means computer-based administration. In PISA 2015, 17 countries and economies used PB, and 56 countries and economies used CB. In PISA 2018, 9 countries and economies used PB, and 70 countries and economies used CB. Only items that are comparable across modes of administration (as shown in the last column of this table) will be used for trend analysis in this report.

References

OECD (2017), *PISA 2015 Technical Report.* [3]

OECD (2009), *Green at Fifteen?: How 15-Year-Olds Perform in Environmental Science and Geoscience in PISA 2006*, PISA, OECD Publishing, Paris, https://doi.org/10.1787/9789264063600-en. [2]

OECD (2009), *PISA 2006 Technical Report*, PISA, OECD Publishing, Paris, https://doi.org/10.1787/9789264048096-en. [1]

ANNEX B

PISA 2018 Data

All tables in Annex B are available on line

Results for countries and economies
https://stat.link/zy2p63
https://stat.link/gra5to
https://stat.link/vg1mh6

ANNEX B

Results for countries and economies

Table B.2.2 [1/4] **Student performance in science and in environmental/non-environmental science items, PISA 2015**

Mean score in science and percentage of students who correctly answered environmental and non-environmental science items (PISA 2015)

		Mean science performance in PISA 2015		Percent correct across science items[1]:				Percentage of students who correctly answered the following environmental science item (PISA 2015)							
				Environmental science items only (11 items)		Non-environmental science items (47 items)		Algae (s268q02)		Earth Temperature (s269q03)		Earth Temperature (s269q04)		Water (s304q03a)	
		Mean score	S.E.	%	S.E.	%	S.E.	%	S.E.	%	S.E.	%	S.E.	%	S.E.
OECD	Australia	510	(1.5)	45.5	(0.6)	55.2	(0.4)	38.0	(1.7)	45.0	(1.4)	29.2	(1.3)	31.4	(1.4)
	Austria	495	(2.4)	45.8	(0.7)	54.3	(0.6)	23.1	(1.3)	37.6	(1.9)	32.5	(1.9)	44.0	(2.0)
	Belgium	502	(2.3)	43.8	(0.6)	52.2	(0.5)	24.2	(1.3)	40.8	(1.7)	25.8	(1.3)	44.8	(1.7)
	Canada	528	(2.1)	51.1	(0.7)	58.3	(0.5)	43.5	(1.5)	51.9	(1.8)	36.6	(1.6)	46.4	(1.5)
	Chile	447	(2.4)	32.9	(0.6)	42.0	(0.6)	23.7	(1.5)	28.6	(1.8)	15.8	(1.2)	28.6	(1.8)
	Colombia	416	(2.4)	m	m	36.3	(0.5)	15.7	(1.5)	13.8	(1.1)	19.2	(1.5)	22.2	(1.5)
	Czech Republic	493	(2.3)	43.8	(0.8)	54.1	(0.6)	16.8	(1.6)	38.1	(2.0)	37.1	(2.1)	34.7	(2.1)
	Denmark	502	(2.4)	45.0	(0.8)	54.1	(0.5)	27.2	(1.8)	32.6	(2.0)	37.2	(2.1)	38.1	(2.2)
	Estonia	534	(2.1)	52.3	(0.8)	61.5	(0.5)	61.1	(2.2)	39.3	(2.1)	29.3	(2.2)	48.7	(1.9)
	Finland	531	(2.4)	52.4	(0.8)	61.6	(0.6)	37.1	(1.8)	46.4	(2.1)	33.5	(2.1)	54.3	(2.2)
	France	495	(2.1)	42.8	(0.7)	m	m	25.2	(1.8)	37.1	(1.8)	28.6	(1.8)	44.5	(2.0)
	Germany	509	(2.7)	48.1	(0.8)	55.3	(0.6)	24.2	(1.8)	45.7	(1.9)	30.7	(1.5)	49.3	(1.9)
	Greece	455	(3.9)	37.3	(0.9)	43.7	(0.8)	32.1	(1.8)	29.2	(2.2)	17.2	(1.8)	31.1	(2.2)
	Hungary	477	(2.4)	43.5	(0.7)	m	m	40.6	(2.2)	29.6	(1.8)	38.5	(2.1)	33.2	(1.7)
	Iceland	473	(1.7)	m	m	48.5	(0.5)	17.4	(2.1)	32.7	(2.5)	24.9	(2.1)	35.3	(2.4)
	Ireland	503	(2.4)	49.6	(0.8)	55.1	(0.6)	39.2	(2.4)	63.6	(2.0)	41.3	(1.9)	39.9	(2.3)
	Israel	467	(3.4)	38.5	(0.9)	47.2	(0.8)	27.9	(2.0)	33.0	(1.9)	21.9	(1.8)	47.9	(2.4)
	Italy	481	(2.5)	40.4	(0.8)	53.0	(0.6)	30.7	(1.8)	33.7	(1.7)	30.8	(1.8)	31.9	(1.9)
	Japan	538	(3.0)	m	m	m	m	49.7	(2.1)	77.6	(1.5)	55.5	(2.1)	30.9	(1.9)
	Korea	516	(3.1)	45.9	(0.9)	m	m	45.6	(2.5)	52.4	(2.4)	44.0	(1.9)	38.1	(2.2)
	Latvia	490	(1.6)	41.6	(0.8)	53.0	(0.4)	28.5	(2.0)	28.3	(2.2)	27.5	(2.0)	30.0	(2.0)
	Lithuania	475	(2.7)	40.0	(0.7)	50.2	(0.6)	29.6	(1.7)	36.9	(2.4)	25.6	(1.6)	32.0	(2.1)
	Luxembourg	483	(1.1)	42.3	(0.7)	51.3	(0.4)	26.8	(2.0)	34.0	(2.0)	25.5	(1.5)	37.3	(2.2)
	Mexico	416	(2.1)	28.1	(0.6)	35.4	(0.5)	29.0	(1.9)	10.5	(1.2)	16.9	(1.4)	29.7	(2.3)
	Netherlands	509	(2.3)	44.3	(0.7)	55.2	(0.5)	29.8	(1.5)	36.9	(2.1)	29.4	(1.8)	42.8	(2.2)
	New Zealand	513	(2.4)	43.7	(0.9)	55.8	(0.6)	33.7	(2.5)	49.5	(2.2)	26.1	(1.9)	34.5	(2.1)
	Norway	498	(2.3)	44.2	(0.8)	53.2	(0.6)	18.7	(2.0)	40.0	(1.9)	33.7	(2.2)	44.4	(2.1)
	Poland	501	(2.5)	49.1	(0.9)	55.4	(0.6)	41.4	(2.1)	44.3	(2.1)	35.9	(2.5)	43.2	(2.3)
	Portugal	501	(2.4)	43.4	(0.7)	53.0	(0.5)	30.6	(1.9)	34.2	(2.1)	31.6	(2.2)	40.0	(1.9)
	Slovak Republic	461	(2.6)	36.7	(0.8)	46.9	(0.7)	19.5	(1.7)	28.2	(1.9)	29.7	(2.2)	29.7	(1.8)
	Slovenia	513	(1.3)	52.6	(0.8)	55.3	(0.4)	45.5	(2.3)	32.6	(2.4)	37.6	(2.4)	48.6	(2.1)
	Spain	493	(2.1)	43.1	(0.6)	52.5	(0.5)	34.7	(1.9)	38.4	(1.7)	30.1	(1.7)	32.8	(1.7)
	Sweden	493	(3.6)	46.9	(0.9)	52.2	(0.8)	27.5	(1.8)	55.0	(2.4)	40.8	(2.5)	39.9	(2.3)
	Switzerland	506	(2.9)	47.5	(0.9)	54.8	(0.6)	35.5	(2.5)	39.5	(2.4)	31.5	(2.3)	41.0	(2.6)
	Türkiye	425	(3.9)	26.9	(0.9)	39.3	(0.9)	18.0	(1.6)	16.0	(1.7)	16.7	(1.8)	17.3	(1.9)
	United Kingdom	509	(2.6)	48.5	(0.7)	56.8	(0.6)	42.9	(2.0)	59.8	(2.0)	44.7	(1.8)	44.8	(2.3)
	United States	496	(3.2)	41.6	(0.7)	51.6	(0.8)	32.5	(2.3)	37.9	(2.1)	28.7	(1.8)	28.8	(1.7)
	OECD average-33	492	(0.4)	43.5	(0.1)	52.2	(0.1)	32.3	(0.3)	38.4	(0.3)	30.6	(0.3)	38.2	(0.4)
	OECD average	491	(0.4)	41.5	(0.1)	49.7	(0.1)	29.9	(0.3)	37.4	(0.3)	28.9	(0.3)	34.6	(0.3)

1. 58 science items are comparable between 2006 and 2015.

StatLink https://stat.link/5me8xs

Table B.2.2 [2/4] **Student performance in science and in environmental/non-environmental science items, PISA 2015**
Mean score in science and percentage of students who correctly answered environmental and non-environmental science items (PISA 2015)

	Percentage of students who correctly answered the following environmental science item (PISA 2015)													
	Wild Oat Grass (s408q04)		Solar Power Generation (s415q02)		Penguin Island (s425q02)		Penguin Island (s425q03)		Penguin Island (s425q04)		Different Climates (s465q04)		Extinction of the Dinosaurs (s527q04)	
	%	S.E.	%	S.E.	%	S.E.	%	S.E.	%	S.E.	%	S.E.	%	S.E.
OECD														
Australia	60.6	(1.5)	80.2	(1.3)	52.9	(1.6)	41.3	(1.8)	21.7	(1.3)	41.4	(1.6)	58.8	(1.5)
Austria	55.0	(1.9)	86.5	(1.4)	48.4	(2.2)	35.9	(1.9)	45.0	(2.4)	35.4	(2.0)	60.6	(2.0)
Belgium	47.5	(1.9)	72.8	(1.9)	55.0	(1.7)	44.5	(1.8)	35.4	(1.6)	39.2	(1.7)	51.5	(1.6)
Canada	58.7	(1.7)	83.5	(1.1)	57.8	(1.7)	43.3	(1.6)	35.2	(1.4)	42.6	(1.3)	62.7	(1.4)
Chile	41.1	(2.0)	70.6	(2.1)	38.6	(2.5)	41.2	(2.1)	21.9	(1.8)	16.9	(1.4)	34.4	(2.1)
Colombia	34.2	(1.5)	61.5	(2.1)	31.8	(2.2)	27.3	(1.8)	9.9	(1.1)	m	m	29.6	(1.9)
Czech Republic	59.5	(2.0)	72.6	(2.7)	45.0	(2.1)	52.3	(2.2)	26.5	(2.4)	41.4	(2.1)	58.3	(2.1)
Denmark	62.5	(2.0)	77.8	(1.6)	54.0	(2.3)	48.4	(2.3)	21.9	(1.8)	37.5	(2.4)	57.5	(2.3)
Estonia	62.8	(2.1)	86.1	(1.7)	50.0	(2.4)	60.7	(2.3)	38.9	(2.3)	52.2	(2.5)	45.8	(2.5)
Finland	64.5	(2.0)	84.8	(2.2)	54.8	(2.4)	45.9	(1.8)	46.9	(2.0)	42.5	(2.0)	65.4	(1.9)
France	49.0	(2.0)	73.8	(1.8)	49.7	(2.0)	47.8	(1.9)	35.1	(2.1)	21.8	(1.6)	57.9	(2.0)
Germany	57.4	(1.8)	82.3	(2.3)	54.3	(1.9)	41.3	(2.1)	41.2	(1.8)	37.5	(1.9)	64.8	(1.7)
Greece	37.6	(2.0)	67.8	(2.3)	49.2	(2.1)	45.5	(2.2)	36.7	(2.0)	27.1	(1.9)	37.4	(1.9)
Hungary	40.9	(2.1)	76.0	(1.7)	46.0	(2.4)	34.7	(2.3)	37.6	(2.2)	46.0	(1.8)	55.1	(1.9)
Iceland	46.6	(2.6)	73.7	(2.3)	51.9	(2.8)	37.3	(2.3)	18.9	(2.3)	m	m	35.9	(2.8)
Ireland	58.0	(2.2)	77.0	(1.9)	55.7	(2.0)	43.0	(2.1)	22.1	(1.9)	44.0	(2.0)	62.1	(1.8)
Israel	48.5	(2.2)	65.3	(1.8)	48.8	(2.6)	33.4	(2.5)	43.1	(2.3)	20.2	(3.3)	33.7	(2.0)
Italy	46.3	(2.0)	75.3	(1.9)	45.5	(2.1)	30.1	(1.8)	30.3	(2.1)	28.0	(2.0)	61.8	(1.8)
Japan	39.1	(1.8)	81.0	(1.4)	58.6	(1.8)	41.6	(1.9)	22.5	(1.6)	m	m	67.2	(2.0)
Korea	37.4	(2.1)	74.7	(1.6)	66.0	(1.9)	43.1	(2.3)	19.6	(1.8)	43.2	(2.0)	41.0	(2.3)
Latvia	55.6	(2.1)	75.5	(2.2)	47.7	(2.2)	46.9	(2.5)	26.3	(2.2)	41.2	(2.0)	50.0	(2.3)
Lithuania	57.4	(2.1)	64.1	(2.0)	38.8	(1.9)	43.6	(1.9)	25.2	(2.0)	44.3	(2.1)	42.4	(1.9)
Luxembourg	48.8	(1.9)	80.1	(1.9)	50.7	(2.0)	42.2	(2.1)	35.3	(2.6)	30.1	(1.9)	54.5	(2.2)
Mexico	20.5	(1.3)	63.9	(2.0)	34.4	(2.0)	33.0	(2.0)	12.6	(1.5)	24.7	(1.8)	34.1	(1.8)
Netherlands	46.9	(2.1)	75.2	(1.5)	57.6	(2.0)	43.1	(2.3)	31.6	(2.1)	39.6	(2.1)	54.6	(1.9)
New Zealand	57.1	(2.5)	78.9	(2.1)	50.0	(2.3)	35.2	(2.1)	27.0	(2.3)	31.0	(2.2)	57.8	(2.4)
Norway	60.3	(2.1)	74.4	(2.1)	55.5	(2.1)	39.7	(2.0)	27.4	(2.2)	37.4	(1.9)	55.1	(2.1)
Poland	67.8	(2.0)	84.5	(1.9)	50.6	(2.3)	51.1	(2.3)	24.5	(1.9)	41.2	(2.6)	55.6	(2.3)
Portugal	53.6	(2.1)	84.5	(1.2)	44.2	(1.9)	40.7	(1.9)	37.5	(2.2)	21.6	(1.8)	58.3	(2.2)
Slovak Republic	48.3	(2.4)	65.8	(2.3)	42.4	(1.7)	27.5	(1.6)	22.6	(1.8)	46.7	(1.9)	43.5	(2.0)
Slovenia	63.1	(2.1)	81.9	(1.3)	48.6	(2.4)	64.5	(2.1)	43.7	(2.9)	52.8	(2.1)	60.1	(2.2)
Spain	49.3	(1.8)	80.2	(1.9)	43.5	(2.3)	39.6	(2.2)	43.3	(2.2)	31.0	(1.7)	51.3	(2.1)
Sweden	59.5	(2.2)	72.5	(2.2)	55.7	(2.4)	40.5	(2.0)	36.5	(2.2)	33.1	(1.9)	55.0	(2.1)
Switzerland	54.3	(1.9)	82.8	(2.7)	54.6	(2.3)	43.6	(2.3)	45.3	(2.4)	33.1	(2.3)	61.5	(2.3)
Türkiye	28.6	(1.7)	46.5	(2.7)	36.7	(2.4)	26.8	(1.6)	16.3	(1.9)	31.1	(2.0)	42.0	(2.2)
United Kingdom	59.0	(1.6)	74.8	(1.7)	49.9	(1.7)	36.0	(1.7)	26.9	(1.8)	31.9	(1.8)	62.8	(1.6)
United States	57.2	(1.9)	75.1	(2.0)	50.7	(2.3)	35.4	(1.8)	21.4	(1.7)	34.3	(2.2)	55.4	(2.2)
OECD average-33	51.9	(0.3)	75.6	(0.3)	49.3	(0.4)	41.9	(0.4)	31.4	(0.4)	35.9	(0.4)	53.0	(0.4)
OECD average	48.5	(0.3)	72.0	(0.3)	47.1	(0.3)	40.2	(0.3)	27.0	(0.3)	35.5	(0.3)	48.6	(0.3)

1. 58 science items are comparable between 2006 and 2015.

StatLink https://stat.link/5me8xs

Table B.2.2 [3/4] **Student performance in science and in environmental/non-environmental science items, PISA 2015**
Mean score in science and percentage of students who correctly answered environmental and non-environmental science items (PISA 2015)

		Mean science performance in PISA 2015		Percent correct across science items[1]:				Percentage of students who correctly answered the following environmental science item (PISA 2015)							
				Environmental science items only (11 items)		Non-environmental science items (47 items)		Algae (s268q02)		Earth Temperature (s269q03)		Earth Temperature (s269q04)		Water (s304q03a)	
		Mean score	S.E.	%	S.E.	%	S.E.	%	S.E.	%	S.E.	%	S.E.	%	S.E.
Partners	Brazil	401	(2.3)	m	m	34.6	(0.4)	9.5	(0.8)	12.2	(1.0)	17.4	(1.2)	19.9	(1.2)
	Bulgaria	446	(4.4)	35.5	(1.0)	43.9	(0.9)	30.6	(2.2)	26.1	(1.8)	16.3	(1.3)	35.3	(2.1)
	Croatia	475	(2.5)	39.5	(0.7)	49.7	(0.6)	20.4	(1.6)	25.4	(1.5)	23.0	(1.9)	32.7	(1.8)
	Hong Kong (China)	523	(2.5)	50.4	(0.8)	61.2	(0.6)	46.2	(2.6)	73.6	(2.0)	48.6	(2.2)	30.5	(2.1)
	Indonesia	403	(2.6)	31.0	(0.5)	m	m	28.9	(1.1)	21.0	(1.0)	9.7	(0.8)	27.3	(1.4)
	Jordan	409	(2.7)	30.3	(0.5)	36.2	(0.5)	7.1	(0.7)	36.3	(1.3)	14.8	(0.9)	34.9	(1.3)
	Macao (China)	529	(1.1)	49.6	(0.8)	57.0	(0.5)	46.2	(2.4)	73.4	(1.9)	42.6	(2.4)	28.5	(2.0)
	Montenegro	411	(1.0)	30.7	(0.8)	35.3	(0.4)	14.8	(1.3)	16.8	(1.6)	21.2	(1.8)	19.0	(2.0)
	Qatar	418	(1.0)	31.8	(0.4)	37.8	(0.3)	17.6	(1.2)	32.2	(1.2)	28.1	(1.1)	24.6	(1.2)
	Romania	435	(3.2)	35.8	(0.8)	41.0	(0.6)	40.8	(1.5)	26.6	(1.5)	18.3	(0.9)	45.4	(1.6)
	Chinese Taipei	532	(2.7)	49.6	(0.7)	57.8	(0.5)	56.8	(1.8)	69.3	(1.7)	36.4	(1.5)	23.3	(1.7)
	Thailand	421	(2.8)	26.6	(0.7)	36.7	(0.6)	0.9	(0.2)	31.8	(1.9)	13.7	(1.5)	10.8	(1.4)
	Tunisia	386	(2.1)	21.1	(0.6)	m	m	17.5	(1.6)	11.3	(1.3)	18.6	(1.7)	9.4	(1.3)
	Uruguay	435	(2.2)	m	m	39.8	(0.5)	20.3	(1.6)	23.2	(1.8)	24.2	(1.8)	30.4	(1.9)

1. 58 science items are comparable between 2006 and 2015.

StatLink https://stat.link/5me8xs

Table B.2.2 [4/4] **Student performance in science and in environmental/non-environmental science items, PISA 2015**
Mean score in science and percentage of students who correctly answered environmental and non-environmental science items (PISA 2015)

		Percentage of students who correctly answered the following environmental science item (PISA 2015)													
		Wild Oat Grass (s408q04)		Solar Power Generation (s415q02)		Penguin Island (s425q02)		Penguin Island (s425q03)		Penguin Island (s425q04)		Different Climates (s465q04)		Extinction of the Dinosaurs (s527q04)	
		%	S.E.	%	S.E.	%	S.E.	%	S.E.	%	S.E.	%	S.E.	%	S.E.
Partners	Brazil	35.5	(1.3)	54.0	(1.7)	33.5	(1.5)	29.0	(1.7)	10.0	(1.0)	m	m	28.4	(1.5)
	Bulgaria	42.9	(1.7)	60.6	(2.4)	43.2	(2.3)	34.3	(2.3)	23.2	(2.5)	37.9	(2.1)	39.7	(2.1)
	Croatia	53.0	(2.0)	72.8	(1.4)	40.4	(2.2)	49.2	(2.1)	19.4	(1.9)	45.1	(1.8)	52.9	(2.1)
	Hong Kong (China)	50.2	(2.6)	81.3	(1.9)	63.2	(2.3)	42.7	(2.5)	27.7	(2.3)	41.2	(2.1)	49.3	(2.2)
	Indonesia	44.8	(1.3)	56.5	(1.5)	38.0	(1.2)	40.5	(1.1)	13.9	(0.9)	30.3	(1.0)	29.9	(1.0)
	Jordan	32.2	(1.2)	60.0	(1.6)	32.7	(1.4)	46.4	(1.4)	12.5	(0.8)	22.2	(1.1)	34.7	(1.2)
	Macao (China)	52.9	(2.1)	82.2	(1.8)	56.8	(2.2)	43.8	(2.3)	27.2	(2.3)	41.3	(2.3)	50.4	(2.3)
	Montenegro	31.1	(1.8)	60.3	(1.9)	35.1	(2.1)	48.2	(2.3)	18.1	(2.0)	37.4	(1.9)	35.2	(2.3)
	Qatar	34.9	(1.2)	58.9	(1.4)	38.5	(1.6)	31.7	(1.2)	13.3	(1.2)	31.2	(1.2)	38.8	(1.4)
	Romania	36.8	(1.4)	61.4	(1.4)	31.7	(1.3)	44.3	(1.7)	19.8	(1.0)	29.8	(1.3)	39.2	(1.4)
	Chinese Taipei	55.0	(1.6)	76.4	(1.5)	63.5	(1.7)	47.0	(1.9)	31.7	(1.7)	43.8	(1.9)	42.9	(1.8)
	Thailand	46.2	(2.0)	58.2	(2.1)	37.0	(2.2)	17.0	(1.6)	14.8	(1.5)	30.7	(1.4)	31.9	(2.2)
	Tunisia	31.8	(2.2)	43.8	(2.1)	28.6	(2.2)	10.6	(1.5)	6.5	(1.2)	21.9	(1.8)	31.8	(2.4)
	Uruguay	30.4	(1.9)	61.6	(2.3)	33.5	(2.2)	35.1	(2.3)	23.1	(2.0)	m	m	37.0	(2.1)

1. 58 science items are comparable between 2006 and 2015.

StatLink https://stat.link/5me8xs

Table B.2.3 [1/4] **Change between PISA 2006 and PISA 2015 in student performance in science and in environmental/non-environmental science items**

Score-point difference in science and percentage-point difference of students who correctly answered environmental and non-environmental science items (PISA 2015-PISA 2006)

		Change in science performance (PISA 2015 - PISA 2006)		Change between 2006 and 2015 in the percent correct across[1]:				Change in the percentage of students who correctly answered the following environmental science item (PISA 2015 - PISA 2006)							
				Environmental science items only (11 items)		Non-environmental science items (47 items)		Algae (s268q02)		Earth Temperature (s269q03)		Earth Temperature (s269q04)		Water (s304q03a)	
		Score dif.	S.E.	% dif.	S.E.	% dif.	S.E.	% dif.	S.E.	% dif.	S.E.	% dif.	S.E.	% dif.	S.E.
OECD	Australia	**-17**	(5.2)	**-3.6**	(0.7)	**-3.9**	(0.6)	-2.6	(1.9)	**-4.3**	(1.7)	**-5.9**	(1.6)	**-9.4**	(1.7)
	Austria	**-16**	(6.4)	-0.6	(1.2)	-1.6	(1.0)	**-4.9**	(1.9)	-3.9	(2.5)	**-6.7**	(2.4)	-0.3	(2.5)
	Belgium	-8	(5.6)	**-1.9**	(0.8)	**-3.7**	(0.7)	**-5.6**	(1.7)	2.8	(2.1)	**-4.5**	(1.7)	-2.4	(2.0)
	Canada	-7	(5.3)	-1.4	(0.8)	**-2.5**	(0.7)	**-8.5**	(1.8)	-1.2	(2.1)	-1.3	(1.9)	**3.8**	(1.7)
	Chile	9	(6.7)	-1.3	(1.0)	-0.7	(1.0)	**-5.1**	(2.0)	**5.4**	(2.3)	**-14.8**	(1.9)	3.1	(2.3)
	Colombia	**28**	(6.1)	m	m	-0.2	(0.9)	-1.4	(2.1)	-3.0	(1.7)	-3.4	(2.1)	**-6.1**	(2.3)
	Czech Republic	**-20**	(6.1)	**-3.0**	(1.1)	**-2.7**	(0.9)	**-18.2**	(2.2)	-1.0	(2.4)	**-10.9**	(2.7)	**-6.6**	(2.7)
	Denmark	6	(5.9)	1.7	(1.1)	1.0	(0.8)	**-10.0**	(2.5)	1.0	(2.4)	1.3	(2.6)	-0.3	(2.6)
	Estonia	3	(5.6)	**2.9**	(1.0)	**1.8**	(0.8)	**11.4**	(2.6)	-0.1	(2.5)	-3.9	(2.6)	**-5.0**	(2.3)
	Finland	**-33**	(5.5)	**-2.8**	(0.9)	**-5.0**	(0.8)	**-10.4**	(2.3)	1.2	(2.6)	-0.1	(2.4)	**-5.2**	(2.6)
	France	0	(6.0)	-1.0	(1.0)	m	m	**-17.1**	(2.4)	-0.1	(2.3)	1.4	(2.1)	-3.3	(2.4)
	Germany	-7	(6.5)	-1.6	(1.2)	**-2.1**	(1.0)	**-6.2**	(2.3)	0.3	(2.5)	**-8.6**	(2.1)	-4.7	(2.4)
	Greece	**-19**	(6.8)	**-2.9**	(1.1)	**-4.7**	(1.0)	**-17.0**	(2.4)	-4.8	(2.7)	-3.5	(2.1)	-3.0	(2.7)
	Hungary	**-27**	(5.8)	**-4.4**	(1.0)	m	m	**-6.0**	(2.7)	**-12.9**	(2.3)	**-5.2**	(2.6)	**-9.1**	(2.2)
	Iceland	**-18**	(5.1)	m	m	**-3.5**	(0.7)	**-10.9**	(2.4)	-3.2	(2.9)	-0.6	(2.4)	4.0	(2.7)
	Ireland	-6	(6.0)	**2.6**	(1.1)	0.4	(0.8)	4.3	(2.8)	-1.4	(2.5)	3.0	(2.3)	**6.4**	(2.6)
	Israel	13	(6.8)	-1.4	(1.1)	1.1	(1.0)	**-10.2**	(2.5)	1.0	(2.5)	-0.9	(2.2)	-1.0	(2.8)
	Italy	5	(5.5)	**3.1**	(0.9)	**2.6**	(0.7)	-3.0	(2.0)	3.6	(2.0)	-1.7	(2.1)	-0.1	(2.1)
	Japan	7	(6.3)	m	m	m	m	0.4	(2.6)	-2.5	(2.0)	-1.7	(2.4)	**-10.6**	(2.3)
	Korea	-6	(6.4)	**-3.4**	(1.2)	m	m	-3.3	(3.0)	-2.4	(2.8)	1.9	(2.4)	**-8.2**	(2.6)
	Latvia	1	(5.6)	1.0	(1.1)	**1.6**	(0.8)	2.7	(2.4)	**6.6**	(2.6)	**4.8**	(2.4)	-3.3	(2.8)
	Lithuania	**-13**	(5.9)	**-3.3**	(1.0)	-0.7	(0.9)	**-11.4**	(2.2)	-2.7	(2.9)	**-5.0**	(2.1)	0.3	(2.6)
	Luxembourg	-4	(4.7)	0.9	(0.8)	-0.2	(0.5)	**-5.3**	(2.2)	4.4	(2.3)	-0.1	(1.8)	-1.9	(2.6)
	Mexico	6	(5.7)	-0.7	(0.8)	m	m	0.7	(2.2)	-0.6	(1.4)	**-10.4**	(1.7)	-0.8	(2.6)
	Netherlands	**-16**	(5.7)	**-2.9**	(0.9)	**-4.4**	(0.8)	1.1	(1.9)	1.7	(2.5)	**-5.8**	(2.2)	**-7.6**	(2.7)
	New Zealand	**-17**	(5.7)	**-4.8**	(1.1)	**-3.9**	(0.8)	**-7.9**	(2.9)	-1.2	(2.6)	-1.8	(2.2)	-4.5	(2.5)
	Norway	**12**	(5.9)	m	m	m	m	m	m	**8.9**	(2.4)	-0.5	(2.7)	**11.5**	(2.4)
	Poland	4	(5.6)	**2.5**	(1.1)	**2.5**	(0.8)	1.3	(2.6)	-4.2	(2.5)	0.1	(2.9)	2.1	(2.7)
	Portugal	**27**	(5.9)	**6.2**	(1.0)	**4.2**	(0.8)	**12.0**	(2.2)	2.7	(2.4)	-0.5	(2.6)	**10.9**	(2.4)
	Slovak Republic	**-28**	(5.8)	**-5.6**	(1.1)	**-4.3**	(0.9)	**-11.0**	(2.4)	**-9.8**	(2.4)	-3.9	(2.7)	-2.8	(2.2)
	Slovenia	-6	(4.8)	**3.1**	(1.0)	0.3	(0.5)	0.5	(2.7)	1.5	(2.8)	-0.2	(2.8)	1.1	(2.5)
	Spain	4	(5.6)	**2.4**	(0.8)	1.1	(0.7)	-0.8	(2.3)	0.6	(2.2)	1.9	(2.0)	-0.6	(2.0)
	Sweden	-10	(6.2)	2.0	(1.1)	m	m	2.0	(2.4)	**7.9**	(2.8)	2.0	(2.8)	3.5	(2.6)
	Switzerland	-6	(6.2)	0.5	(1.2)	-1.6	(0.9)	-1.1	(2.8)	1.8	(2.8)	-0.6	(2.6)	-4.5	(2.8)
	Türkiye	2	(7.1)	-1.5	(1.2)	0.5	(1.2)	**-4.4**	(2.1)	-3.4	(2.3)	2.8	(2.3)	-2.9	(2.5)
	United Kingdom	-6	(5.6)	**2.1**	(0.9)	-0.7	(0.7)	3.4	(2.3)	4.2	(2.3)	1.3	(2.1)	**10.1**	(2.6)
	United States	7	(6.9)	-0.7	(1.1)	-0.3	(1.1)	-3.1	(2.7)	-3.3	(2.5)	0.0	(2.2)	0.7	(2.3)
	OECD average-33	**-6**	(1.0)	**-0.5**	(0.2)	**-0.9**	(0.2)	**-4.1**	(0.4)	-0.3	(0.4)	**-2.3**	(0.4)	**-1.4**	(0.4)
	OECD average	**-4**	(1.0)	**-0.3**	(0.2)	**-0.3**	(0.1)	**-3.4**	(0.3)	-0.4	(0.3)	**-2.0**	(0.3)	**-0.9**	(0.3)

Note: Statistically significant differences are marked in bold.

1. 58 science items are comparable between 2006 and 2015.

StatLink https://stat.link/nh7c28

Table B.2.3 [2/4] **Change between PISA 2006 and PISA 2015 in student performance in science and in environmental/non-environmental science items**

Score-point difference in science and percentage-point difference of students who correctly answered environmental and non-environmental science items (PISA 2015-PISA 2006)

	Change in the percentage of students who correctly answered the following environmental science item (PISA 2015 - PISA 2006)														
		Wild Oat Grass (s408q04)		Solar Power Generation (s415q02)		Penguin Island (s425q02)		Penguin Island (s425q03)		Penguin Island (s425q04)		Different Climates (s465q04)		Extinction of the Dinosaurs (s527q04)	
		% dif.	S.E.	% dif.	S.E.	% dif.	S.E.	% dif.	S.E.	% dif.	S.E.	% dif.	S.E.	% dif.	S.E.
OECD	**Australia**	-1.7	(1.7)	-1.4	(1.5)	-1.2	(1.9)	**-5.1**	(2.1)	**-5.7**	(1.5)	0.0	(1.9)	-2.7	(1.7)
	Austria	0.3	(2.4)	0.6	(1.7)	**6.7**	(2.6)	**-5.3**	(2.3)	**5.6**	(2.9)	-1.2	(2.5)	2.8	(2.5)
	Belgium	1.6	(2.2)	**-4.6**	(2.1)	0.8	(2.0)	**-5.0**	(2.1)	**-4.3**	(1.9)	0.9	(2.1)	-0.7	(2.0)
	Canada	**5.5**	(2.0)	**-3.0**	(1.3)	0.8	(2.0)	**-4.7**	(1.9)	-2.2	(1.7)	**-4.5**	(1.6)	-0.1	(1.7)
	Chile	-0.9	(2.5)	-2.3	(2.5)	**6.0**	(3.0)	0.5	(2.6)	-0.9	(2.2)	-0.7	(1.8)	-4.4	(2.6)
	Colombia	4.3	(2.5)	**-8.2**	(2.7)	2.9	(2.8)	-0.6	(2.8)	**-8.4**	(1.6)	m	m	3.4	(2.6)
	Czech Republic	**5.5**	(2.6)	**-9.8**	(2.9)	3.7	(2.5)	**7.5**	(2.7)	-3.6	(2.8)	-3.2	(2.5)	3.9	(2.4)
	Denmark	1.9	(2.4)	0.3	(2.0)	**10.2**	(2.8)	**7.1**	(2.8)	-2.1	(2.2)	-2.2	(2.8)	**11.1**	(2.8)
	Estonia	**5.6**	(2.5)	**6.6**	(2.1)	**9.8**	(2.9)	**5.5**	(2.7)	4.7	(2.9)	-1.3	(3.0)	-1.1	(2.8)
	Finland	-2.5	(2.3)	**-4.8**	(2.4)	2.6	(2.8)	-1.2	(2.4)	**-5.2**	(2.5)	**-5.3**	(2.5)	0.1	(2.3)
	France	-1.9	(2.4)	**10.7**	(2.3)	2.7	(2.5)	**5.4**	(2.4)	-1.9	(2.4)	**-6.2**	(2.0)	-0.7	(2.5)
	Germany	0.0	(2.3)	**-6.0**	(2.5)	**9.4**	(2.4)	-2.8	(2.5)	-0.5	(2.3)	-1.5	(2.4)	3.1	(2.2)
	Greece	-3.7	(2.5)	**-10.8**	(2.7)	**7.3**	(2.6)	5.2	(2.7)	2.9	(2.6)	3.7	(2.4)	**-7.6**	(2.3)
	Hungary	-2.3	(2.5)	0.4	(2.1)	**8.6**	(2.8)	**-13.1**	(2.8)	2.5	(2.6)	**-8.0**	(2.4)	-3.7	(2.5)
	Iceland	1.5	(3.0)	-1.0	(2.6)	1.6	(3.2)	2.8	(2.7)	-2.5	(2.7)	m	m	-4.3	(3.2)
	Ireland	-1.8	(2.6)	-0.1	(2.3)	**11.6**	(2.4)	**6.9**	(2.5)	**6.8**	(2.2)	-3.4	(2.4)	-3.7	(2.4)
	Israel	0.0	(2.6)	-0.2	(2.4)	3.3	(2.9)	**-7.7**	(2.9)	3.1	(2.9)	-3.9	(3.6)	0.8	(2.6)
	Italy	**10.8**	(2.3)	0.9	(2.2)	**9.8**	(2.3)	2.8	(2.0)	**10.1**	(2.2)	-2.7	(2.4)	3.9	(2.1)
	Japan	**-6.0**	(2.2)	0.6	(1.7)	-0.6	(2.4)	**-8.2**	(2.2)	-3.5	(2.1)	m	m	**10.8**	(2.4)
	Korea	2.3	(2.5)	-2.9	(2.0)	-0.9	(2.3)	**-7.6**	(2.8)	**-6.5**	(2.4)	-4.9	(2.5)	**-5.3**	(2.7)
	Latvia	3.7	(2.7)	0.4	(2.6)	**11.2**	(2.6)	**-6.6**	(3.2)	**-6.0**	(2.6)	-1.5	(2.5)	-0.6	(3.0)
	Lithuania	-1.5	(2.5)	-4.1	(2.5)	**4.8**	(2.4)	-4.3	(2.5)	**-7.0**	(2.4)	**-6.0**	(2.5)	1.1	(2.6)
	Luxembourg	-0.4	(2.4)	2.4	(2.1)	**7.4**	(2.3)	1.0	(2.5)	-2.4	(2.9)	0.2	(2.2)	4.6	(2.6)
	Mexico	0.4	(1.6)	**-5.2**	(2.5)	2.8	(2.3)	**7.3**	(2.2)	-2.5	(1.7)	2.2	(2.0)	-1.2	(2.2)
	Netherlands	**-6.0**	(2.5)	**-7.6**	(2.0)	2.3	(2.3)	-3.4	(2.7)	**-9.4**	(2.6)	2.8	(2.4)	-0.4	(2.5)
	New Zealand	**-5.7**	(2.7)	**-5.1**	(2.3)	-2.6	(2.7)	**-12.2**	(2.4)	-1.1	(2.6)	-2.4	(2.5)	**-7.9**	(2.7)
	Norway	-2.6	(2.5)	-2.8	(2.5)	**17.4**	(2.6)	**5.5**	(2.4)	0.1	(2.6)	-1.0	(2.3)	**9.9**	(2.5)
	Poland	**9.3**	(2.4)	**4.4**	(2.2)	**7.8**	(2.7)	**7.2**	(2.6)	-3.1	(2.3)	-0.5	(2.9)	2.7	(2.6)
	Portugal	**11.0**	(2.6)	1.5	(1.8)	**8.7**	(2.4)	1.5	(2.4)	**13.0**	(2.6)	**5.5**	(2.0)	1.8	(2.6)
	Slovak Republic	-3.3	(2.8)	**-15.4**	(2.6)	**5.6**	(2.3)	**-11.6**	(2.0)	**-6.7**	(2.3)	0.4	(2.3)	-3.5	(2.5)
	Slovenia	**5.6**	(2.6)	3.4	(1.8)	5.0	(2.8)	**9.3**	(2.5)	1.6	(3.2)	2.6	(2.5)	3.3	(2.5)
	Spain	2.3	(2.2)	0.3	(2.1)	**6.2**	(2.5)	-0.9	(2.4)	**13.5**	(2.4)	1.3	(2.0)	3.0	(2.5)
	Sweden	-1.3	(2.6)	-4.0	(2.5)	4.8	(2.8)	-4.2	(2.5)	**8.8**	(2.6)	1.9	(2.3)	0.6	(2.5)
	Switzerland	2.8	(2.3)	-1.7	(2.8)	4.0	(2.6)	2.5	(2.6)	-0.7	(2.7)	-1.4	(2.8)	4.5	(2.6)
	Türkiye	**-7.7**	(2.3)	-2.1	(3.0)	0.9	(2.8)	**-10.6**	(2.3)	2.6	(2.2)	-0.9	(2.5)	**8.8**	(2.6)
	United Kingdom	-0.4	(2.1)	**-5.9**	(1.9)	**5.3**	(2.1)	2.7	(2.0)	-0.4	(2.2)	2.3	(2.0)	0.2	(2.1)
	United States	2.7	(2.3)	0.7	(2.4)	3.5	(2.8)	-1.9	(2.4)	0.6	(2.0)	-5.0	(2.7)	-1.9	(2.6)
	OECD average-33	**0.9**	(0.4)	**-1.9**	(0.4)	**5.1**	(0.4)	**-1.1**	(0.4)	0.1	(0.4)	**-1.3**	(0.4)	0.3	(0.4)
	OECD average	**0.9**	(0.3)	**-1.1**	(0.3)	**4.9**	(0.4)	**-1.6**	(0.3)	**-0.8**	(0.3)	**-0.8**	(0.3)	**1.0**	(0.3)

Note: Statistically significant differences are marked in bold.

1. 58 science items are comparable between 2006 and 2015.

StatLink https://stat.link/nh7c28

Table B.2.3 [3/4] **Change between PISA 2006 and PISA 2015 in student performance in science and in environmental/non-environmental science items**

Score-point difference in science and percentage-point difference of students who correctly answered environmental and non-environmental science items (PISA 2015-PISA 2006)

		Change in science performance (PISA 2015 - PISA 2006)		Change between 2006 and 2015 in the percent correct across[1]:				Change in the percentage of students who correctly answered the following environmental science item (PISA 2015 - PISA 2006)							
				Environmental science items only (11 items)		Non-environmental science items (47 items)		Algae (s268q02)		Earth Temperature (s269q03)		Earth Temperature (s269q04)		Water (s304q03a)	
		Score dif.	S.E.	% dif.	S.E.	% dif.	S.E.	% dif.	S.E.	% dif.	S.E.	% dif.	S.E.	% dif.	S.E.
Partners	Brazil	10	(5.8)	m	m	1.1	(0.7)	**-14.4**	(1.4)	-1.5	(1.5)	-1.4	(1.6)	-2.7	(1.7)
	Bulgaria	12	(8.7)	1.2	(1.5)	2.3	(1.5)	-1.3	(2.9)	2.6	(2.5)	0.8	(1.7)	-0.9	(3.0)
	Croatia	**-18**	(5.7)	-1.2	(0.9)	**-1.6**	(0.8)	**-7.9**	(1.9)	**-4.7**	(2.0)	**-8.2**	(2.2)	-0.3	(2.2)
	Hong Kong (China)	**-19**	(5.7)	**-5.3**	(1.0)	0.0	(0.8)	-4.2	(2.9)	**-8.5**	(2.4)	**-5.9**	(2.9)	**-5.4**	(2.5)
	Indonesia	10	(7.7)	**3.7**	(1.2)	m	m	**8.0**	(1.7)	3.2	(2.3)	1.7	(1.1)	**10.6**	(3.0)
	Jordan	**-13**	(5.9)	**-4.1**	(0.8)	-1.5	(0.8)	**-7.4**	(1.3)	-3.0	(1.7)	**-4.2**	(1.6)	-2.8	(2.0)
	Macao (China)	**18**	(4.7)	0.2	(1.0)	**1.8**	(0.6)	4.4	(2.7)	-2.2	(2.4)	-5.4	(2.8)	-0.9	(2.4)
	Montenegro	0	(4.7)	0.0	(0.9)	0.6	(0.5)	**-7.3**	(1.8)	-2.0	(2.0)	3.7	(2.2)	1.6	(2.4)
	Qatar	**68**	(4.7)	**11.6**	(0.5)	**12.6**	(0.3)	**8.3**	(1.4)	**16.7**	(1.5)	**12.6**	(1.4)	**12.1**	(1.4)
	Romania	**16**	(6.9)	**6.6**	(1.1)	**4.9**	(1.0)	**26.6**	(1.9)	0.6	(2.9)	**-4.1**	(1.9)	**18.0**	(2.3)
	Chinese Taipei	0	(6.3)	-0.3	(1.0)	-1.0	(0.9)	-2.5	(2.2)	-2.9	(2.1)	**-4.6**	(1.9)	**-10.4**	(2.0)
	Thailand	0	(5.7)	**-3.5**	(0.9)	-0.5	(0.7)	**-16.4**	(1.1)	**5.5**	(2.3)	3.0	(1.7)	**-7.5**	(1.9)
	Tunisia	1	(5.8)	**-4.9**	(0.9)	m	m	-1.6	(2.0)	**-9.7**	(2.1)	1.8	(2.1)	**-7.2**	(1.7)
	Uruguay	7	(5.7)	m	m	**-2.4**	(0.7)	**-8.9**	(2.1)	-4.2	(2.2)	**-8.6**	(2.2)	**-5.3**	(2.4)

Note: Statistically significant differences are marked in bold.

1. 58 science items are comparable between 2006 and 2015.

StatLink https://stat.link/nh7c28

Table B.2.3 [4/4] **Change between PISA 2006 and PISA 2015 in student performance in science and in environmental/non-environmental science items**

Score-point difference in science and percentage-point difference of students who correctly answered environmental and non-environmental science items (PISA 2015-PISA 2006)

		Change in the percentage of students who correctly answered the following environmental science item (PISA 2015 - PISA 2006)													
		Wild Oat Grass (s408q04)		Solar Power Generation (s415q02)		Penguin Island (s425q02)		Penguin Island (s425q03)		Penguin Island (s425q04)		Different Climates (s465q04)		Extinction of the Dinosaurs (s527q04)	
		% dif.	S.E.	% dif.	S.E.	% dif.	S.E.	% dif.	S.E.	% dif.	S.E.	% dif.	S.E.	% dif.	S.E.
Partbers	Brazil	-3.6	(1.9)	0.0	(2.2)	**4.3**	(1.9)	-1.5	(2.2)	-0.1	(1.4)	m	m	-0.7	(1.9)
	Bulgaria	1.5	(2.4)	-3.4	(3.0)	**13.3**	(2.7)	-2.4	(3.0)	-1.5	(3.0)	2.2	(2.6)	2.0	(2.6)
	Croatia	-0.7	(2.4)	-2.5	(1.8)	3.4	(2.5)	**8.4**	(2.5)	**-6.3**	(2.2)	2.4	(2.2)	3.2	(2.6)
	Hong Kong (China)	4.3	(3.0)	-3.1	(2.1)	-0.3	(2.8)	**-9.2**	(2.8)	**-15.7**	(2.7)	**-7.7**	(2.5)	-3.1	(2.6)
	Indonesia	**6.9**	(1.8)	**-6.8**	(2.3)	**6.8**	(1.8)	**10.2**	(2.2)	-2.7	(1.5)	1.1	(1.5)	1.4	(1.9)
	Jordan	-2.4	(1.6)	-2.1	(2.3)	0.4	(1.9)	**-11.0**	(2.0)	**-4.6**	(1.3)	**-5.2**	(1.6)	-2.6	(1.9)
	Macao (China)	**6.9**	(2.6)	**4.7**	(2.1)	1.7	(2.6)	**-10.9**	(2.8)	2.1	(2.6)	-0.4	(2.8)	2.4	(2.7)
	Montenegro	-3.5	(2.3)	-4.4	(2.4)	**7.6**	(2.5)	4.1	(2.7)	-0.9	(2.4)	-0.3	(2.3)	1.8	(2.6)
	Qatar	**12.9**	(1.6)	**20.0**	(1.8)	**12.4**	(1.9)	**15.6**	(1.4)	**6.8**	(1.3)	**5.7**	(1.7)	**4.7**	(1.9)
	Romania	-2.5	(2.7)	**12.6**	(2.9)	**3.9**	(1.9)	**7.7**	(2.2)	**3.8**	(1.6)	**5.8**	(2.0)	0.1	(2.1)
	Chinese Taipei	0.4	(1.9)	**22.5**	(1.8)	-0.7	(2.1)	**-10.4**	(2.3)	3.8	(2.1)	-4.3	(2.6)	**5.6**	(2.2)
	Thailand	**-5.2**	(2.5)	-1.8	(2.5)	4.2	(2.6)	**-19.8**	(2.1)	**-5.2**	(2.1)	**4.8**	(1.8)	0.3	(2.5)
	Tunisia	-0.9	(2.6)	**-5.9**	(2.9)	-2.2	(2.8)	**-25.0**	(1.9)	**-4.5**	(1.6)	3.6	(2.1)	-1.9	(2.8)
	Uruguay	4.5	(2.4)	**-9.8**	(2.8)	2.3	(2.6)	-1.8	(2.8)	-3.4	(2.4)	m	m	**7.1**	(2.5)

Note: Statistically significant differences are marked in bold.

1. 58 science items are comparable between 2006 and 2015.

StatLink https://stat.link/nh7c28

Table B.2.31 **Difference in the percentage of students who correctly responded to the two first sub-items of the Rising Sea Levels Item 5**

		Percentage of students who responded to the following sub-items of the Rising Sea Levels Item 5 "Is this proposal a short-term (A) or long-term (B) response to rising sea levels?"								Difference between correct response to item DG122Q01RA and correct response to item DG122Q01RB	
		Building sea defences such as dams and sea walls (DG122Q01RA)				Reducing greenhouse gases that are warming the planet (DG122Q01RB)					
		A (correct response)		B		A		B (correct response)			
		%	S.E.	%	S.E.	%	S.E.	%	S.E.	% dif.	S.E.
OECD	Canada	72.3	(1.3)	27.7	(1.3)	14.0	(0.9)	86.0	(0.9)	**13.7**	(1.6)
	Chile	49.3	(2.1)	50.7	(2.1)	33.3	(2.0)	66.7	(2.0)	**17.4**	(2.9)
	Colombia	53.5	(1.6)	46.5	(1.6)	37.9	(1.9)	62.1	(1.9)	**8.5**	(2.5)
	Costa Rica	54.2	(2.1)	45.8	(2.1)	34.4	(1.9)	65.6	(1.9)	**11.3**	(2.8)
	Greece	60.3	(1.6)	39.7	(1.6)	31.1	(1.5)	68.9	(1.5)	**8.6**	(2.2)
	Israel	68.7	(1.9)	31.3	(1.9)	27.6	(1.8)	72.4	(1.8)	3.7	(2.6)
	Korea	82.2	(1.3)	17.8	(1.3)	15.4	(1.2)	84.6	(1.2)	2.4	(1.8)
	Latvia	57.1	(1.9)	42.9	(1.9)	33.9	(2.2)	66.1	(2.2)	**9.0**	(2.9)
	Lithuania	66.2	(1.7)	33.8	(1.7)	29.6	(1.8)	70.4	1.8	4.3	(2.5)
	Scotland (United Kingdom)	65.9	(3.0)	34.1	(3.0)	20.2	(2.0)	79.8	(2.0)	**13.9**	(3.6)
	Slovak Republic	64.8	(2.0)	35.2	(2.0)	22.4	(1.7)	77.6	(1.7)	**12.8**	(2.6)
	Spain*	60.9	(1.3)	39.1	(1.3)	25.2	(0.9)	74.8	(0.9)	**14.0**	(1.6)
Partners	Albania	59.1	(1.9)	40.9	(1.9)	36.0	(2.2)	64.0	(2.2)	4.9	(2.8)
	Brunei Darussalam	39.6	(1.6)	60.4	(1.6)	44.1	(1.4)	55.9	(1.4)	**16.3**	(2.1)
	Croatia	72.6	(1.5)	27.4	(1.5)	21.1	(1.4)	78.9	(1.4)	**6.3**	(2.1)
	Hong Kong (China)	68.6	(1.7)	31.4	(1.7)	13.5	(1.2)	86.5	(1.2)	**18.0**	(2.0)
	Indonesia	40.8	(2.0)	59.2	(2.0)	49.1	(1.9)	50.9	(1.9)	**10.1**	(2.8)
	Kazakhstan	53.2	(1.2)	46.8	(1.2)	44.3	(1.3)	55.7	(1.3)	2.5	(1.8)
	Malta	50.9	(2.5)	49.1	(2.5)	26.1	(1.9)	73.9	(1.9)	**23.0**	(3.2)
	Morocco	49.4	(1.7)	50.6	(1.7)	38.2	(1.9)	61.8	(1.9)	**12.4**	(2.5)
	Panama	51.2	(2.5)	48.8	(2.5)	41.0	(2.1)	59.0	(2.1)	**7.8**	(3.3)
	Philippines	50.4	(1.7)	49.6	(1.7)	37.7	(1.6)	62.3	(1.6)	**12.0**	(2.3)
	Serbia	78.2	(1.5)	21.8	(1.5)	28.7	(1.7)	71.3	(1.7)	**-6.9**	(2.2)
	Singapore	68.2	(1.5)	31.8	(1.5)	15.4	(1.4)	84.6	(1.4)	**16.3**	(2.1)
	Chinese Taipei	79.2	(1.3)	20.8	(1.3)	8.3	(1.0)	91.7	(1.0)	**12.5**	(1.6)
	Thailand	44.0	(2.0)	56.0	(2.0)	34.9	(1.9)	65.1	(1.9)	**21.1**	(2.7)
	Overall average	60.0	(0.4)	40.0	(0.4)	29.4	(0.3)	70.6	(0.3)	**10.6**	(0.5)

* In 2018, some regions in Spain conducted their high-stakes exams for tenth-grade students earlier in the year than in the past, which resulted in the testing period for these exams coinciding with the end of the PISA testing window. Because of this overlap, a number of students were negatively disposed towards the PISA test and did not try their best to demonstrate their proficiency. Although the data of only a minority of students show clear signs of lack of engagement (see PISA 2018 Results Volume I, Annex A9), the comparability of PISA 2018 data for Spain with those from earlier PISA assessments cannot be fully ensured.

StatLink https://stat.link/v9uqf5

Table B.3.1 [1/2] **Environmental awareness, by student background**

	Percentage of students who reported knowing about or being very familiar with climate change and global warming																	
			Students' socio-economic status[1]										Gender					
	All students		Bottom quarter of ESCS[1] (disadvantaged students)		2nd quarter of ESCS		3rd quarter of ESCS		Top quarter of ESCS (advantaged students)		Difference (Top - Bottom quarter of ESCS)		Boys		Girls		Difference (Girls - Boys)	
	%	S.E.	%	S.E.	%	S.E.	%	S.E.	%	S.E.	% dif.	S.E.	%	S.E.	%	S.E.	% dif.	S.E.
OECD																		
Australia	82.6	(0.5)	73.6	(1.0)	78.6	(0.9)	86.8	(0.8)	91.5	(0.6)	**17.8**	(1.1)	83.1	(0.6)	82.1	(0.7)	-0.9	(0.8)
Austria	78.0	(0.8)	63.4	(1.6)	77.4	(1.5)	80.2	(1.3)	90.1	(0.8)	**26.6**	(1.9)	79.8	(1.0)	76.3	(1.2)	**-3.6**	(1.5)
Belgium	80.7	(1.2)	65.6	(2.8)	76.0	(1.5)	84.0	(1.2)	92.4	(0.8)	**26.8**	(2.6)	81.5	(1.4)	79.9	(1.3)	-1.6	(1.5)
Canada	87.4	(0.4)	80.0	(0.9)	86.3	(0.6)	90.0	(0.6)	93.1	(0.6)	**13.0**	(0.9)	87.2	(0.5)	87.5	(0.6)	0.3	(0.8)
Chile	72.0	(1.0)	59.5	(1.6)	70.1	(1.2)	74.5	(1.4)	83.2	(1.1)	**23.7**	(1.7)	74.3	(1.1)	69.7	(1.2)	**-4.6**	(1.3)
Colombia	71.8	(0.9)	65.6	(1.9)	68.5	(1.6)	71.6	(1.4)	80.2	(1.4)	**14.6**	(2.3)	72.4	(1.2)	71.3	(1.2)	-1.1	(1.4)
Costa Rica	73.6	(0.9)	63.3	(1.6)	69.5	(1.2)	75.5	(1.3)	85.8	(1.0)	**22.5**	(1.9)	75.3	(1.0)	72.0	(1.2)	**-3.3**	(1.3)
Estonia	81.4	(0.7)	72.6	(1.6)	78.3	(1.4)	85.0	(1.2)	89.5	(0.8)	**17.0**	(1.9)	82.3	(0.8)	80.4	(1.0)	-1.9	(1.2)
France	80.9	(0.7)	67.2	(1.5)	75.7	(1.4)	85.6	(1.0)	94.0	(0.6)	**26.9**	(1.6)	83.0	(0.8)	78.9	(1.0)	**-4.1**	(1.2)
Germany	82.6	(0.8)	69.6	(1.7)	81.5	(1.6)	84.9	(1.3)	93.4	(0.7)	**23.8**	(2.0)	84.1	(0.9)	81.0	(1.2)	**-3.1**	(1.4)
Greece	72.5	(0.8)	61.1	(1.5)	67.4	(1.2)	76.5	(1.2)	84.6	(1.0)	**23.5**	(1.7)	71.8	(1.2)	73.2	(1.1)	1.4	(1.4)
Hungary	76.0	(0.7)	59.3	(1.9)	74.3	(1.3)	79.4	(1.3)	90.0	(0.8)	**30.7**	(2.0)	78.2	(1.1)	73.9	(0.9)	**-4.2**	(1.4)
Iceland	76.8	(0.8)	63.1	(2.0)	72.6	(1.6)	81.2	(1.2)	89.3	(1.0)	**26.2**	(2.2)	78.3	(1.0)	75.3	(1.1)	-3.0	(1.5)
Ireland	86.5	(0.5)	77.3	(1.3)	85.5	(1.1)	89.6	(0.7)	93.9	(0.6)	**16.6**	(1.5)	86.4	(0.6)	86.7	(0.7)	0.3	(0.9)
Israel	68.2	(0.9)	56.0	(1.6)	65.1	(1.4)	72.5	(1.2)	78.2	(1.4)	**22.2**	(2.0)	69.4	(1.2)	67.3	(1.2)	-2.1	(1.6)
Italy	77.9	(0.6)	71.0	(1.4)	78.7	(1.2)	77.8	(1.3)	83.9	(1.2)	**12.9**	(1.8)	77.4	(0.9)	78.4	(0.9)	1.0	(1.2)
Korea	88.1	(0.5)	81.2	(1.2)	86.5	(0.9)	90.2	(0.8)	94.8	(0.5)	**13.6**	(1.3)	87.9	(0.7)	88.2	(0.9)	0.2	(1.3)
Latvia	75.8	(0.7)	64.9	(1.5)	73.6	(1.4)	80.8	(1.1)	83.8	(1.1)	**18.9**	(1.8)	74.1	(1.0)	77.4	(0.9)	**3.2**	(1.2)
Lithuania	80.4	(0.6)	69.6	(1.4)	78.7	(1.1)	84.4	(1.0)	89.1	(0.9)	**19.5**	(1.9)	78.0	(0.9)	83.0	(0.8)	**5.0**	(1.2)
Mexico	77.0	(0.8)	69.3	(1.8)	72.7	(1.2)	77.4	(1.2)	85.4	(1.1)	**16.1**	(1.9)	76.4	(1.0)	77.6	(1.0)	1.2	(1.2)
Netherlands	85.0	(0.6)	78.0	(1.5)	79.9	(1.4)	87.7	(1.0)	92.6	(0.9)	**14.6**	(1.7)	88.0	(0.7)	82.2	(1.0)	**-5.8**	(1.2)
New Zealand	80.5	(0.6)	70.4	(1.4)	77.6	(1.0)	83.9	(1.2)	90.3	(0.7)	**19.8**	(1.5)	81.9	(0.8)	79.2	(0.9)	**-2.7**	(1.2)
Poland	75.4	(0.8)	64.8	(1.6)	74.6	(1.2)	77.3	(1.2)	84.5	(1.2)	**19.7**	(1.8)	76.7	(1.1)	74.2	(1.0)	**-2.5**	(1.2)
Portugal	83.4	(0.7)	71.4	(1.7)	80.8	(1.2)	88.0	(1.1)	93.7	(0.8)	**22.2**	(1.8)	85.0	(0.8)	81.8	(1.1)	**-3.1**	(1.3)
Scotland (United Kingdom)	78.4	(0.9)	65.5	(2.0)	74.0	(1.7)	84.2	(1.5)	91.7	(1.1)	**26.2**	(2.4)	81.2	(1.2)	75.8	(1.3)	**-5.4**	(1.6)
Slovak Republic	69.4	(0.7)	52.8	(1.5)	67.0	(1.4)	73.9	(1.3)	81.5	(1.1)	**28.7**	(2.0)	67.9	(0.9)	70.7	(1.0)	**2.8**	(1.4)
Slovenia	77.7	(0.6)	67.1	(1.4)	74.9	(1.4)	78.9	(1.2)	89.4	(1.1)	**22.3**	(1.9)	77.7	(0.8)	77.7	(0.9)	0.1	(1.2)
Spain	81.0	(0.5)	72.1	(1.1)	78.8	(0.9)	83.6	(0.6)	89.1	(0.5)	**17.0**	(1.1)	80.9	(0.6)	81.2	(0.6)	0.4	(0.8)
Switzerland	78.7	(1.0)	65.9	(2.1)	76.7	(1.5)	81.0	(1.2)	90.2	(1.1)	**24.2**	(2.3)	79.4	(1.2)	78.0	(1.2)	-1.4	(1.3)
Türkiye	78.8	(0.7)	75.6	(1.3)	78.4	(1.0)	76.5	(1.1)	84.6	(1.1)	**8.9**	(1.7)	74.6	(1.0)	83.0	(0.7)	**8.4**	(1.1)
OECD average	78.6	(0.1)	67.9	(0.3)	76.0	(0.2)	81.4	(0.2)	88.4	(0.2)	**20.6**	(0.3)	79.1	(0.2)	78.1	(0.2)	**-1.0**	(0.2)

Note: Values that are statistically significant are indicated in bold.

1. Students' socio-economic status is measured by the PISA index of economic, social and cultural status (ESCS).

StatLink https://stat.link/iwfu6l

Table B.3.1 [2/2] **Environmental awareness, by student background**

		Percentage of students who reported knowing about or being very familiar with climate change and global warming																	
				Students' socio-economic status[1]										Gender					
		All students		Bottom quarter of ESCS[1] (disadvantaged students)		2nd quarter of ESCS		3rd quarter of ESCS		Top quarter of ESCS (advantaged students)		Difference (Top - Bottom quarter of ESCS)		Boys		Girls		Difference (Girls - Boys)	
		%	S.E.	%	S.E.	%	S.E.	%	S.E.	%	S.E.	% dif.	S.E.	%	S.E.	%	S.E.	% dif.	S.E.
Partners	Albania	82.1	(0.7)	75.0	(1.5)	82.5	(1.2)	82.1	(1.2)	88.6	(0.9)	**13.5**	(1.7)	75.8	(1.1)	88.3	(0.7)	**12.6**	(1.4)
	Argentina	49.7	(0.8)	35.2	(1.4)	44.3	(1.4)	52.3	(1.6)	64.2	(1.2)	**29.0**	(1.8)	50.6	(1.2)	48.8	(0.9)	-1.9	(1.5)
	Baku (Azerbaijan)	69.3	(0.9)	62.6	(1.5)	66.4	(1.3)	70.0	(1.6)	77.9	(1.5)	**15.3**	(1.9)	68.9	(1.2)	69.8	(1.2)	0.9	(1.6)
	Bosnia and Herzegovina	64.5	(0.9)	52.5	(1.5)	64.4	(1.8)	67.0	(1.2)	73.5	(1.5)	**21.0**	(2.0)	62.5	(1.1)	66.5	(1.3)	**4.0**	(1.4)
	Brazil	61.1	(0.9)	46.7	(1.5)	53.4	(1.3)	61.6	(1.3)	78.5	(1.1)	**31.8**	(1.7)	61.5	(1.1)	60.8	(1.0)	-0.7	(1.2)
	Brunei Darussalam	71.7	(0.5)	56.6	(1.2)	69.4	(1.2)	74.1	(0.9)	85.3	(0.8)	**28.8**	(1.6)	70.4	(0.7)	72.9	(0.8)	**2.4**	(1.1)
	Bulgaria	69.8	(1.0)	56.4	(1.6)	66.8	(1.6)	71.8	(1.7)	83.2	(1.2)	**26.8**	(1.8)	66.2	(1.5)	73.5	(1.1)	**7.3**	(1.5)
	Croatia	77.8	(0.7)	69.2	(1.5)	73.4	(1.2)	80.4	(1.1)	88.2	(0.9)	**19.0**	(1.7)	77.4	(1.0)	78.2	(0.8)	0.8	(1.2)
	Cyprus	65.7	(0.6)	54.0	(1.4)	62.4	(1.3)	67.8	(1.5)	77.9	(1.3)	**24.0**	(1.9)	65.5	(1.0)	65.8	(0.9)	0.3	(1.3)
	Dominican Republic	66.2	(1.2)	58.0	(2.5)	62.2	(2.0)	65.2	(2.1)	74.2	(2.0)	**16.2**	(3.1)	64.4	(1.5)	67.8	(1.5)	3.4	(1.8)
	Hong Kong (China)	90.6	(0.6)	87.0	(0.8)	90.7	(0.9)	91.4	(1.0)	93.7	(0.9)	**6.6**	(1.2)	89.2	(0.8)	92.0	(0.6)	**2.8**	(0.9)
	Indonesia	56.6	(1.2)	47.1	(1.8)	51.5	(1.6)	58.1	(1.8)	70.2	(1.9)	**23.1**	(2.7)	55.1	(1.5)	58.1	(1.5)	3.0	(1.7)
	Jordan	69.8	(1.0)	62.0	(2.0)	69.2	(1.5)	70.2	(1.6)	78.4	(2.0)	**16.4**	(2.8)	58.1	(1.7)	80.7	(1.0)	**22.6**	(1.9)
	Kazakhstan	74.4	(0.4)	69.8	(1.1)	73.1	(0.8)	75.0	(0.8)	79.4	(0.7)	**9.6**	(1.4)	69.9	(0.7)	79.1	(0.5)	**9.2**	(0.9)
	Kosovo	67.8	(0.7)	60.7	(1.6)	66.7	(1.4)	65.9	(1.7)	77.6	(1.3)	**16.9**	(2.3)	62.3	(1.2)	72.9	(1.0)	**10.6**	(1.8)
	Lebanon	58.2	(1.5)	49.1	(2.3)	54.6	(2.0)	58.9	(2.2)	70.6	(1.8)	**21.5**	(2.6)	55.1	(1.8)	61.0	(1.5)	**5.9**	(1.5)
	Macao (China)	87.2	(0.5)	82.0	(1.3)	85.9	(1.2)	89.2	(0.9)	92.2	(0.9)	**10.3**	(1.7)	86.1	(0.8)	88.4	(0.7)	**2.3**	(1.1)
	Malaysia	68.2	(0.9)	59.6	(1.6)	63.7	(1.5)	68.1	(1.3)	81.5	(1.3)	**21.9**	(2.0)	67.2	(1.0)	69.2	(1.2)	2.1	(1.3)
	Malta	83.4	(0.6)	74.6	(1.6)	81.7	(1.4)	85.3	(1.2)	91.4	(1.1)	**16.8**	(1.9)	80.6	(1.0)	86.1	(0.8)	**5.5**	(1.3)
	Moldova	71.9	(0.7)	57.8	(1.7)	68.5	(1.3)	76.7	(1.4)	83.8	(1.1)	**26.1**	(1.9)	70.6	(1.0)	73.2	(1.0)	**2.6**	(1.3)
	Montenegro	69.8	(0.7)	62.4	(1.5)	67.4	(1.2)	71.9	(1.2)	77.3	(1.1)	**15.0**	(1.8)	66.5	(1.0)	73.0	(0.9)	**6.5**	(1.4)
	Morocco	57.6	(1.4)	48.7	(2.2)	54.8	(1.9)	54.8	(2.0)	68.6	(1.7)	**19.9**	(2.5)	56.4	(1.5)	59.0	(1.6)	2.6	(1.5)
	North Macedonia	69.1	(0.7)	54.3	(1.6)	66.6	(1.5)	72.3	(1.1)	83.4	(1.1)	**29.1**	(2.0)	65.5	(0.9)	73.1	(0.9)	**7.6**	(1.3)
	Panama	67.9	(1.1)	54.1	(2.3)	65.0	(1.8)	67.8	(1.9)	78.3	(1.5)	**24.2**	(2.6)	68.4	(1.6)	67.3	(1.4)	-1.1	(2.0)
	Peru	82.2	(0.8)	78.5	(1.9)	79.3	(1.4)	81.2	(1.5)	86.7	(1.1)	**8.2**	(2.2)	82.5	(1.1)	81.8	(1.1)	-0.6	(1.3)
	Philippines	72.9	(0.8)	60.9	(1.5)	73.8	(1.2)	73.2	(1.3)	83.4	(1.1)	**22.5**	(1.9)	67.2	(1.2)	77.9	(0.8)	**10.7**	(1.2)
	Romania	60.9	(1.3)	47.3	(1.6)	56.2	(1.7)	63.9	(1.5)	75.6	(1.7)	**28.3**	(2.1)	60.3	(1.4)	61.5	(1.7)	1.2	(1.7)
	Saudi Arabia	40.2	(0.9)	31.4	(1.6)	37.6	(1.6)	41.2	(1.3)	50.9	(1.5)	**19.4**	(2.0)	35.5	(1.4)	44.8	(1.1)	**9.3**	(1.7)
	Serbia	73.6	(1.0)	65.1	(1.7)	70.6	(1.6)	76.8	(1.3)	81.5	(1.7)	**16.4**	(2.4)	71.8	(1.3)	75.4	(1.1)	**3.5**	(1.3)
	Singapore	89.4	(0.4)	81.7	(0.9)	87.4	(0.8)	93.5	(0.6)	94.9	(0.6)	**13.2**	(1.2)	90.1	(0.5)	88.6	(0.6)	-1.5	(0.8)
	Chinese Taipei	85.8	(0.5)	77.0	(1.1)	85.8	(0.8)	87.2	(0.9)	93.4	(0.7)	**16.4**	(1.3)	84.1	(0.7)	87.5	(0.6)	**3.4**	(0.9)
	Thailand	77.4	(0.8)	72.2	(1.0)	74.9	(1.5)	78.6	(1.3)	84.1	(1.3)	**11.9**	(1.7)	72.1	(1.1)	82.1	(0.8)	**10.0**	(1.1)
	Ukraine	74.0	(1.0)	63.0	(1.8)	71.1	(1.4)	77.3	(1.2)	83.8	(1.1)	**20.8**	(2.1)	71.4	(1.3)	76.8	(1.1)	**5.4**	(1.4)
	United Arab Emirates	74.4	(0.4)	60.0	(0.9)	69.0	(0.9)	80.5	(0.7)	87.5	(0.6)	**27.5**	(1.2)	70.8	(0.6)	77.6	(0.6)	**6.8**	(0.9)
	Uruguay	67.4	(0.9)	55.3	(1.7)	64.5	(1.9)	69.8	(1.7)	77.3	(1.4)	**22.0**	(2.2)	67.3	(1.5)	67.6	(1.1)	0.3	(1.9)
	Viet Nam	74.8	(1.1)	64.7	(1.8)	73.1	(1.5)	77.5	(1.3)	83.8	(1.5)	**19.2**	(2.3)	73.8	(1.4)	75.7	(1.2)	1.9	(1.3)
	Overall average	74.3	(0.1)	64.1	(0.2)	71.6	(0.2)	76.4	(0.2)	84.2	(0.1)	**20.1**	(0.2)	73.3	(0.1)	75.3	(0.1)	**2.0**	(0.2)

Note: Values that are statistically significant are indicated in bold.

1. Students' socio-economic status is measured by the PISA index of economic, social and cultural status (ESCS).

StatLink https://stat.link/iwfu61

Table B.3.3 [1/2] **Self-efficacy in environmental understanding, by student background**

	Percentage of students who reported they could explain how carbon-dioxide emissions affect global climate change easily or with a bit of effort																	
	All students		Students' socio-economic status[1]										Gender					
			Bottom quarter of ESCS[1] (disadvantaged students)		2nd quarter of ESCS		3rd quarter of ESCS		Top quarter of ESCS (advantaged students)		Difference (Top - Bottom quarter of ESCS)		Boys		Girls		Difference (Girls - Boys)	
	%	S.E.	%	S.E.	%	S.E.	%	S.E.	%	S.E.	% dif.	S.E.	%	S.E.	%	S.E.	% dif.	S.E.
OECD																		
Australia	69.8	(0.6)	59.2	(1.1)	64.9	(1.2)	74.3	(0.9)	81.1	(0.8)	**21.8**	(1.3)	73.0	(0.8)	66.6	(0.7)	**-6.4**	(0.9)
Austria	53.3	(0.9)	41.5	(1.3)	50.2	(1.7)	55.5	(1.6)	64.9	(1.5)	**23.5**	(1.9)	61.4	(1.0)	45.5	(1.3)	**-15.9**	(1.6)
Belgium	m	m	m	m	m	m	m	m	m	m	m	m	m	m	m	m	m	m
Canada	73.3	(0.6)	63.8	(0.9)	68.9	(0.9)	77.4	(0.9)	82.7	(0.9)	**19.0**	(1.2)	76.5	(0.8)	70.2	(0.8)	**-6.3**	(1.0)
Chile	65.0	(0.8)	56.6	(1.4)	64.0	(1.6)	67.1	(1.4)	71.3	(1.4)	**14.7**	(1.8)	67.1	(0.9)	62.9	(1.1)	**-4.3**	(1.2)
Colombia	70.9	(1.0)	64.8	(1.6)	68.4	(1.9)	70.2	(1.2)	79.1	(1.4)	**14.3**	(2.1)	71.5	(1.1)	70.4	(1.2)	-1.1	(1.3)
Costa Rica	63.7	(0.8)	57.3	(1.2)	60.2	(1.3)	64.6	(1.5)	72.4	(1.2)	**15.1**	(1.7)	64.2	(0.9)	63.2	(1.1)	-0.9	(1.3)
Estonia	59.5	(0.8)	49.0	(1.8)	54.0	(1.6)	61.9	(1.5)	72.9	(1.4)	**23.9**	(2.2)	63.2	(1.1)	55.9	(1.1)	**-7.3**	(1.5)
France	66.5	(0.8)	52.2	(1.3)	60.6	(1.7)	68.8	(1.4)	83.0	(1.0)	**30.7**	(1.7)	71.8	(0.9)	61.3	(1.0)	**-10.5**	(1.1)
Germany	60.6	(0.9)	48.3	(1.7)	57.1	(1.9)	62.4	(2.2)	72.7	(1.5)	**24.5**	(2.2)	66.0	(1.1)	54.7	(1.3)	**-11.3**	(1.5)
Greece	45.1	(0.7)	35.4	(1.5)	42.5	(1.3)	45.8	(1.4)	56.2	(1.5)	**20.8**	(2.3)	47.7	(1.1)	42.6	(1.0)	**-5.1**	(1.5)
Hungary	66.9	(0.8)	55.2	(1.5)	63.9	(1.5)	68.3	(1.6)	79.6	(1.1)	**24.4**	(1.8)	70.5	(1.1)	63.4	(1.1)	**-7.1**	(1.5)
Iceland	63.7	(0.9)	49.2	(1.7)	58.8	(1.8)	66.6	(1.7)	79.5	(1.5)	**30.3**	(2.3)	66.7	(1.3)	61.0	(1.2)	**-5.7**	(1.9)
Ireland	72.3	(0.8)	60.1	(1.2)	70.9	(1.3)	73.0	(1.4)	85.2	(1.1)	**25.1**	(1.6)	75.0	(0.9)	69.7	(1.1)	**-5.3**	(1.4)
Israel	64.1	(0.8)	55.2	(1.2)	60.9	(1.5)	68.2	(1.2)	73.4	(1.4)	**18.2**	(1.9)	63.7	(1.2)	64.5	(1.1)	0.8	(1.6)
Italy	57.8	(0.7)	50.2	(1.5)	57.0	(1.2)	60.2	(1.4)	63.3	(1.5)	**13.0**	(1.9)	58.7	(1.0)	56.9	(0.9)	-1.8	(1.3)
Korea	81.3	(0.7)	70.3	(1.7)	81.1	(1.0)	84.9	(0.9)	89.3	(0.8)	**19.0**	(1.7)	80.7	(0.9)	82.0	(1.0)	1.4	(1.3)
Latvia	63.7	(0.7)	51.9	(1.6)	60.9	(1.5)	67.9	(1.4)	74.1	(1.4)	**22.2**	(2.2)	66.1	(1.0)	61.5	(0.9)	**-4.6**	(1.3)
Lithuania	62.1	(0.8)	50.5	(1.6)	61.0	(1.3)	63.3	(1.5)	74.0	(1.2)	**23.5**	(1.8)	64.7	(1.0)	59.4	(1.1)	**-5.2**	(1.3)
Mexico	66.7	(0.9)	60.4	(1.8)	63.6	(1.4)	67.8	(1.3)	72.3	(1.2)	**12.0**	(2.2)	67.8	(1.1)	65.6	(1.2)	-2.2	(1.5)
Netherlands	m	m	m	m	m	m	m	m	m	m	m	m	m	m	m	m	m	m
New Zealand	68.7	(0.7)	55.7	(1.2)	64.2	(1.3)	73.7	(1.4)	81.1	(0.9)	**25.3**	(1.7)	73.0	(0.8)	64.5	(1.0)	**-8.6**	(1.2)
Poland	62.6	(0.9)	48.4	(1.4)	61.5	(1.4)	62.9	(1.4)	77.2	(1.3)	**28.8**	(2.1)	63.6	(1.2)	61.7	(1.1)	-1.9	(1.4)
Portugal	64.4	(0.9)	48.2	(1.8)	59.8	(1.6)	70.4	(1.6)	79.0	(1.1)	**30.8**	(1.9)	66.8	(1.1)	61.9	(1.2)	**-4.9**	(1.4)
Scotland (United Kingdom)	61.4	(1.0)	47.6	(1.9)	57.3	(1.7)	64.5	(1.9)	79.2	(1.3)	**31.6**	(2.5)	67.4	(1.3)	55.8	(1.4)	**-11.6**	(1.9)
Slovak Republic	41.5	(0.8)	28.8	(1.4)	39.6	(1.4)	42.2	(1.5)	53.8	(1.6)	**25.0**	(2.1)	46.7	(1.1)	36.5	(1.2)	**-10.3**	(1.6)
Slovenia	64.2	(0.7)	52.2	(1.4)	61.7	(1.4)	66.2	(1.5)	76.0	(1.4)	**23.8**	(2.0)	65.1	(1.0)	63.2	(1.0)	-1.8	(1.4)
Spain	58.2	(0.5)	48.3	(1.1)	54.0	(1.0)	59.6	(0.8)	70.1	(0.9)	**21.7**	(1.3)	61.0	(0.6)	55.5	(0.8)	**-5.5**	(0.9)
Switzerland	57.7	(1.2)	48.4	(1.9)	53.2	(1.8)	57.6	(1.7)	70.4	(1.8)	**22.0**	(2.6)	62.6	(1.3)	52.3	(1.5)	**-10.3**	(1.6)
Türkiye	58.9	(0.8)	53.8	(1.3)	57.2	(1.3)	57.2	(1.4)	67.3	(1.5)	**13.5**	(1.8)	54.4	(0.9)	63.4	(1.2)	**9.0**	(1.3)
OECD average	63.0	(0.2)	52.2	(0.3)	59.9	(0.3)	65.1	(0.3)	74.3	(0.2)	**22.1**	(0.4)	65.6	(0.2)	60.4	(0.2)	**-5.2**	(0.3)

Note: Values that are statistically significant are indicated in bold.

1. Students' socio-economic status is measured by the PISA index of economic, social and cultural status (ESCS).

StatLink https://stat.link/hag5i7

Table B.3.3 [2/2] **Self-efficacy in environmental understanding, by student background**

	Percentage of students who reported they could explain how carbon-dioxide emissions affect global climate change easily or with a bit of effort																	
	All students		Students' socio-economic status[1]										Gender					
			Bottom quarter of ESCS[1] (disadvantaged students)		2nd quarter of ESCS		3rd quarter of ESCS		Top quarter of ESCS (advantaged students)		Difference (Top - Bottom quarter of ESCS)		Boys		Girls		Difference (Girls - Boys)	
	%	S.E.	%	S.E.	%	S.E.	%	S.E.	%	S.E.	% dif.	S.E.	%	S.E.	%	S.E.	% dif.	S.E.
Partners																		
Albania	74.9	(0.7)	68.6	(1.6)	74.2	(1.1)	74.4	(1.3)	82.5	(1.1)	**13.9**	(1.8)	68.3	(1.0)	81.5	(0.8)	**13.1**	(1.2)
Argentina	45.4	(0.8)	36.4	(1.5)	41.9	(1.4)	46.9	(1.4)	55.2	(1.3)	**18.8**	(2.0)	45.2	(1.1)	45.6	(1.0)	0.4	(1.6)
Baku (Azerbaijan)	50.2	(0.8)	44.5	(1.3)	46.5	(1.7)	52.4	(1.4)	56.9	(1.6)	**12.5**	(2.0)	52.8	(1.2)	47.7	(1.0)	**-5.0**	(1.4)
Bosnia and Herzegovina	46.7	(1.1)	36.5	(1.3)	44.9	(1.5)	47.9	(1.5)	56.7	(1.6)	**20.2**	(1.9)	45.7	(1.1)	47.6	(1.4)	1.8	(1.5)
Brazil	44.9	(0.8)	33.5	(1.2)	39.5	(1.2)	46.3	(1.3)	57.0	(1.4)	**23.5**	(1.9)	45.8	(1.0)	43.9	(1.0)	-1.9	(1.2)
Brunei Darussalam	64.5	(0.6)	51.6	(1.3)	59.6	(1.4)	66.7	(1.2)	78.8	(1.0)	**27.2**	(1.7)	62.4	(0.7)	66.6	(0.8)	**4.1**	(1.1)
Bulgaria	58.3	(1.0)	48.5	(1.7)	54.1	(1.7)	59.5	(1.9)	70.6	(1.5)	**22.1**	(2.2)	57.4	(1.3)	59.2	(1.2)	1.8	(1.5)
Croatia	63.7	(0.8)	53.8	(1.6)	58.5	(1.3)	66.7	(1.4)	75.6	(1.0)	**21.7**	(1.8)	64.1	(1.1)	63.4	(1.0)	-0.7	(1.4)
Cyprus	51.7	(0.7)	41.7	(1.5)	46.2	(1.5)	53.1	(1.4)	64.7	(1.5)	**23.0**	(2.3)	53.0	(1.0)	50.4	(1.1)	-2.6	(1.5)
Dominican Republic	66.4	(1.1)	58.7	(2.4)	66.7	(1.8)	62.9	(1.9)	73.4	(1.7)	**14.7**	(2.8)	64.3	(1.4)	68.5	(1.5)	**4.2**	(1.8)
Hong Kong (China)	79.1	(0.7)	74.0	(1.1)	77.2	(1.3)	80.8	(1.1)	84.9	(1.2)	**10.8**	(1.6)	77.0	(0.9)	81.3	(0.8)	**4.3**	(1.1)
Indonesia	33.9	(0.8)	28.9	(1.5)	31.3	(1.2)	36.8	(1.4)	38.7	(1.7)	**9.8**	(2.2)	33.1	(1.0)	34.6	(1.2)	1.5	(1.6)
Jordan	48.3	(0.9)	36.9	(1.7)	47.9	(1.5)	48.4	(1.6)	60.1	(1.3)	**23.2**	(2.2)	41.1	(1.1)	55.0	(1.4)	**13.9**	(1.8)
Kazakhstan	52.0	(0.5)	45.4	(1.1)	50.0	(1.0)	53.6	(0.9)	58.6	(1.0)	**13.2**	(1.4)	52.6	(0.7)	51.4	(0.7)	-1.2	(0.9)
Kosovo	34.2	(0.9)	27.3	(1.7)	30.9	(1.4)	32.9	(1.5)	45.7	(1.8)	**18.4**	(2.5)	35.6	(1.2)	33.0	(1.2)	-2.6	(1.6)
Lebanon	58.4	(1.1)	52.8	(2.2)	57.3	(1.8)	57.2	(1.7)	66.0	(1.5)	**13.2**	(2.7)	54.6	(1.3)	61.6	(1.4)	**7.0**	(1.6)
Macao (China)	60.9	(0.8)	50.4	(1.6)	56.7	(1.6)	64.3	(1.7)	72.4	(1.4)	**22.0**	(2.1)	58.1	(1.1)	63.7	(1.0)	**5.5**	(1.5)
Malaysia	64.3	(0.8)	53.7	(1.6)	61.2	(1.6)	64.9	(1.3)	77.3	(1.4)	**23.6**	(2.1)	62.0	(1.0)	66.5	(1.0)	**4.5**	(1.2)
Malta	68.4	(0.8)	54.2	(2.1)	66.0	(2.0)	71.5	(1.6)	80.9	(1.2)	**26.7**	(2.6)	66.6	(1.2)	70.1	(1.1)	**3.6**	(1.6)
Moldova	51.5	(0.7)	41.1	(1.9)	46.7	(1.6)	53.9	(1.2)	63.5	(1.5)	**22.4**	(2.4)	52.7	(1.0)	50.4	(0.9)	-2.3	(1.2)
Montenegro	53.8	(0.6)	44.6	(1.2)	51.5	(1.3)	56.4	(1.3)	62.0	(1.1)	**17.4**	(1.7)	52.5	(0.9)	55.0	(1.0)	2.4	(1.4)
Morocco	40.2	(1.0)	34.9	(1.5)	35.0	(1.7)	39.9	(1.7)	48.5	(1.9)	**13.6**	(2.4)	41.1	(1.3)	39.2	(1.3)	-2.0	(1.5)
North Macedonia	40.9	(0.8)	28.2	(1.6)	38.9	(1.5)	42.0	(1.7)	53.6	(1.6)	**25.4**	(2.2)	39.6	(1.1)	42.3	(1.2)	2.7	(1.6)
Panama	63.8	(1.1)	59.2	(2.3)	61.5	(1.9)	60.9	(1.9)	70.4	(1.6)	**11.2**	(2.7)	62.8	(1.4)	64.7	(1.5)	1.9	(2.0)
Peru	69.4	(0.9)	61.1	(2.1)	65.3	(1.5)	70.4	(1.4)	75.5	(1.4)	**14.4**	(2.4)	68.7	(1.1)	70.0	(1.2)	1.3	(1.5)
Philippines	62.3	(0.8)	53.5	(1.3)	62.7	(1.4)	61.0	(1.3)	71.6	(1.4)	**18.0**	(1.9)	58.4	(1.2)	65.7	(0.7)	**7.3**	(1.1)
Romania	39.7	(1.1)	28.8	(1.5)	35.6	(1.5)	41.9	(1.6)	52.2	(1.8)	**23.4**	(2.1)	41.8	(1.2)	37.5	(1.3)	**-4.3**	(1.2)
Saudi Arabia	39.9	(0.7)	35.2	(1.3)	37.6	(1.4)	39.4	(1.2)	47.6	(1.3)	**12.4**	(1.8)	37.0	(0.9)	42.7	(1.0)	**5.7**	(1.3)
Serbia	54.0	(0.8)	45.5	(1.4)	51.2	(1.5)	55.8	(1.7)	62.8	(1.7)	**17.3**	(2.1)	54.2	(1.2)	53.7	(1.0)	-0.5	(1.5)
Singapore	85.2	(0.5)	76.1	(1.1)	83.0	(1.0)	88.8	(0.8)	93.1	(0.7)	**17.0**	(1.3)	86.2	(0.6)	84.3	(0.7)	**-1.9**	(0.8)
Chinese Taipei	77.1	(0.6)	69.6	(1.3)	75.7	(1.2)	77.4	(1.1)	85.5	(1.0)	**15.9**	(1.7)	75.8	(0.8)	78.4	(0.9)	**2.6**	(1.1)
Thailand	67.3	(0.8)	60.7	(1.5)	64.7	(1.4)	66.6	(1.2)	77.2	(1.4)	**16.5**	(1.9)	63.9	(1.2)	70.3	(1.1)	**6.4**	(1.6)
Ukraine	57.4	(1.2)	45.7	(1.8)	54.2	(1.5)	58.3	(1.7)	70.4	(1.3)	**24.7**	(2.0)	57.5	(1.5)	57.2	(1.4)	-0.2	(1.7)
United Arab Emirates	71.5	(0.4)	58.5	(0.9)	66.9	(0.9)	76.7	(0.8)	83.2	(0.7)	**24.7**	(1.2)	67.6	(0.5)	75.0	(0.6)	**7.4**	(0.8)
Uruguay	51.0	(0.8)	45.3	(2.0)	47.5	(1.5)	52.7	(1.5)	56.9	(1.5)	**11.7**	(2.4)	53.1	(1.2)	49.2	(1.0)	**-3.9**	(1.6)
Viet Nam	69.1	(1.2)	61.9	(1.7)	67.8	(1.6)	69.0	(1.6)	77.6	(1.6)	**15.7**	(1.9)	65.2	(1.4)	72.8	(1.2)	**7.6**	(1.1)
Overall average	59.8	(0.1)	50.2	(0.2)	56.8	(0.2)	61.3	(0.2)	70.1	(0.2)	**20.0**	(0.3)	60.2	(0.1)	59.3	(0.1)	**-1.0**	(0.2)

Note: Values that are statistically significant are indicated in bold.

1. Students' socio-economic status is measured by the PISA index of economic, social and cultural status (ESCS).

StatLink https://stat.link/hag5i7

Table B.3.5 [1/2] **Environmental sense-of-purpose, by student background**

	Percentage of students who reported that looking after the global environment is important to them																	
			Students' socio-economic status[1]										Gender					
	All students		Bottom quarter of ESCS[1] (disadvantaged students)		2nd quarter of ESCS		3rd quarter of ESCS		Top quarter of ESCS (advantaged students)		Difference (Top - Bottom quarter of ESCS)		Boys		Girls		Difference (Girls - Boys)	
	%	S.E.	%	S.E.	%	S.E.	%	S.E.	%	S.E.	% dif.	S.E.	%	S.E.	%	S.E.	% dif.	S.E.
OECD																		
Australia	76.7	(0.5)	70.2	(1.0)	73.8	(0.8)	80.4	(0.9)	82.5	(0.8)	**12.3**	(1.3)	72.2	(0.6)	81.4	(0.6)	**9.2**	(0.8)
Austria	69.0	(0.7)	62.8	(1.4)	68.1	(1.6)	70.3	(1.5)	73.9	(1.3)	**11.2**	(2.0)	65.6	(1.0)	72.1	(0.9)	**6.5**	(1.4)
Belgium	m	m	m	m	m	m	m	m	m	m	m	m	m	m	m	m	m	m
Canada	79.4	(0.4)	73.6	(0.9)	77.8	(1.0)	82.1	(0.7)	83.7	(0.7)	**10.1**	(1.1)	75.2	(0.7)	83.4	(0.6)	**8.3**	(0.9)
Chile	84.5	(0.7)	82.5	(1.0)	84.1	(1.4)	84.7	(1.2)	87.1	(1.0)	**4.6**	(1.5)	82.1	(0.9)	87.0	(0.8)	**4.9**	(1.1)
Colombia	87.7	(0.6)	85.4	(1.4)	87.7	(1.1)	87.5	(0.9)	89.6	(0.9)	**4.1**	(1.7)	84.9	(0.8)	90.5	(0.7)	**5.6**	(1.0)
Costa Rica	90.7	(0.5)	90.2	(0.8)	89.6	(0.9)	90.5	(0.9)	92.5	(0.8)	**2.3**	(1.1)	88.8	(0.7)	92.6	(0.5)	**3.9**	(0.8)
Estonia	71.3	(0.8)	62.4	(1.6)	71.6	(1.2)	71.3	(1.5)	79.9	(1.0)	**17.5**	(1.9)	67.3	(1.1)	75.2	(1.0)	**8.0**	(1.5)
France	76.3	(0.7)	67.8	(1.4)	72.7	(1.5)	78.5	(1.2)	85.1	(1.1)	**17.3**	(1.7)	75.3	(0.8)	77.3	(0.9)	**2.0**	(1.0)
Germany	67.4	(1.0)	62.0	(2.0)	63.6	(1.7)	66.1	(1.9)	77.0	(1.6)	**14.9**	(2.4)	63.4	(1.4)	71.9	(1.2)	**8.5**	(1.7)
Greece	81.4	(0.7)	76.4	(1.3)	81.2	(1.1)	82.5	(1.1)	85.3	(1.1)	**9.0**	(1.7)	76.9	(1.0)	85.7	(0.7)	**8.8**	(1.2)
Hungary	83.9	(0.7)	77.2	(1.4)	84.2	(1.2)	84.1	(1.1)	89.5	(1.1)	**12.3**	(1.7)	80.7	(1.0)	86.8	(0.8)	**6.1**	(1.3)
Iceland	73.7	(0.8)	66.4	(1.9)	69.5	(2.0)	76.9	(1.6)	81.0	(1.3)	**14.6**	(2.3)	70.1	(1.3)	77.1	(1.1)	**7.1**	(1.7)
Ireland	70.8	(0.8)	62.4	(1.5)	68.8	(1.4)	70.8	(1.5)	81.2	(1.0)	**18.8**	(1.8)	66.1	(1.1)	75.5	(1.0)	**9.4**	(1.4)
Israel	m	m	m	m	m	m	m	m	m	m	m	m	m	m	m	m	m	m
Italy	71.8	(0.7)	66.8	(1.5)	72.1	(1.5)	73.0	(1.5)	75.0	(1.4)	**8.2**	(2.2)	68.9	(1.0)	74.9	(1.0)	**6.0**	(1.5)
Korea	89.4	(0.5)	88.0	(1.0)	89.3	(0.7)	89.1	(0.9)	91.3	(0.7)	**3.4**	(1.2)	87.7	(0.7)	91.3	(0.5)	**3.6**	(0.8)
Latvia	71.4	(0.7)	63.1	(1.6)	71.3	(1.4)	73.5	(1.2)	78.1	(1.3)	**15.0**	(2.1)	67.0	(1.2)	75.6	(0.9)	**8.6**	(1.5)
Lithuania	81.0	(0.5)	75.5	(1.3)	80.6	(1.4)	82.6	(1.0)	85.9	(0.9)	**10.4**	(1.5)	75.1	(0.8)	87.1	(0.6)	**12.0**	(1.0)
Mexico	85.3	(0.7)	81.3	(1.7)	82.8	(1.1)	84.7	(1.3)	89.9	(1.0)	**8.6**	(1.9)	81.7	(1.1)	88.7	(0.8)	**6.9**	(1.2)
Netherlands	m	m	m	m	m	m	m	m	m	m	m	m	m	m	m	m	m	m
New Zealand	80.1	(0.6)	74.4	(1.2)	78.2	(1.2)	81.6	(1.1)	86.1	(0.8)	**11.6**	(1.5)	75.7	(0.9)	84.4	(0.8)	**8.7**	(1.1)
Poland	76.3	(0.7)	70.3	(1.5)	77.6	(1.1)	75.8	(1.3)	81.1	(1.1)	**10.8**	(1.9)	71.3	(0.9)	81.1	(0.9)	**9.9**	(1.3)
Portugal	94.0	(0.4)	93.1	(0.8)	93.6	(0.7)	93.7	(0.8)	95.7	(0.6)	**2.7**	(1.0)	92.5	(0.6)	95.5	(0.5)	**3.0**	(0.8)
Scotland (United Kingdom)	71.6	(1.0)	62.6	(1.8)	69.5	(1.7)	76.5	(1.7)	79.9	(2.0)	**17.3**	(2.9)	65.6	(1.6)	77.3	(1.2)	**11.7**	(2.0)
Slovak Republic	64.3	(0.8)	54.6	(1.6)	63.6	(1.3)	64.7	(1.4)	73.2	(1.3)	**18.6**	(2.1)	61.0	(1.0)	67.6	(1.2)	**6.6**	(1.6)
Slovenia	78.6	(0.8)	74.5	(1.5)	76.8	(1.4)	81.1	(1.4)	81.8	(1.4)	**7.3**	(2.0)	74.5	(1.2)	82.7	(0.9)	**8.1**	(1.5)
Spain	83.5	(0.4)	80.7	(0.8)	82.6	(0.6)	84.4	(0.7)	86.3	(0.6)	**5.6**	(0.9)	81.8	(0.5)	85.3	(0.5)	**3.5**	(0.7)
Switzerland	74.7	(1.0)	66.8	(2.1)	72.4	(1.9)	76.1	(1.4)	82.6	(1.2)	**15.8**	(2.3)	71.9	(1.3)	77.7	(1.3)	**5.8**	(1.6)
Türkiye	80.8	(0.6)	81.4	(1.0)	79.3	(1.1)	79.9	(1.2)	82.5	(1.0)	1.1	(1.4)	76.4	(0.9)	85.1	(0.7)	**8.8**	(1.0)
OECD average	78.4	(0.1)	73.0	(0.3)	77.1	(0.3)	79.4	(0.2)	83.6	(0.2)	**10.6**	(0.3)	74.8	(0.2)	81.9	(0.2)	**7.1**	(0.2)

Note: Values that are statistically significant are indicated in bold.

1. Students' socio-economic status is measured by the PISA index of economic, social and cultural status (ESCS).

StatLink https://stat.link/3wkgpq

Table B.3.5 [2/2] **Environmental sense-of-purpose, by student background**

	Percentage of students who reported that looking after the global environment is important to them																	
	All students		Students' socio-economic status[1]										Gender					
			Bottom quarter of ESCS[1] (disadvantaged students)		2nd quarter of ESCS		3rd quarter of ESCS		Top quarter of ESCS (advantaged students)		Difference (Top - Bottom quarter of ESCS)		Boys		Girls		Difference (Girls - Boys)	
	%	S.E.	%	S.E.	%	S.E.	%	S.E.	%	S.E.	% dif.	S.E.	%	S.E.	%	S.E.	% dif.	S.E.
Partners Albania	90.4	(0.4)	89.6	(0.9)	90.2	(0.9)	91.1	(0.9)	90.7	(0.8)	1.1	(1.3)	87.2	(0.6)	93.5	(0.5)	**6.3**	(0.7)
Argentina	78.4	(0.7)	72.5	(1.7)	79.4	(1.3)	78.4	(1.2)	82.5	(1.0)	**9.9**	(2.0)	73.7	(1.0)	83.0	(0.8)	**9.3**	(1.2)
Baku (Azerbaijan)	76.9	(0.6)	76.2	(1.6)	76.8	(1.3)	75.5	(1.2)	79.0	(1.3)	2.9	(2.1)	74.7	(1.1)	79.0	(1.0)	**4.2**	(1.6)
Bosnia and Herzegovina	65.5	(0.7)	63.6	(1.4)	63.0	(1.4)	66.4	(1.4)	68.9	(1.6)	**5.3**	(2.3)	64.6	(1.0)	66.5	(1.1)	1.8	(1.4)
Brazil	81.5	(0.5)	79.8	(1.1)	80.0	(1.1)	81.8	(1.2)	84.0	(1.0)	**4.2**	(1.7)	77.2	(0.8)	85.6	(0.6)	**8.4**	(1.0)
Brunei Darussalam	76.8	(0.4)	70.5	(1.3)	76.2	(1.2)	76.7	(1.0)	82.6	(0.8)	**12.2**	(1.6)	73.1	(0.7)	80.3	(0.7)	**7.2**	(1.1)
Bulgaria	74.6	(0.9)	68.4	(1.7)	73.6	(1.8)	73.3	(1.6)	82.5	(1.1)	**14.2**	(2.0)	68.2	(1.3)	81.2	(1.0)	**13.0**	(1.5)
Croatia	74.5	(0.6)	68.4	(1.3)	75.7	(1.2)	75.8	(1.2)	77.9	(1.0)	**9.5**	(1.7)	72.5	(0.8)	76.4	(0.8)	**3.9**	(1.1)
Cyprus	75.5	(0.6)	74.4	(1.4)	74.6	(1.3)	76.4	(1.2)	76.9	(1.3)	2.5	(2.1)	70.7	(1.0)	80.1	(0.8)	**9.4**	(1.3)
Dominican Republic	79.8	(1.1)	74.3	(2.4)	76.7	(2.1)	77.2	(1.9)	86.1	(1.6)	**11.8**	(2.9)	75.6	(1.5)	83.9	(1.5)	**8.3**	(2.0)
Hong Kong (China)	85.0	(0.6)	83.8	(1.1)	85.6	(1.0)	84.9	(1.0)	86.1	(1.2)	2.2	(1.6)	82.9	(0.8)	87.3	(0.7)	**4.4**	(1.0)
Indonesia	84.7	(0.7)	82.3	(1.3)	85.0	(1.2)	84.6	(1.3)	87.2	(1.2)	**4.9**	(1.8)	81.9	(1.1)	87.5	(0.7)	**5.6**	(1.2)
Jordan	79.3	(0.6)	77.7	(1.3)	79.3	(1.0)	77.1	(1.1)	83.5	(1.2)	**5.8**	(1.8)	72.4	(0.9)	85.8	(0.7)	**13.3**	(1.1)
Kazakhstan	77.7	(0.4)	76.9	(0.9)	77.6	(0.9)	76.9	(0.8)	79.5	(0.7)	**2.6**	(1.0)	74.1	(0.7)	81.4	(0.5)	**7.3**	(0.8)
Kosovo	84.7	(0.6)	83.9	(1.2)	85.1	(1.3)	82.6	(1.2)	87.1	(1.1)	3.3	(1.7)	82.1	(0.8)	87.1	(0.8)	**5.0**	(1.1)
Lebanon	72.8	(0.9)	69.7	(1.7)	72.5	(1.4)	73.3	(1.6)	76.2	(1.3)	**6.5**	(2.1)	69.4	(1.2)	75.8	(1.2)	**6.5**	(1.6)
Macao (China)	90.0	(0.5)	90.3	(0.9)	90.3	(0.9)	90.3	(0.9)	89.1	(1.0)	-1.2	(1.4)	87.2	(0.7)	92.9	(0.6)	**5.7**	(0.9)
Malaysia	80.4	(0.6)	76.8	(1.4)	78.6	(1.3)	80.9	(1.2)	85.3	(1.1)	**8.5**	(1.8)	77.7	(0.9)	83.0	(0.8)	**5.3**	(1.0)
Malta	81.9	(0.7)	77.5	(1.5)	81.9	(1.3)	81.4	(1.4)	86.6	(1.1)	**9.1**	(1.9)	78.6	(1.0)	85.1	(0.8)	**6.5**	(1.3)
Moldova	78.6	(0.7)	73.3	(1.4)	78.7	(1.4)	79.6	(1.0)	82.6	(1.0)	**9.3**	(1.6)	73.8	(1.1)	83.4	(0.8)	**9.6**	(1.3)
Montenegro	74.5	(0.6)	70.8	(1.3)	75.1	(1.1)	74.9	(1.2)	77.1	(1.1)	**6.3**	(1.7)	72.4	(1.1)	76.6	(0.9)	**4.2**	(1.4)
Morocco	78.7	(0.9)	76.0	(1.9)	80.1	(1.7)	77.0	(1.5)	80.7	(1.5)	4.7	(2.4)	74.1	(1.1)	83.9	(1.1)	**9.8**	(1.5)
North Macedonia	84.7	(0.5)	79.7	(1.3)	85.6	(1.1)	86.6	(1.1)	87.2	(1.1)	**7.5**	(1.7)	80.9	(0.8)	88.9	(0.7)	**8.0**	(1.2)
Panama	80.6	(1.1)	78.8	(2.2)	78.2	(2.0)	80.6	(1.9)	83.4	(1.9)	4.5	(2.9)	78.7	(1.4)	82.5	(1.2)	**3.7**	(1.5)
Peru	87.9	(0.6)	84.2	(1.9)	91.8	(1.0)	87.8	(1.2)	86.9	(1.0)	2.8	(2.1)	86.0	(0.9)	90.0	(0.8)	**3.9**	(1.1)
Philippines	83.1	(0.6)	77.3	(1.1)	83.1	(1.0)	83.6	(0.8)	88.0	(0.7)	**10.7**	(1.4)	80.5	(0.9)	85.5	(0.6)	**5.0**	(1.1)
Romania	83.0	(0.9)	78.0	(1.7)	81.1	(1.2)	84.2	(1.3)	88.5	(1.1)	**10.4**	(2.0)	78.2	(1.1)	88.0	(0.8)	**9.8**	(1.1)
Saudi Arabia	69.7	(0.7)	68.8	(1.6)	69.0	(1.5)	69.3	(1.1)	71.6	(1.3)	2.8	(2.1)	63.7	(1.0)	75.6	(0.9)	**11.9**	(1.3)
Serbia	65.3	(0.8)	62.2	(1.7)	65.1	(1.5)	64.9	(1.6)	68.9	(1.4)	**6.7**	(2.3)	64.0	(1.2)	66.6	(0.9)	**2.5**	(1.3)
Singapore	86.7	(0.5)	84.7	(0.8)	87.1	(0.9)	87.8	(0.8)	87.1	(1.0)	**2.4**	(1.2)	84.7	(0.6)	88.8	(0.6)	**4.0**	(0.9)
Chinese Taipei	88.9	(0.4)	87.9	(0.9)	88.8	(0.8)	90.0	(0.7)	88.8	(0.9)	0.9	(1.2)	87.1	(0.6)	90.6	(0.5)	**3.5**	(0.8)
Thailand	85.4	(0.6)	82.0	(1.0)	84.7	(1.0)	86.0	(0.9)	88.8	(0.9)	**6.8**	(1.3)	82.7	(0.9)	87.7	(0.7)	**5.0**	(1.0)
Ukraine	69.4	(0.7)	62.9	(1.8)	68.3	(1.4)	70.2	(1.4)	75.7	(1.1)	**12.7**	(2.3)	63.2	(0.9)	76.0	(0.8)	**12.8**	(1.1)
United Arab Emirates	m	m	m	m	m	m	m	m	m	m	m	m	m	m	m	m	m	m
Uruguay	79.3	(0.6)	77.2	(1.5)	77.7	(1.4)	79.0	(1.4)	82.4	(1.1)	**5.1**	(1.9)	76.5	(1.2)	81.7	(0.9)	**5.2**	(1.6)
Viet Nam	73.2	(0.7)	70.9	(1.5)	72.0	(1.1)	72.8	(1.4)	77.0	(1.1)	**6.1**	(2.0)	72.2	(1.0)	74.0	(0.9)	1.8	(1.3)
Overall average	79.0	(0.1)	74.9	(0.2)	78.2	(0.2)	79.4	(0.2)	83.0	(0.1)	**8.1**	(0.2)	75.5	(0.1)	82.3	(0.1)	**6.8**	(0.2)

Note: Values that are statistically significant are indicated in bold.

1. Students' socio-economic status is measured by the PISA index of economic, social and cultural status (ESCS).

StatLink https://stat.link/3wkgpg

Table B.3.12 [1/2] **Overlap of environmental attitudes**

	Percentage of students who display the following combinations of environmental attitudes:															
	Environmentally enthusiastic (shows awareness, self-efficacy and sense-of-purpose)		Awareness and self-efficacy but no sense-of-purpose		Awareness and sense-of-purpose but no self-efficacy		Awareness but no self-efficacy nor sense-of-purpose		No awareness yet shows self-efficacy and sense-of-purpose		No awareness and no sense-of-purpose yet shows self-efficacy		No awareness and no self-efficacy yet sense-of-purpose		Environmentally indifferent (does not identify with any of the environmental attitudes)	
	%	S.E.	%	S.E.	%	S.E.	%	S.E.	%	S.E.	%	S.E.	%	S.E.	%	S.E.
OECD																
Australia	54.2	(0.7)	11.8	(0.4)	12.5	(0.3)	4.7	(0.2)	3.0	(0.2)	1.4	(0.1)	7.2	(0.3)	5.4	(0.3)
Austria	38.5	(0.9)	11.6	(0.5)	19.6	(0.8)	9.1	(0.4)	2.0	(0.2)	1.8	(0.2)	9.1	(0.5)	8.3	(0.4)
Belgium	m	m	m	m	m	m	m	m	m	m	m	m	m	m	m	m
Canada	58.1	(0.6)	11.9	(0.3)	13.2	(0.3)	4.5	(0.2)	2.6	(0.2)	1.1	(0.1)	5.5	(0.2)	3.1	(0.2)
Chile	48.2	(1.2)	6.2	(0.4)	15.0	(0.6)	2.9	(0.3)	9.1	(0.5)	2.0	(0.2)	12.4	(0.6)	4.2	(0.4)
Colombia	53.4	(1.2)	4.9	(0.3)	11.9	(0.6)	2.0	(0.2)	11.4	(0.6)	2.0	(0.2)	11.1	(0.5)	3.2	(0.3)
Costa Rica	50.6	(0.9)	3.9	(0.3)	17.7	(0.5)	1.9	(0.2)	9.0	(0.3)	0.8	(0.1)	13.6	(0.6)	2.5	(0.2)
Estonia	43.3	(0.8)	11.7	(0.6)	18.4	(0.7)	8.4	(0.4)	2.8	(0.2)	1.8	(0.2)	6.9	(0.5)	6.7	(0.4)
France	51.6	(0.9)	10.2	(0.4)	14.2	(0.6)	5.8	(0.4)	3.6	(0.3)	1.9	(0.2)	7.2	(0.4)	5.4	(0.4)
Germany	43.4	(1.0)	14.5	(0.6)	17.4	(0.7)	8.5	(0.5)	1.6	(0.3)	2.2	(0.3)	5.5	(0.4)	7.0	(0.5)
Greece	34.1	(0.8)	5.0	(0.4)	28.6	(0.7)	5.5	(0.3)	4.5	(0.3)	1.6	(0.2)	14.3	(0.5)	6.3	(0.4)
Hungary	53.6	(1.0)	6.3	(0.4)	13.8	(0.6)	3.2	(0.2)	6.0	(0.4)	1.7	(0.2)	10.8	(0.6)	4.7	(0.4)
Iceland	47.9	(0.9)	11.2	(0.6)	13.7	(0.7)	4.4	(0.3)	2.8	(0.3)	2.3	(0.3)	9.2	(0.5)	8.3	(0.5)
Ireland	53.2	(0.9)	16.3	(0.5)	11.2	(0.5)	6.3	(0.3)	1.9	(0.2)	1.3	(0.2)	4.6	(0.3)	5.3	(0.3)
Israel	m	m	m	m	m	m	m	m	m	m	m	m	m	m	m	m
Italy	42.3	(0.7)	10.6	(0.4)	17.9	(0.6)	7.7	(0.4)	3.2	(0.3)	2.4	(0.3)	8.8	(0.4)	7.1	(0.4)
Korea	70.3	(0.8)	6.2	(0.3)	10.1	(0.5)	1.7	(0.2)	3.9	(0.3)	0.9	(0.1)	5.1	(0.3)	1.7	(0.2)
Latvia	44.0	(0.8)	11.9	(0.5)	13.5	(0.5)	6.5	(0.4)	4.8	(0.3)	3.1	(0.3)	9.3	(0.5)	6.9	(0.5)
Lithuania	49.2	(0.8)	8.0	(0.4)	19.5	(0.6)	4.0	(0.3)	3.8	(0.3)	1.8	(0.2)	8.8	(0.4)	4.9	(0.3)
Mexico	51.2	(1.0)	6.8	(0.5)	17.1	(0.6)	2.5	(0.2)	7.4	(0.5)	1.9	(0.3)	9.8	(0.4)	3.5	(0.3)
Netherlands	m	m	m	m	m	m	m	m	m	m	m	m	m	m	m	m
New Zealand	54.2	(0.7)	9.8	(0.5)	13.4	(0.5)	3.5	(0.3)	3.8	(0.3)	1.7	(0.2)	8.6	(0.4)	5.0	(0.3)
Poland	44.7	(1.0)	10.2	(0.4)	15.3	(0.6)	5.5	(0.3)	6.1	(0.3)	2.3	(0.2)	10.4	(0.5)	5.6	(0.4)
Portugal	59.0	(1.0)	2.4	(0.2)	21.1	(0.6)	1.4	(0.2)	3.2	(0.2)	0.3	(0.1)	10.8	(0.5)	1.8	(0.2)
Scotland (United Kingdom)	45.9	(1.2)	11.8	(0.6)	15.2	(0.6)	6.3	(0.5)	3.1	(0.4)	1.6	(0.2)	8.1	(0.7)	8.1	(0.5)
Slovak Republic	26.8	(0.7)	9.0	(0.4)	22.2	(0.6)	11.7	(0.5)	3.5	(0.3)	2.5	(0.2)	12.2	(0.5)	12.1	(0.5)
Slovenia	48.3	(0.8)	8.7	(0.5)	16.2	(0.6)	4.7	(0.3)	5.4	(0.4)	2.0	(0.2)	8.9	(0.4)	5.8	(0.3)
Spain	48.4	(0.6)	6.3	(0.2)	22.5	(0.4)	4.4	(0.2)	3.3	(0.1)	1.1	(0.1)	9.6	(0.3)	4.6	(0.2)
Switzerland	42.8	(1.2)	10.2	(0.6)	19.8	(0.8)	6.3	(0.5)	2.9	(0.3)	2.3	(0.3)	9.4	(0.6)	6.4	(0.5)
Türkiye	45.5	(0.9)	6.9	(0.3)	21.5	(0.6)	5.2	(0.3)	4.7	(0.3)	2.1	(0.2)	9.1	(0.4)	5.0	(0.3)
OECD average	48.2	(0.2)	9.0	(0.1)	16.7	(0.1)	5.1	(0.1)	4.4	(0.1)	1.8	(0.0)	9.1	(0.1)	5.5	(0.1)

StatLink https://stat.link/udoz73

Table B.3.12 [2/2] **Overlap of environmental attitudes**

	Percentage of students who display the following combinations of environmental attitudes:															
	Environmentally enthusiastic (shows awareness, self-efficacy and sense-of-purpose)		Awareness and self-efficacy but no sense-of-purpose		Awareness and sense-of-purpose but no self-efficacy		Awareness but no self-efficacy nor sense-of-purpose		No awareness yet shows self-efficacy and sense-of-purpose		No awareness and no sense-of-purpose yet shows self-efficacy		No awareness and no self-efficacy yet sense-of-purpose		Environmentally indifferent (does not identify with any of the environmental attitudes)	
	%	S.E.	%	S.E.	%	S.E.	%	S.E.	%	S.E.	%	S.E.	%	S.E.	%	S.E.
Partners																
Albania	64.5	(0.8)	4.0	(0.3)	12.4	(0.5)	1.7	(0.2)	5.6	(0.3)	1.3	(0.2)	7.9	(0.4)	2.6	(0.2)
Argentina	27.4	(0.7)	4.1	(0.2)	15.5	(0.6)	3.6	(0.3)	11.5	(0.6)	3.0	(0.3)	24.3	(0.7)	10.5	(0.5)
Baku (Azerbaijan)	35.3	(0.9)	7.5	(0.5)	21.6	(0.6)	6.2	(0.4)	6.0	(0.4)	2.1	(0.2)	14.1	(0.7)	7.1	(0.4)
Bosnia and Herzegovina	28.6	(0.9)	10.2	(0.5)	17.3	(0.5)	9.7	(0.5)	5.2	(0.3)	3.2	(0.3)	14.5	(0.6)	11.3	(0.6)
Brazil	33.0	(0.8)	4.2	(0.3)	21.8	(0.6)	4.0	(0.2)	6.7	(0.3)	1.8	(0.2)	20.4	(0.6)	8.2	(0.4)
Brunei Darussalam	47.2	(0.6)	9.0	(0.3)	11.8	(0.4)	4.6	(0.3)	6.8	(0.3)	2.5	(0.2)	11.1	(0.5)	7.1	(0.3)
Bulgaria	42.0	(1.2)	8.0	(0.5)	15.5	(0.7)	5.3	(0.4)	6.2	(0.5)	2.9	(0.4)	11.5	(0.6)	8.7	(0.6)
Croatia	46.5	(0.8)	11.3	(0.4)	14.5	(0.5)	6.1	(0.3)	4.4	(0.3)	2.3	(0.2)	9.3	(0.4)	5.6	(0.3)
Cyprus	35.4	(0.6)	8.1	(0.4)	17.7	(0.6)	5.1	(0.4)	6.1	(0.4)	2.4	(0.2)	16.3	(0.6)	8.8	(0.4)
Dominican Republic	45.0	(1.5)	7.5	(0.7)	11.8	(0.8)	2.6	(0.4)	11.4	(0.9)	2.8	(0.4)	12.2	(0.9)	6.6	(0.7)
Hong Kong (China)	66.0	(0.8)	9.7	(0.5)	12.3	(0.5)	2.7	(0.2)	2.7	(0.3)	0.7	(0.1)	4.0	(0.3)	1.8	(0.2)
Indonesia	20.9	(0.7)	3.2	(0.2)	28.9	(0.9)	3.7	(0.3)	8.3	(0.5)	1.4	(0.2)	26.5	(0.9)	7.0	(0.4)
Jordan	39.9	(0.8)	4.4	(0.2)	21.4	(0.6)	5.1	(0.3)	3.4	(0.3)	1.4	(0.2)	15.0	(0.6)	9.5	(0.5)
Kazakhstan	37.7	(0.6)	8.5	(0.3)	23.0	(0.4)	5.8	(0.2)	4.5	(0.2)	1.9	(0.1)	12.6	(0.3)	6.0	(0.2)
Kosovo	26.7	(0.8)	2.1	(0.2)	35.1	(0.7)	4.9	(0.3)	4.2	(0.3)	1.1	(0.1)	19.5	(0.7)	6.5	(0.5)
Lebanon	35.8	(1.2)	6.1	(0.4)	12.5	(0.7)	4.7	(0.5)	11.9	(0.8)	4.8	(0.4)	13.0	(0.7)	11.1	(0.7)
Macao (China)	53.2	(0.7)	4.9	(0.4)	26.3	(0.7)	2.9	(0.3)	2.4	(0.3)	0.4	(0.1)	8.2	(0.4)	1.8	(0.2)
Malaysia	46.2	(1.0)	6.8	(0.4)	12.1	(0.4)	3.4	(0.2)	8.7	(0.4)	2.8	(0.2)	13.4	(0.6)	6.5	(0.4)
Malta	58.8	(0.8)	7.2	(0.5)	14.2	(0.7)	4.1	(0.3)	2.3	(0.3)	1.4	(0.2)	6.9	(0.5)	5.1	(0.4)
Moldova	37.9	(0.6)	6.7	(0.4)	22.3	(0.6)	5.8	(0.4)	5.5	(0.4)	1.8	(0.2)	13.2	(0.5)	6.8	(0.4)
Montenegro	38.1	(0.7)	8.0	(0.4)	18.3	(0.5)	6.7	(0.4)	5.6	(0.3)	2.6	(0.2)	13.0	(0.5)	7.7	(0.4)
Morocco	27.8	(1.1)	4.2	(0.3)	22.3	(0.9)	4.6	(0.4)	6.4	(0.4)	2.8	(0.3)	22.5	(1.0)	9.3	(0.7)
North Macedonia	31.7	(0.8)	2.6	(0.2)	31.2	(0.8)	4.8	(0.3)	5.3	(0.3)	1.5	(0.2)	16.8	(0.6)	6.2	(0.4)
Panama	42.9	(1.3)	7.7	(0.7)	15.3	(1.0)	3.3	(0.4)	11.2	(0.7)	3.2	(0.4)	11.4	(0.8)	5.0	(0.6)
Peru	57.3	(1.0)	6.3	(0.4)	16.4	(0.8)	2.4	(0.3)	6.6	(0.5)	0.9	(0.2)	7.7	(0.6)	2.5	(0.3)
Philippines	48.3	(1.0)	5.4	(0.3)	16.5	(0.5)	3.3	(0.2)	6.8	(0.3)	2.1	(0.2)	11.6	(0.4)	5.9	(0.4)
Romania	28.8	(1.1)	3.5	(0.3)	25.3	(0.7)	4.4	(0.4)	6.0	(0.4)	1.8	(0.2)	23.2	(0.8)	7.1	(0.5)
Saudi Arabia	18.8	(0.6)	4.7	(0.3)	12.5	(0.4)	4.7	(0.3)	12.6	(0.5)	4.3	(0.3)	25.7	(0.7)	16.6	(0.6)
Serbia	36.2	(0.9)	12.9	(0.6)	16.2	(0.6)	9.9	(0.4)	3.5	(0.3)	2.3	(0.3)	9.6	(0.5)	9.4	(0.5)
Singapore	71.3	(0.6)	9.4	(0.4)	7.3	(0.4)	1.4	(0.1)	3.5	(0.2)	1.0	(0.2)	4.6	(0.3)	1.4	(0.2)
Chinese Taipei	65.1	(0.7)	6.0	(0.3)	13.0	(0.5)	1.8	(0.2)	5.0	(0.3)	1.0	(0.1)	5.8	(0.3)	2.3	(0.2)
Thailand	53.3	(1.0)	5.4	(0.3)	15.7	(0.5)	3.1	(0.2)	6.8	(0.3)	1.9	(0.2)	9.7	(0.4)	4.1	(0.3)
Ukraine	38.9	(1.1)	11.5	(0.4)	16.3	(0.7)	7.9	(0.5)	4.7	(0.3)	2.9	(0.3)	9.7	(0.5)	8.1	(0.5)
United Arab Emirates	m	m	m	m	m	m	m	m	m	m	m	m	m	m	m	m
Uruguay	36.9	(0.8)	6.3	(0.4)	20.9	(0.6)	5.0	(0.4)	7.1	(0.5)	2.1	(0.3)	14.5	(0.7)	7.3	(0.6)
Viet Nam	44.8	(1.1)	13.6	(0.6)	12.1	(0.6)	4.4	(0.3)	7.8	(0.5)	3.0	(0.3)	8.5	(0.6)	5.8	(0.4)
Overall average	44.7	(0.1)	7.8	(0.1)	17.4	(0.1)	4.8	(0.0)	5.5	(0.0)	2.0	(0.0)	11.5	(0.1)	6.2	(0.1)

StatLink https://stat.link/udoz73

Table B.3.24 [1/6] **Likelihood of being an environmentally enthusiastic student, by student, school and parental characteristics**

	Increased likelihood of being an environmentally enthusiastic student[1]															
	Socio-economically Advantaged Student[2] (reference: Socio-economically disadvantaged)				Baseline Proficiency Level 2 in science						Girls (reference: boys)					
	Before accounting for other variables		After accounting for other variables		Before accounting for socio-economic status		After accounting for socio-economic status		After accounting for socio-economic status and other variables		Before accounting for socio-economic status		After accounting for socio-economic status		After accounting for socio-economic status and other variables	
	Odds ratio	S.E.	Odds ratio	S.E.	Odds ratio	S.E.	Odds ratio	S.E.	Odds ratio	S.E.	Odds ratio	S.E.	Odds ratio	S.E.	Odds ratio	S.E.
OECD Australia	**2.82**	(0.21)	**2.25**	(0.17)	**3.52**	(0.29)	**3.06**	(0.26)	**2.76**	(0.25)	**1.11**	(0.05)	**1.11**	(0.05)	**1.10**	(0.05)
Austria	**3.06**	(0.30)	**2.41**	(0.25)	**3.99**	(0.49)	**3.38**	(0.41)	**3.34**	(0.41)	**0.75**	(0.05)	**0.75**	(0.04)	**0.72**	(0.04)
Belgium	m	m	m	m	m	m	m	m	m	m	m	m	m	m	m	m
Canada	**2.54**	(0.14)	**2.26**	(0.13)	**3.21**	(0.28)	**2.88**	(0.26)	**2.70**	(0.24)	1.04	(0.05)	1.03	(0.05)	1.00	(0.05)
Chile	**2.35**	(0.21)	**1.47**	(0.16)	**2.61**	(0.27)	**2.35**	(0.25)	**2.07**	(0.23)	0.90	(0.07)	0.92	(0.07)	0.91	(0.07)
Colombia	**2.02**	(0.23)	**1.47**	(0.17)	**2.56**	(0.22)	**2.38**	(0.22)	**2.16**	(0.22)	1.00	(0.06)	1.04	(0.06)	1.09	(0.06)
Costa Rica	**2.41**	(0.21)	**1.61**	(0.14)	**2.72**	(0.22)	**2.42**	(0.20)	**2.27**	(0.19)	0.98	(0.06)	0.99	(0.06)	1.03	(0.06)
Estonia	**3.37**	(0.32)	**3.10**	(0.30)	**3.64**	(0.62)	**3.13**	(0.52)	**3.03**	(0.50)	1.00	(0.07)	1.01	(0.07)	0.99	(0.07)
France	**4.17**	(0.42)	**3.30**	(0.34)	**4.89**	(0.64)	**3.71**	(0.47)	**3.66**	(0.47)	**0.75**	(0.04)	**0.72**	(0.04)	**0.71**	(0.04)
Germany	**4.09**	(0.70)	**3.46**	(0.65)	**4.01**	(1.59)	**3.40**	(1.42)	**3.31**	(1.40)	0.92	(0.13)	0.89	(0.13)	0.90	(0.14)
Greece	**2.61**	(0.24)	**1.97**	(0.18)	**3.42**	(0.38)	**3.02**	(0.34)	**2.95**	(0.33)	1.00	(0.07)	1.01	(0.07)	0.95	(0.06)
Hungary	**3.84**	(0.41)	**2.60**	(0.29)	**4.42**	(0.59)	**3.56**	(0.49)	**3.36**	(0.47)	0.94	(0.07)	0.93	(0.06)	0.93	(0.07)
Iceland	**3.96**	(0.47)	**3.23**	(0.40)	**4.08**	(0.66)	**3.52**	(0.58)	**3.28**	(0.55)	1.02	(0.08)	1.03	(0.09)	0.96	(0.08)
Ireland	**3.41**	(0.36)	**2.59**	(0.28)	**3.94**	(0.47)	**3.44**	(0.41)	**3.06**	(0.37)	**1.18**	(0.08)	**1.17**	(0.08)	**1.18**	(0.08)
Israel	m	m	m	m	m	m	m	m	m	m	m	m	m	m	m	m
Italy	**1.79**	(0.19)	**1.36**	(0.16)	**3.31**	(0.48)	**3.11**	(0.46)	**2.98**	(0.45)	1.13	(0.07)	**1.15**	(0.08)	1.13	(0.07)
Korea	**2.62**	(0.25)	**1.94**	(0.18)	**3.79**	(0.31)	**3.38**	(0.27)	**3.18**	(0.25)	**1.20**	(0.09)	**1.17**	(0.09)	**1.22**	(0.09)
Latvia	**2.97**	(0.31)	**2.43**	(0.26)	**4.17**	(0.56)	**3.66**	(0.48)	**3.41**	(0.44)	**1.18**	(0.07)	**1.21**	(0.08)	**1.15**	(0.08)
Lithuania	**3.06**	(0.27)	**2.50**	(0.23)	**2.65**	(0.27)	**2.25**	(0.24)	**2.14**	(0.23)	1.07	(0.06)	1.07	(0.06)	1.03	(0.05)
Mexico	**2.21**	(0.23)	**1.49**	(0.17)	**2.39**	(0.18)	**2.17**	(0.17)	**2.11**	(0.17)	1.04	(0.07)	1.06	(0.08)	1.12	(0.08)
Netherlands	m	m	m	m	m	m	m	m	m	m	m	m	m	m	m	m
New Zealand	**3.59**	(0.32)	**2.70**	(0.25)	**4.12**	(0.44)	**3.35**	(0.38)	**2.88**	(0.34)	0.93	(0.05)	0.91	(0.05)	**0.89**	(0.05)
Poland	**3.45**	(0.35)	**2.90**	(0.30)	**4.61**	(0.57)	**3.88**	(0.50)	**3.84**	(0.49)	1.09	(0.06)	1.10	(0.06)	1.07	(0.06)
Portugal	**4.00**	(0.42)	**2.25**	(0.27)	**5.05**	(0.65)	**4.03**	(0.54)	**3.65**	(0.47)	0.93	(0.06)	0.92	(0.06)	0.93	(0.06)
Scotland (United Kingdom)	**4.75**	(0.68)	**3.78**	(0.56)	**3.76**	(0.94)	**3.07**	(0.79)	**2.91**	(0.78)	0.86	(0.09)	0.91	(0.10)	0.93	(0.11)
Slovak Republic	**4.32**	(0.53)	**3.25**	(0.41)	**3.83**	(0.75)	**3.06**	(0.62)	**3.04**	(0.62)	0.89	(0.07)	0.89	(0.06)	**0.85**	(0.06)
Slovenia	**2.91**	(0.33)	**2.34**	(0.27)	**5.11**	(0.86)	**4.31**	(0.75)	**4.15**	(0.73)	1.00	(0.07)	1.00	(0.08)	0.95	(0.08)
Spain*	**2.53**	(0.14)	**2.10**	(0.11)	**3.56**	(0.29)	**3.15**	(0.26)	**3.09**	(0.25)	**0.90**	(0.03)	**0.89**	(0.03)	**0.88**	(0.03)
Switzerland	**3.48**	(0.40)	**2.83**	(0.32)	**3.84**	(0.58)	**3.13**	(0.49)	**3.18**	(0.49)	**0.81**	(0.07)	**0.76**	(0.07)	**0.74**	(0.06)
Türkiye	**1.73**	(0.14)	**1.50**	(0.12)	**2.67**	(0.23)	**2.51**	(0.22)	**2.39**	(0.20)	**1.65**	(0.09)	**1.69**	(0.09)	**1.63**	(0.10)
OECD average	**3.11**	(0.07)	**2.41**	(0.06)	**3.70**	(0.11)	**3.16**	(0.10)	**3.00**	(0.10)	1.01	(0.01)	1.01	(0.01)	1.00	(0.01)

Note: Values that are statistically significant are indicated in bold.

* In 2018, some regions in Spain conducted their high-stakes exams for tenth-grade students earlier in the year than in the past, which resulted in the testing period for these exams coinciding with the end of the PISA testing window. Because of this overlap, a number of students were negatively disposed towards the PISA test and did not try their best to demonstrate their proficiency. Although the data of only a minority of students show clear signs of lack of engagement (see PISA 2018 Results Volume I, Annex A9), the comparability of PISA 2018 data for Spain with those from earlier PISA assessments cannot be fully ensured.

1. All regression models reported in this table use the same sample: students who had no missing data on any of the variables included in the analyses. For the countries without parental characteristics data, parental variables are not accounted for in the model after accounting for socio-economic status and other variables.

2. Students' socio-economic status is measured by the PISA index of economic, social and cultural status (ESCS).

3. For North Macedonia and Romania, the variable on whether school covers climate change in the curriculum is not included in the model after accounting for socio-economic status and other variables.

StatLink https://stat.link/lv3dsm

Table B.3.24 [2/6] Likelihood of being an environmentally enthusiastic student, by student, school and parental characteristics

	Increased likelihood of being an environmentally enthusiastic student[1]															
	Socio-economically Advantaged Student[2] (reference: Socio-economically disadvantaged)				Baseline Proficiency Level 2 in science						Girls (reference: boys)					
	Before accounting for other variables		After accounting for other variables		Before accounting for socio-economic status		After accounting for socio-economic status		After accounting for socio-economic status and other variables		Before accounting for socio-economic status		After accounting for socio-economic status		After accounting for socio-economic status and other variables	
	Odds ratio	S.E.	Odds ratio	S.E.	Odds ratio	S.E.	Odds ratio	S.E.	Odds ratio	S.E.	Odds ratio	S.E.	Odds ratio	S.E.	Odds ratio	S.E.
Partners																
Albania	**2.01**	(0.20)	**1.59**	(0.16)	**3.19**	(0.25)	**3.03**	(0.24)	**2.86**	(0.21)	**2.25**	(0.15)	**2.30**	(0.15)	**2.19**	(0.15)
Argentina	**3.18**	(0.33)	**2.06**	(0.25)	**3.17**	(0.36)	**2.67**	(0.33)	**2.63**	(0.33)	1.04	(0.08)	1.06	(0.08)	1.07	(0.08)
Baku (Azerbaijan)	**2.00**	(0.25)	**1.79**	(0.22)	**1.89**	(0.19)	**1.77**	(0.18)	**1.78**	(0.18)	0.98	(0.09)	0.95	(0.09)	0.96	(0.09)
Bosnia and Herzegovina	**2.68**	(0.27)	**2.07**	(0.22)	**2.74**	(0.23)	**2.49**	(0.21)	**2.41**	(0.21)	1.05	(0.09)	1.07	(0.09)	1.07	(0.09)
Brazil	**3.24**	(0.38)	**1.57**	(0.22)	**3.95**	(0.41)	**3.32**	(0.35)	**2.87**	(0.31)	1.08	(0.08)	1.12	(0.08)	**1.17**	(0.10)
Brunei Darussalam	**3.86**	(0.29)	**2.46**	(0.21)	**4.54**	(0.34)	**3.83**	(0.30)	**3.45**	(0.29)	**1.29**	(0.07)	**1.31**	(0.07)	**1.26**	(0.08)
Bulgaria	**3.49**	(0.39)	**2.52**	(0.30)	**2.66**	(0.29)	**2.16**	(0.24)	**2.12**	(0.24)	**1.33**	(0.09)	**1.35**	(0.09)	**1.28**	(0.08)
Croatia	**2.71**	(0.24)	**2.02**	(0.19)	**3.62**	(0.36)	**3.19**	(0.33)	**2.94**	(0.30)	1.08	(0.06)	**1.13**	(0.07)	1.10	(0.07)
Cyprus	**2.66**	(0.26)	**2.04**	(0.21)	**3.01**	(0.37)	**2.67**	(0.35)	**2.61**	(0.34)	1.04	(0.07)	1.03	(0.07)	0.95	(0.07)
Dominican Republic	**2.29**	(0.39)	**1.53**	(0.30)	**2.41**	(0.36)	**2.15**	(0.34)	**2.06**	(0.36)	**1.27**	(0.13)	**1.30**	(0.14)	**1.24**	(0.14)
Hong Kong (China)	**1.84**	(0.22)	**1.48**	(0.19)	**3.09**	(0.40)	**2.91**	(0.38)	**2.83**	(0.39)	**1.45**	(0.10)	**1.39**	(0.09)	**1.38**	(0.09)
Indonesia	**1.98**	(0.26)	**1.71**	(0.23)	**1.58**	(0.17)	**1.43**	(0.16)	**1.36**	(0.16)	1.06	(0.09)	1.07	(0.09)	1.03	(0.09)
Jordan	**2.69**	(0.30)	**2.15**	(0.27)	**3.71**	(0.33)	**3.42**	(0.31)	**3.13**	(0.29)	**1.97**	(0.14)	**2.05**	(0.14)	**1.86**	(0.13)
Kazakhstan	**1.65**	(0.10)	**1.45**	(0.10)	**2.30**	(0.15)	**2.23**	(0.14)	**2.20**	(0.14)	**1.21**	(0.05)	**1.21**	(0.05)	**1.19**	(0.05)
Kosovo	**2.65**	(0.35)	**2.13**	(0.29)	**3.21**	(0.41)	**2.88**	(0.36)	**2.94**	(0.38)	1.01	(0.09)	1.04	(0.09)	1.04	(0.10)
Lebanon	**2.51**	(0.38)	**1.72**	(0.27)	**4.06**	(0.43)	**3.75**	(0.42)	**3.74**	(0.42)	**1.21**	(0.10)	**1.28**	(0.10)	**1.24**	(0.11)
Macao (China)	**2.40**	(0.22)	**2.17**	(0.21)	**4.27**	(0.93)	**4.29**	(0.95)	**4.02**	(0.91)	**1.30**	(0.08)	**1.26**	(0.08)	**1.27**	(0.08)
Malaysia	**3.03**	(0.32)	**1.83**	(0.20)	**4.49**	(0.38)	**3.94**	(0.33)	**3.69**	(0.31)	**1.29**	(0.07)	**1.30**	(0.07)	**1.27**	(0.07)
Malta	**2.84**	(0.35)	**1.61**	(0.24)	**4.87**	(0.60)	**4.37**	(0.56)	**3.88**	(0.50)	**1.40**	(0.11)	**1.42**	(0.11)	**1.35**	(0.13)
Moldova	**2.67**	(0.26)	**1.71**	(0.18)	**3.60**	(0.28)	**3.20**	(0.26)	**2.97**	(0.25)	**1.15**	(0.07)	**1.17**	(0.07)	1.12	(0.07)
Montenegro	**2.28**	(0.21)	**1.87**	(0.18)	**2.96**	(0.25)	**2.76**	(0.24)	**2.77**	(0.25)	**1.23**	(0.07)	**1.27**	(0.08)	**1.28**	(0.08)
Morocco	**2.19**	(0.34)	**1.60**	(0.23)	**3.62**	(0.38)	**3.36**	(0.35)	**3.07**	(0.35)	1.08	(0.10)	1.10	(0.10)	1.02	(0.10)
North Macedonia[3]	**3.66**	(0.40)	**2.73**	(0.32)	**3.70**	(0.39)	**3.22**	(0.36)	**3.19**	(0.35)	**1.26**	(0.08)	**1.29**	(0.09)	**1.19**	(0.09)
Panama	**2.20**	(0.44)	1.20	(0.26)	**2.63**	(0.47)	**2.41**	(0.48)	**2.30**	(0.48)	1.03	(0.13)	1.06	(0.13)	1.02	(0.14)
Peru	**1.77**	(0.23)	1.13	(0.16)	**2.61**	(0.27)	**2.52**	(0.28)	**2.30**	(0.27)	1.08	(0.08)	1.07	(0.08)	1.13	(0.09)
Philippines	**2.85**	(0.25)	**1.94**	(0.16)	**4.38**	(0.34)	**3.81**	(0.31)	**3.89**	(0.34)	**1.49**	(0.07)	**1.55**	(0.07)	**1.52**	(0.08)
Romania[3]	**3.50**	(0.40)	**2.30**	(0.28)	**3.86**	(0.43)	**3.23**	(0.36)	**3.19**	(0.35)	**0.89**	(0.05)	**0.90**	(0.05)	**0.87**	(0.05)
Saudi Arabia	**2.36**	(0.28)	**1.77**	(0.21)	**2.50**	(0.22)	**2.25**	(0.20)	**2.13**	(0.21)	**1.42**	(0.13)	**1.41**	(0.12)	**1.27**	(0.11)
Serbia	**2.17**	(0.19)	**1.77**	(0.17)	**2.39**	(0.23)	**2.17**	(0.22)	**2.16**	(0.21)	1.07	(0.07)	1.08	(0.07)	1.08	(0.07)
Singapore	**2.75**	(0.21)	**2.19**	(0.18)	**4.32**	(0.52)	**3.52**	(0.45)	**3.14**	(0.41)	1.04	(0.05)	0.99	(0.05)	0.98	(0.05)
Chinese Taipei	**2.25**	(0.21)	**1.88**	(0.18)	**2.84**	(0.23)	**2.52**	(0.21)	**2.42**	(0.21)	**1.27**	(0.07)	**1.28**	(0.07)	**1.31**	(0.08)
Thailand	**2.44**	(0.24)	**1.73**	(0.15)	**3.46**	(0.22)	**3.18**	(0.19)	**2.88**	(0.17)	**1.50**	(0.10)	**1.55**	(0.09)	**1.38**	(0.08)
Ukraine	**2.73**	(0.27)	**2.08**	(0.20)	**3.04**	(0.36)	**2.65**	(0.31)	**2.56**	(0.30)	**1.34**	(0.08)	**1.31**	(0.08)	**1.31**	(0.08)
United Arab Emirates	m	m	m	m	m	m	m	m	m	m	m	m	m	m	m	m
Uruguay	**1.93**	(0.21)	**1.45**	(0.16)	**2.37**	(0.26)	**2.17**	(0.24)	**2.05**	(0.23)	0.91	(0.07)	0.90	(0.06)	0.92	(0.07)
Viet Nam	m	m	m	m	m	m	m	m	m	m	m	m	m	m	m	m
Overall average	**2.81**	(0.04)	**2.10**	(0.03)	**3.46**	(0.06)	**3.03**	(0.05)	**2.88**	(0.05)	**1.14**	(0.01)	**1.15**	(0.01)	**1.12**	(0.01)

Note: Values that are statistically significant are indicated in bold.

* In 2018, some regions in Spain conducted their high-stakes exams for tenth-grade students earlier in the year than in the past, which resulted in the testing period for these exams coinciding with the end of the PISA testing window. Because of this overlap, a number of students were negatively disposed towards the PISA test and did not try their best to demonstrate their proficiency. Although the data of only a minority of students show clear signs of lack of engagement (see PISA 2018 Results Volume I, Annex A9), the comparability of PISA 2018 data for Spain with those from earlier PISA assessments cannot be fully ensured.

1. All regression models reported in this table use the same sample: students who had no missing data on any of the variables included in the analyses. For the countries without parental characteristics data, parental variables are not accounted for in the model after accounting for socio-economic status and other variables.

2. Students' socio-economic status is measured by the PISA index of economic, social and cultural status (ESCS).

3. For North Macedonia and Romania, the variable on whether school covers climate change in the curriculum is not included in the model after accounting for socio-economic status and other variables.

StatLink https://stat.link/lv3dsm

Table B.3.24 [3/6] **Likelihood of being an environmentally enthusiastic student, by student, school and parental characteristics**

	Increased likelihood of being an environmentally enthusiastic student [1]																	
	Student has a Growth Mindset (reference: does not have it)						School covers climate change in the curriculum (reference: does not cover it it)						Parents are environmentally aware (reference: they are not)					
	Before accounting for socio-economic status		After accounting for socio-economic status		After accounting for socio-economic status and other variables		Before accounting for socio-economic status		After accounting for socio-economic status		After accounting for socio-economic status and other variables		Before accounting for socio-economic status		After accounting for socio-economic status		After accounting for socio-economic status and other variables	
	Odds ratio	S.E.	Odds ratio	S.E.	Odds ratio	S.E.	Odds ratio	S.E.	Odds ratio	S.E.	Odds ratio	S.E.	Odds ratio	S.E.	Odds ratio	S.E.	Odds ratio	S.E.
OECD																		
Australia	**1.98**	(0.10)	**1.80**	(0.09)	**1.53**	(0.08)	**1.35**	(0.15)	**1.38**	(0.15)	**1.38**	(0.15)	m	m	m	m	m	m
Austria	**1.30**	(0.09)	**1.26**	(0.09)	**1.22**	(0.09)	**1.37**	(0.20)	1.24	(0.17)	1.17	(0.13)	m	m	m	m	m	m
Belgium	m	m	m	m	m	m	m	m	m	m	m	m	m	m	m	m	m	m
Canada	**1.65**	(0.08)	**1.58**	(0.07)	**1.47**	(0.07)	1.15	(0.09)	1.12	(0.08)	1.11	(0.08)	m	m	m	m	m	m
Chile	**1.75**	(0.12)	**1.63**	(0.11)	**1.37**	(0.10)	0.91	(0.09)	0.92	(0.09)	0.96	(0.09)	**1.92**	(0.13)	**1.63**	(0.12)	**1.46**	(0.12)
Colombia	**1.91**	(0.12)	**1.76**	(0.11)	**1.37**	(0.10)	**1.26**	(0.11)	**1.20**	(0.10)	1.12	(0.10)	m	m	m	m	m	m
Costa Rica	**1.75**	(0.11)	**1.61**	(0.10)	**1.38**	(0.08)	1.11	(0.20)	1.07	(0.15)	1.00	(0.13)	m	m	m	m	m	m
Estonia	**1.52**	(0.12)	**1.45**	(0.11)	**1.40**	(0.11)	0.95	(0.18)	0.91	(0.19)	0.92	(0.19)	m	m	m	m	m	m
France	**1.33**	(0.10)	**1.27**	(0.10)	**1.18**	(0.09)	1.34	(0.47)	1.26	(0.37)	1.12	(0.32)	m	m	m	m	m	m
Germany	1.12	(0.13)	1.18	(0.12)	1.16	(0.13)	1.69	(0.46)	1.33	(0.41)	1.28	(0.40)	**1.85**	(0.40)	1.20	(0.29)	1.04	(0.27)
Greece	**1.32**	(0.08)	**1.31**	(0.08)	**1.18**	(0.08)	1.21	(0.14)	1.15	(0.12)	1.10	(0.10)	m	m	m	m	m	m
Hungary	**1.70**	(0.12)	**1.54**	(0.11)	**1.31**	(0.10)	1.04	(0.26)	1.09	(0.22)	1.09	(0.19)	m	m	m	m	m	m
Iceland	**1.93**	(0.20)	**1.75**	(0.20)	**1.44**	(0.17)	1.06	(0.15)	1.10	(0.16)	1.15	(0.17)	m	m	m	m	m	m
Ireland	**2.14**	(0.17)	**2.03**	(0.16)	**1.84**	(0.15)	1.13	(0.16)	1.11	(0.19)	1.16	(0.20)	**1.94**	(0.17)	**1.51**	(0.14)	**1.35**	(0.13)
Israel	m	m	m	m	m	m	m	m	m	m	m	m	m	m	m	m	m	m
Italy	**1.43**	(0.11)	**1.41**	(0.11)	**1.33**	(0.11)	0.88	(0.08)	0.89	(0.07)	0.90	(0.06)	**1.57**	(0.17)	**1.38**	(0.15)	1.19	(0.13)
Korea	**1.74**	(0.10)	**1.70**	(0.11)	**1.65**	(0.10)	c	c	c	c	c	c	**1.66**	(0.12)	**1.48**	(0.10)	**1.38**	(0.10)
Latvia	**1.84**	(0.15)	**1.71**	(0.14)	**1.53**	(0.13)	1.02	(0.15)	1.02	(0.14)	1.10	(0.16)	m	m	m	m	m	m
Lithuania	**1.60**	(0.10)	**1.44**	(0.09)	**1.26**	(0.09)	0.91	(0.21)	0.83	(0.19)	0.77	(0.19)	m	m	m	m	m	m
Mexico	**1.50**	(0.10)	**1.38**	(0.10)	**1.17**	(0.09)	1.10	(0.11)	1.11	(0.11)	1.15	(0.10)	**1.75**	(0.11)	**1.50**	(0.10)	**1.44**	(0.10)
Netherlands	m	m	m	m	m	m	m	m	m	m	m	m	m	m	m	m	m	m
New Zealand	**2.25**	(0.14)	**1.98**	(0.13)	**1.66**	(0.11)	1.06	(0.15)	1.05	(0.13)	1.03	(0.12)	m	m	m	m	m	m
Poland	**1.25**	(0.08)	**1.18**	(0.07)	1.12	(0.07)	c	c	c	c	c	c	m	m	m	m	m	m
Portugal	**1.60**	(0.12)	**1.53**	(0.11)	**1.35**	(0.10)	0.81	(0.09)	0.84	(0.09)	0.88	(0.09)	**2.88**	(0.26)	**2.02**	(0.20)	**1.83**	(0.20)
Scotland (United Kingdom)	**1.86**	(0.19)	**1.64**	(0.17)	**1.51**	(0.16)	0.90	(0.18)	0.93	(0.15)	0.93	(0.15)	m	m	m	m	m	m
Slovak Republic	**1.38**	(0.11)	**1.26**	(0.10)	1.18	(0.10)	1.09	(0.29)	1.08	(0.25)	1.10	(0.25)	m	m	m	m	m	m
Slovenia	**1.67**	(0.13)	**1.59**	(0.12)	**1.51**	(0.12)	1.22	(0.19)	1.13	(0.17)	1.17	(0.18)	m	m	m	m	m	m
Spain*	**1.32**	(0.05)	**1.29**	(0.05)	**1.20**	(0.05)	1.03	(0.15)	1.13	(0.15)	1.18	(0.15)	m	m	m	m	m	m
Switzerland	1.01	(0.07)	1.00	(0.07)	0.97	(0.07)	1.04	(0.20)	1.00	(0.18)	1.01	(0.17)	m	m	m	m	m	m
Türkiye	**1.47**	(0.08)	**1.47**	(0.08)	**1.33**	(0.08)	1.68	(0.53)	1.61	(0.52)	1.56	(0.43)	m	m	m	m	m	m
OECD average	**1.60**	(0.02)	**1.51**	(0.02)	**1.36**	(0.02)	**1.13**	(0.05)	**1.10**	(0.04)	**1.09**	(0.04)	**1.94**	(0.08)	**1.53**	(0.06)	**1.38**	(0.06)

Note: Values that are statistically significant are indicated in bold.

* In 2018, some regions in Spain conducted their high-stakes exams for tenth-grade students earlier in the year than in the past, which resulted in the testing period for these exams coinciding with the end of the PISA testing window. Because of this overlap, a number of students were negatively disposed towards the PISA test and did not try their best to demonstrate their proficiency. Although the data of only a minority of students show clear signs of lack of engagement (see PISA 2018 Results Volume I, Annex A9), the comparability of PISA 2018 data for Spain with those from earlier PISA assessments cannot be fully ensured.

1. All regression models reported in this table use the same sample: students who had no missing data on any of the variables included in the analyses. For the countries without parental characteristics data, parental variables are not accounted for in the model after accounting for socio-economic status and other variables.

2. Students' socio-economic status is measured by the PISA index of economic, social and cultural status (ESCS).

3. For North Macedonia and Romania, the variable on whether school covers climate change in the curriculum is not included in the model after accounting for socio-economic status and other variables.

StatLink https://stat.link/lv3dsm

Table B.3.24 [4/6] **Likelihood of being an environmentally enthusiastic student, by student, school and parental characteristics**

	Increased likelihood of being an environmentally enthusiastic student[1]																	
	Student has a Growth Mindset (reference: does not have it)						School covers climate change in the curriculum (reference: does not cover it it)						Parents are environmentally aware (reference: they are not)					
	Before accounting for socio-economic status		After accounting for socio-economic status		After accounting for socio-economic status and other variables		Before accounting for socio-economic status		After accounting for socio-economic status		After accounting for socio-economic status and other variables		Before accounting for socio-economic status		After accounting for socio-economic status		After accounting for socio-economic status and other variables	
	Odds ratio	S.E.	Odds ratio	S.E.	Odds ratio	S.E.	Odds ratio	S.E.	Odds ratio	S.E.	Odds ratio	S.E.	Odds ratio	S.E.	Odds ratio	S.E.	Odds ratio	S.E.
Partners Albania	**1.36**	(0.09)	**1.34**	(0.09)	**1.19**	(0.09)	**1.31**	(0.17)	1.27	(0.15)	1.10	(0.13)	m	m	m	m	m	m
Argentina	**1.51**	(0.10)	**1.32**	(0.09)	1.08	(0.08)	0.93	(0.16)	0.96	(0.15)	1.02	(0.16)	m	m	m	m	m	m
Baku (Azerbaijan)	1.13	(0.12)	1.08	(0.11)	0.97	(0.10)	1.03	(0.11)	1.02	(0.10)	1.04	(0.10)	m	m	m	m	m	m
Bosnia and Herzegovina	**1.45**	(0.10)	**1.37**	(0.09)	**1.25**	(0.09)	**1.33**	(0.10)	**1.29**	(0.09)	**1.24**	(0.09)	m	m	m	m	m	m
Brazil	**2.24**	(0.17)	**1.97**	(0.16)	**1.53**	(0.13)	1.42	(0.26)	1.27	(0.18)	1.12	(0.12)	**2.37**	(0.18)	**1.83**	(0.15)	**1.53**	(0.13)
Brunei Darussalam	**2.27**	(0.13)	**2.03**	(0.13)	**1.53**	(0.10)	c	c	c	c	c	c	m	m	m	m	m	m
Bulgaria	**1.29**	(0.09)	**1.18**	(0.09)	1.03	(0.08)	1.10	(0.13)	1.07	(0.10)	1.04	(0.10)	m	m	m	m	m	m
Croatia	**1.57**	(0.08)	**1.56**	(0.08)	**1.41**	(0.08)	**1.22**	(0.12)	**1.22**	(0.11)	1.14	(0.09)	**2.07**	(0.23)	**1.68**	(0.19)	**1.45**	(0.17)
Cyprus	**1.40**	(0.10)	**1.34**	(0.09)	**1.22**	(0.09)	**1.31**	(0.14)	1.22	(0.14)	1.22	(0.15)	m	m	m	m	m	m
Dominican Republic	**1.26**	(0.13)	1.18	(0.13)	0.97	(0.11)	**1.21**	(0.25)	1.22	(0.28)	1.15	(0.29)	**2.02**	(0.18)	**1.80**	(0.17)	**1.68**	(0.16)
Hong Kong (China)	**1.33**	(0.09)	**1.34**	(0.09)	**1.34**	(0.09)	c	c	c	c	c	c	**1.37**	(0.09)	**1.25**	(0.09)	**1.21**	(0.09)
Indonesia	**1.35**	(0.11)	**1.27**	(0.11)	1.18	(0.10)	**1.36**	(0.17)	1.25	(0.16)	1.21	(0.15)	m	m	m	m	m	m
Jordan	**1.58**	(0.10)	**1.50**	(0.10)	**1.30**	(0.09)	**1.46**	(0.17)	**1.50**	(0.19)	1.20	(0.13)	m	m	m	m	m	m
Kazakhstan	**1.25**	(0.05)	**1.22**	(0.05)	1.07	(0.05)	1.00	(0.05)	0.99	(0.05)	1.00	(0.05)	m	m	m	m	m	m
Kosovo	1.18	(0.11)	1.09	(0.10)	0.90	(0.09)	1.11	(0.10)	1.07	(0.09)	0.98	(0.09)	m	m	m	m	m	m
Lebanon	1.05	(0.10)	1.00	(0.09)	0.99	(0.09)	0.87	(0.09)	0.95	(0.10)	1.00	(0.13)	m	m	m	m	m	m
Macao (China)	**1.39**	(0.10)	**1.40**	(0.10)	**1.38**	(0.10)	m	m	m	m	m	m	**1.51**	(0.10)	**1.31**	(0.09)	**1.29**	(0.10)
Malaysia	**1.87**	(0.12)	**1.72**	(0.10)	**1.45**	(0.09)	0.92	(0.21)	1.02	(0.20)	1.07	(0.17)	m	m	m	m	m	m
Malta	**1.92**	(0.16)	**1.84**	(0.16)	**1.51**	(0.14)	c	c	c	c	c	c	**2.25**	(0.21)	**1.89**	(0.20)	**1.66**	(0.19)
Moldova	**1.82**	(0.08)	**1.62**	(0.08)	**1.28**	(0.07)	**1.26**	(0.11)	**1.23**	(0.10)	1.11	(0.09)	m	m	m	m	m	m
Montenegro	**1.19**	(0.07)	**1.17**	(0.07)	1.07	(0.07)	1.05	(0.06)	1.00	(0.06)	0.90	(0.06)	m	m	m	m	m	m
Morocco	**1.93**	(0.21)	**1.88**	(0.21)	**1.42**	(0.18)	0.94	(0.28)	1.01	(0.32)	1.10	(0.23)	m	m	m	m	m	m
North Macedonia[3]	0.94	(0.08)	0.91	(0.08)	0.88	(0.08)	m	m	m	m	m	m	m	m	m	m	m	m
Panama	1.02	(0.13)	0.91	(0.12)	0.77	(0.11)	0.94	(0.16)	0.86	(0.15)	0.88	(0.16)	**2.11**	(0.31)	**1.89**	(0.29)	**1.69**	(0.28)
Peru	**1.89**	(0.16)	**1.80**	(0.16)	**1.47**	(0.14)	c	c	c	c	c	c	m	m	m	m	m	m
Philippines	**1.40**	(0.11)	**1.26**	(0.09)	0.92	(0.07)	1.14	(0.16)	1.09	(0.13)	0.98	(0.11)	m	m	m	m	m	m
Romania[3]	**1.49**	(0.10)	**1.30**	(0.09)	1.08	(0.08)	m	m	m	m	m	m	m	m	m	m	m	m
Saudi Arabia	**1.42**	(0.09)	**1.33**	(0.09)	1.11	(0.08)	1.15	(0.15)	1.14	(0.15)	1.06	(0.13)	m	m	m	m	m	m
Serbia	1.09	(0.07)	1.08	(0.07)	1.01	(0.06)	0.84	(0.09)	0.88	(0.09)	0.91	(0.08)	m	m	m	m	m	m
Singapore	1.82	(0.11)	**1.70**	(0.11)	**1.52**	(0.10)	1.11	(0.13)	1.17	(0.14)	1.09	(0.14)	m	m	m	m	m	m
Chinese Taipei	1.63	(0.09)	**1.61**	(0.08)	**1.59**	(0.08)	1.25	(0.38)	1.15	(0.32)	1.02	(0.22)	m	m	m	m	m	m
Thailand	1.83	(0.11)	**1.69**	(0.10)	**1.36**	(0.08)	c	c	c	c	c	c	m	m	m	m	m	m
Ukraine	1.56	(0.12)	**1.41**	(0.10)	**1.20**	(0.09)	1.11	(0.17)	1.06	(0.15)	1.08	(0.15)	m	m	m	m	m	m
United Arab Emirates	m	m	m	m	m	m	m	m	m	m	m	m	m	m	m	m	m	m
Uruguay	**1.50**	(0.14)	**1.43**	(0.14)	**1.28**	(0.12)	0.89	(0.11)	0.93	(0.10)	0.97	(0.11)	m	m	m	m	m	m
Viet Nam	m	m	m	m	m	m	m	m	m	m	m	m	m	m	m	m	m	m
Overall average	**1.54**	(0.01)	**1.45**	(0.01)	**1.28**	(0.01)	**1.13**	(0.03)	**1.10**	(0.03)	**1.08**	(0.02)	**1.95**	(0.06)	**1.60**	(0.05)	**1.44**	(0.04)

Note: Values that are statistically significant are indicated in bold.

* In 2018, some regions in Spain conducted their high-stakes exams for tenth-grade students earlier in the year than in the past, which resulted in the testing period for these exams coinciding with the end of the PISA testing window. Because of this overlap, a number of students were negatively disposed towards the PISA test and did not try their best to demonstrate their proficiency. Although the data of only a minority of students show clear signs of lack of engagement (see PISA 2018 Results Volume I, Annex A9), the comparability of PISA 2018 data for Spain with those from earlier PISA assessments cannot be fully ensured.

1. All regression models reported in this table use the same sample: students who had no missing data on any of the variables included in the analyses. For the countries without parental characteristics data, parental variables are not accounted for in the model after accounting for socio-economic status and other variables.

2. Students' socio-economic status is measured by the PISA index of economic, social and cultural status (ESCS).

3. For North Macedonia and Romania, the variable on whether school covers climate change in the curriculum is not included in the model after accounting for socio-economic status and other variables.

StatLink https://stat.link/lv3dsm

Table B.3.24 [5/6] **Likelihood of being an environmentally enthusiastic student, by student, school and parental characteristics**

	Increased likelihood of being an environmentally enthusiastic student [1]											
	Parents save energy at home to protect the environment (reference: parents do not do this)						Parents boycott products or companies for political, ethical or environmental reasons (reference: parents do not do this)					
	Before accounting for socio-economic status		After accounting for socio-economic status		After accounting for socio-economic status and other variables		Before accounting for socio-economic status		After accounting for socio-economic status		After accounting for socio-economic status and other variables	
	Odds ratio	S.E.	Odds ratio	S.E.	Odds ratio	S.E.	Odds ratio	S.E.	Odds ratio	S.E.	Odds ratio	S.E.
OECD Australia	m	m	m	m	m	m	m	m	m	m	m	m
Austria	m	m	m	m	m	m	m	m	m	m	m	m
Belgium	m	m	m	m	m	m	m	m	m	m	m	m
Canada	m	m	m	m	m	m	m	m	m	m	m	m
Chile	1.23	(0.13)	1.18	(0.13)	1.16	(0.13)	**1.40**	(0.13)	**1.29**	(0.12)	**1.27**	(0.13)
Colombia	m	m	m	m	m	m	m	m	m	m	m	m
Costa Rica	m	m	m	m	m	m	m	m	m	m	m	m
Estonia	m	m	m	m	m	m	m	m	m	m	m	m
France	m	m	m	m	m	m	m	m	m	m	m	m
Germany	1.51	(0.44)	1.36	(0.46)	1.27	(0.44)	**1.58**	(0.17)	**1.29**	(0.15)	**1.27**	(0.15)
Greece	m	m	m	m	m	m	m	m	m	m	m	m
Hungary	m	m	m	m	m	m	m	m	m	m	m	m
Iceland	m	m	m	m	m	m	m	m	m	m	m	m
Ireland	**1.33**	(0.17)	**1.32**	(0.17)	1.26	(0.17)	**1.38**	(0.09)	**1.24**	(0.08)	**1.16**	(0.08)
Israel	m	m	m	m	m	m	m	m	m	m	m	m
Italy	1.22	(0.13)	1.17	(0.13)	1.08	(0.12)	**1.30**	(0.11)	**1.20**	(0.10)	1.18	(0.11)
Korea	**1.27**	(0.11)	1.18	(0.11)	1.10	(0.10)	**1.37**	(0.08)	**1.22**	(0.07)	1.10	(0.07)
Latvia	m	m	m	m	m	m	m	m	m	m	m	m
Lithuania	m	m	m	m	m	m	m	m	m	m	m	m
Mexico	1.05	(0.13)	0.96	(0.12)	0.88	(0.11)	1.09	(0.12)	1.05	(0.13)	1.10	(0.14)
Netherlands	m	m	m	m	m	m	m	m	m	m	m	m
New Zealand	m	m	m	m	m	m	m	m	m	m	m	m
Poland	m	m	m	m	m	m	m	m	m	m	m	m
Portugal	**1.74**	(0.24)	**1.59**	(0.24)	1.34	(0.23)	**1.44**	(0.12)	1.14	(0.09)	1.03	(0.09)
Scotland (United Kingdom)	m	m	m	m	m	m	m	m	m	m	m	m
Slovak Republic	m	m	m	m	m	m	m	m	m	m	m	m
Slovenia	m	m	m	m	m	m	m	m	m	m	m	m
Spain*	m	m	m	m	m	m	m	m	m	m	m	m
Switzerland	m	m	m	m	m	m	m	m	m	m	m	m
Türkiye	m	m	m	m	m	m	m	m	m	m	m	m
OECD average	**1.34**	(0.08)	**1.25**	(0.09)	**1.16**	(0.08)	**1.36**	(0.05)	**1.21**	(0.04)	**1.16**	(0.04)

Note: Values that are statistically significant are indicated in bold.

* In 2018, some regions in Spain conducted their high-stakes exams for tenth-grade students earlier in the year than in the past, which resulted in the testing period for these exams coinciding with the end of the PISA testing window. Because of this overlap, a number of students were negatively disposed towards the PISA test and did not try their best to demonstrate their proficiency. Although the data of only a minority of students show clear signs of lack of engagement (see PISA 2018 Results Volume I, Annex A9), the comparability of PISA 2018 data for Spain with those from earlier PISA assessments cannot be fully ensured.

1. All regression models reported in this table use the same sample: students who had no missing data on any of the variables included in the analyses. For the countries without parental characteristics data, parental variables are not accounted for in the model after accounting for socio-economic status and other variables.

2. Students' socio-economic status is measured by the PISA index of economic, social and cultural status (ESCS).

3. For North Macedonia and Romania, the variable on whether school covers climate change in the curriculum is not included in the model after accounting for socio-economic status and other variables.

StatLink https://stat.link/1v3dsm

Table B.3.24 [6/6] **Likelihood of being an environmentally enthusiastic student, by student, school and parental characteristics**

		Increased likelihood of being an environmentally enthusiastic student[1]											
		Parents save energy at home to protect the environment (reference: parents do not do this)						Parents boycott products or companies for political, ethical or environmental reasons (reference: parents do not do this)					
		Before accounting for socio-economic status		After accounting for socio-economic status		After accounting for socio-economic status and other variables		Before accounting for socio-economic status		After accounting for socio-economic status		After accounting for socio-economic status and other variables	
		Odds ratio	S.E.	Odds ratio	S.E.	Odds ratio	S.E.	Odds ratio	S.E.	Odds ratio	S.E.	Odds ratio	S.E.
Partners	**Albania**	m	m	m	m	m	m	m	m	m	m	m	m
	Argentina	m	m	m	m	m	m	m	m	m	m	m	m
	Baku (Azerbaijan)	m	m	m	m	m	m	m	m	m	m	m	m
	Bosnia and Herzegovina	m	m	m	m	m	m	m	m	m	m	m	m
	Brazil	**1.35**	(0.21)	1.25	(0.20)	1.20	(0.20)	**1.57**	(0.14)	**1.28**	(0.11)	**1.20**	(0.11)
	Brunei Darussalam	m	m	m	m	m	m	m	m	m	m	m	m
	Bulgaria	m	m	m	m	m	m	m	m	m	m	m	m
	Croatia	**1.55**	(0.18)	**1.40**	(0.16)	1.27	(0.16)	**1.45**	(0.11)	**1.26**	(0.09)	**1.18**	(0.09)
	Cyprus	m	m	m	m	m	m	m	m	m	m	m	m
	Dominican Republic	1.54	(0.53)	1.38	(0.47)	1.28	(0.44)	0.96	(0.16)	0.99	(0.16)	0.96	(0.15)
	Hong Kong (China)	**1.37**	(0.16)	**1.30**	(0.15)	1.17	(0.14)	1.12	(0.08)	1.06	(0.07)	1.06	(0.08)
	Indonesia	m	m	m	m	m	m	m	m	m	m	m	m
	Jordan	m	m	m	m	m	m	m	m	m	m	m	m
	Kazakhstan	m	m	m	m	m	m	m	m	m	m	m	m
	Kosovo	m	m	m	m	m	m	m	m	m	m	m	m
	Lebanon	m	m	m	m	m	m	m	m	m	m	m	m
	Macao (China)	1.18	(0.16)	1.14	(0.16)	1.04	(0.15)	**1.16**	(0.08)	1.10	(0.08)	1.05	(0.08)
	Malaysia	m	m	m	m	m	m	m	m	m	m	m	m
	Malta	0.99	(0.24)	0.97	(0.23)	0.89	(0.23)	**1.73**	(0.18)	**1.62**	(0.17)	**1.60**	(0.17)
	Moldova	m	m	m	m	m	m	m	m	m	m	m	m
	Montenegro	m	m	m	m	m	m	m	m	m	m	m	m
	Morocco	m	m	m	m	m	m	m	m	m	m	m	m
	North Macedonia[3]	m	m	m	m	m	m	m	m	m	m	m	m
	Panama	**2.83**	(0.87)	**2.51**	(0.74)	**2.08**	(0.63)	0.90	(0.13)	0.89	(0.13)	0.87	(0.13)
	Peru	m	m	m	m	m	m	m	m	m	m	m	m
	Philippines	m	m	m	m	m	m	m	m	m	m	m	m
	Romania[3]	m	m	m	m	m	m	m	m	m	m	m	m
	Saudi Arabia	m	m	m	m	m	m	m	m	m	m	m	m
	Serbia	m	m	m	m	m	m	m	m	m	m	m	m
	Singapore	m	m	m	m	m	m	m	m	m	m	m	m
	Chinese Taipei	m	m	m	m	m	m	m	m	m	m	m	m
	Thailand	m	m	m	m	m	m	m	m	m	m	m	m
	Ukraine	m	m	m	m	m	m	m	m	m	m	m	m
	United Arab Emirates	m	m	m	m	m	m	m	m	m	m	m	m
	Uruguay	m	m	m	m	m	m	m	m	m	m	m	m
	Viet Nam	m	m	m	m	m	m	m	m	m	m	m	m
	Overall average	**1.44**	(0.09)	**1.34**	(0.08)	**1.22**	(0.07)	**1.32**	(0.03)	**1.19**	(0.03)	**1.14**	(0.03)

Note: Values that are statistically significant are indicated in bold.

* In 2018, some regions in Spain conducted their high-stakes exams for tenth-grade students earlier in the year than in the past, which resulted in the testing period for these exams coinciding with the end of the PISA testing window. Because of this overlap, a number of students were negatively disposed towards the PISA test and did not try their best to demonstrate their proficiency. Although the data of only a minority of students show clear signs of lack of engagement (see PISA 2018 Results Volume I, Annex A9), the comparability of PISA 2018 data for Spain with those from earlier PISA assessments cannot be fully ensured.

1. All regression models reported in this table use the same sample: students who had no missing data on any of the variables included in the analyses. For the countries without parental characteristics data, parental variables are not accounted for in the model after accounting for socio-economic status and other variables.

2. Students' socio-economic status is measured by the PISA index of economic, social and cultural status (ESCS).

3. For North Macedonia and Romania, the variable on whether school covers climate change in the curriculum is not included in the model after accounting for socio-economic status and other variables.

StatLink https://stat.link/lv3dsm

Table B.4.11 [1/4] **Students reducing the energy they use at home to protect the environment, by student environmental attitudes and proficiency in science**

		Increased likelihood of students reducing the energy they use at home to protect the environment[1]																
		Environmental awareness[2]						Self-efficacy in environmental understanding[3]						Environmental sense-of-purpose[4]				
		Before accounting for other variables		After accounting for environmental attitudes		After accounting for environmental attitudes and student characteristics		Before accounting for other variables		After accounting for environmental attitudes		After accounting for environmental attitudes and student characteristics		Before accounting for other variables		After accounting for environmental attitudes		After accounting for environmental attitudes and student characteristics	
		Odds ratio	S.E.	Odds ratio	S.E.	Odds ratio	S.E.	Odds ratio	S.E.	Odds ratio	S.E.	Odds ratio	S.E.	Odds ratio	S.E.	Odds ratio	S.E.	Odds ratio	S.E.
OECD	Australia	**1.59**	(0.09)	1.10	(0.08)	1.08	(0.08)	**1.67**	(0.08)	**1.41**	(0.08)	**1.44**	(0.08)	**2.77**	(0.16)	**2.59**	(0.15)	**2.46**	(0.15)
	Austria	**1.48**	(0.11)	1.15	(0.10)	1.06	(0.10)	**1.35**	(0.08)	**1.16**	(0.08)	**1.18**	(0.09)	**2.52**	(0.19)	**2.41**	(0.19)	**2.30**	(0.18)
	Canada	**1.58**	(0.09)	**1.19**	(0.07)	**1.16**	(0.08)	**1.59**	(0.07)	**1.40**	(0.07)	**1.42**	(0.07)	**2.44**	(0.12)	**2.31**	(0.11)	**2.17**	(0.11)
	Chile	**1.45**	(0.11)	**1.27**	(0.11)	**1.40**	(0.12)	**1.41**	(0.12)	**1.24**	(0.12)	**1.30**	(0.12)	**1.85**	(0.16)	**1.73**	(0.15)	**1.77**	(0.16)
	Colombia	**1.37**	(0.13)	1.20	(0.12)	1.17	(0.11)	**1.43**	(0.12)	**1.28**	(0.12)	**1.25**	(0.12)	**1.85**	(0.20)	**1.72**	(0.19)	**1.66**	(0.18)
	Costa Rica	**1.46**	(0.13)	**1.28**	(0.11)	**1.39**	(0.13)	**1.46**	(0.11)	**1.31**	(0.10)	**1.34**	(0.09)	**2.01**	(0.24)	**1.89**	(0.23)	**1.82**	(0.23)
	Estonia	**1.49**	(0.13)	1.21	(0.12)	1.20	(0.12)	**1.32**	(0.10)	1.13	(0.10)	1.12	(0.10)	**2.16**	(0.14)	**2.06**	(0.14)	**1.99**	(0.14)
	France	**1.66**	(0.11)	**1.24**	(0.10)	**1.23**	(0.11)	**1.51**	(0.08)	**1.20**	(0.08)	**1.17**	(0.08)	**3.04**	(0.23)	**2.83**	(0.23)	**2.78**	(0.23)
	Germany	**1.77**	(0.20)	1.28	(0.17)	1.22	(0.17)	**1.36**	(0.09)	1.12	(0.08)	1.15	(0.08)	**2.89**	(0.20)	**2.73**	(0.20)	**2.55**	(0.20)
	Greece	**1.18**	(0.08)	1.00	(0.07)	1.03	(0.08)	**1.36**	(0.08)	**1.31**	(0.08)	**1.31**	(0.08)	**1.75**	(0.12)	**1.70**	(0.12)	**1.73**	(0.12)
	Hungary	**1.74**	(0.14)	**1.38**	(0.13)	**1.29**	(0.13)	**1.60**	(0.11)	**1.29**	(0.11)	**1.28**	(0.11)	**2.56**	(0.22)	**2.30**	(0.22)	**2.15**	(0.20)
	Iceland	1.09	(0.11)	0.89	(0.10)	0.92	(0.11)	1.13	(0.10)	1.09	(0.11)	1.12	(0.11)	**1.78**	(0.15)	**1.80**	(0.16)	**1.71**	(0.17)
	Ireland	**1.81**	(0.17)	1.19	(0.14)	1.15	(0.14)	**1.82**	(0.14)	**1.48**	(0.13)	**1.51**	(0.13)	**2.70**	(0.20)	**2.48**	(0.20)	**2.34**	(0.19)
	Italy	**1.25**	(0.09)	1.01	(0.08)	1.06	(0.09)	**1.34**	(0.08)	**1.23**	(0.08)	**1.26**	(0.08)	**1.96**	(0.13)	**1.90**	(0.13)	**1.92**	(0.13)
	Korea	**1.60**	(0.16)	**1.27**	(0.13)	**1.29**	(0.14)	**1.43**	(0.12)	1.19	(0.11)	1.19	(0.11)	**3.04**	(0.28)	**2.87**	(0.27)	**2.79**	(0.27)
	Latvia	**1.27**	(0.08)	1.07	(0.07)	1.07	(0.08)	**1.33**	(0.09)	**1.21**	(0.08)	**1.22**	(0.08)	**1.79**	(0.12)	**1.72**	(0.12)	**1.68**	(0.12)
	Lithuania	**1.24**	(0.09)	1.04	(0.09)	1.06	(0.10)	**1.40**	(0.08)	**1.36**	(0.09)	**1.40**	(0.09)	**1.31**	(0.11)	**1.25**	(0.11)	**1.20**	(0.10)
	Mexico	**1.67**	(0.13)	**1.49**	(0.12)	**1.43**	(0.12)	**1.32**	(0.12)	1.14	(0.11)	1.14	(0.11)	**1.94**	(0.24)	**1.79**	(0.22)	**1.68**	(0.21)
	New Zealand	**1.68**	(0.13)	**1.37**	(0.11)	**1.36**	(0.11)	**1.37**	(0.08)	1.10	(0.07)	1.11	(0.07)	**2.63**	(0.18)	**2.46**	(0.17)	**2.28**	(0.16)
	Poland	**1.34**	(0.09)	**1.17**	(0.09)	**1.20**	(0.09)	**1.25**	(0.08)	1.08	(0.07)	1.11	(0.08)	**2.53**	(0.19)	**2.46**	(0.18)	**2.43**	(0.18)
	Portugal	**1.75**	(0.18)	**1.41**	(0.17)	**1.45**	(0.17)	**1.61**	(0.12)	**1.40**	(0.13)	**1.43**	(0.14)	**1.97**	(0.26)	**1.71**	(0.24)	**1.66**	(0.23)
	Scotland (United Kingdom)	**1.74**	(0.18)	**1.26**	(0.14)	**1.27**	(0.15)	**1.55**	(0.14)	**1.22**	(0.12)	**1.25**	(0.13)	**3.00**	(0.24)	**2.78**	(0.23)	**2.61**	(0.22)
	Slovak Republic	**1.22**	(0.09)	1.02	(0.08)	1.00	(0.08)	**1.32**	(0.09)	**1.21**	(0.09)	**1.21**	(0.09)	**1.96**	(0.13)	**1.90**	(0.13)	**1.85**	(0.12)
	Slovenia	**1.73**	(0.15)	**1.52**	(0.14)	**1.46**	(0.14)	**1.35**	(0.10)	1.11	(0.10)	1.08	(0.10)	**1.81**	(0.14)	**1.64**	(0.14)	**1.60**	(0.13)
	Spain*	**1.66**	(0.08)	**1.23**	(0.07)	**1.21**	(0.07)	**1.56**	(0.05)	**1.34**	(0.05)	**1.33**	(0.05)	**2.97**	(0.15)	**2.74**	(0.14)	**2.70**	(0.14)
	Switzerland	**1.46**	(0.13)	1.12	(0.11)	1.06	(0.11)	**1.40**	(0.12)	**1.27**	(0.11)	**1.30**	(0.11)	**2.41**	(0.18)	**2.31**	(0.18)	**2.16**	(0.18)
	Türkiye	**1.61**	(0.16)	**1.26**	(0.13)	1.22	(0.13)	**1.47**	(0.11)	**1.26**	(0.09)	**1.25**	(0.10)	**2.56**	(0.22)	**2.37**	(0.21)	**2.25**	(0.20)
	OECD average	**1.52**	(0.02)	**1.21**	(0.02)	**1.20**	(0.02)	**1.43**	(0.02)	**1.24**	(0.02)	**1.25**	(0.02)	**2.30**	(0.04)	**2.16**	(0.03)	**2.08**	(0.03)

Note: Values that are statistically significant are marked in bold.

* In 2018, some regions in Spain conducted their high-stakes exams for tenth-grade students earlier in the year than in the past, which resulted in the testing period for these exams coinciding with the end of the PISA testing window. Because of this overlap, a number of students were negatively disposed towards the PISA test and did not try their best to demonstrate their proficiency. Although the data of only a minority of students show clear signs of lack of engagement (see PISA 2018 Results Volume I, Annex A9), the comparability of PISA 2018 data for Spain with those from earlier PISA assessments cannot be fully ensured.

1. All regression models reported in this table use the same sample: students who had no missing data on any of the variables included in the analyses.

2. Results come from three logistic regression models in which the outcome variable is whether a student responded Yes (response value = 1) or No (response value = 0) to the statement "I reduce the energy I use at home to protect the environment". The first model includes only student awareness of climate change and global warming as a predictor. The second model includes all three environmental attitudes as predictors. The third model includes also the following variables: a dummy variable for whether the student scored above the baseline Level 2 in science (plausible values), student socio-economic status (value in the PISA index of economic, social and cultural status [ESCS]) and student gender (girl=1, boy=0).

3. Same as above, but in this case the first model includes only student self-efficacy regarding climate change (i.e. student can explain how carbon-dioxide emissions affect global climate change) as a predictor.

4. Same as above, but in this case the first model includes only student sense-of-purpose regarding environmental issues (i.e. student reported that looking after the global environment is important to them) as a predictor.

5. Same as above, but in this case the first model includes two dummy variables indicating a student proficiency level in science: whether she/he scored in science at Levels 2, 3 or 4 (response value = 1, otherwise=0) and whether she/he scored at Levels 5 or 6 (response value = 1, 0 otherwise).

StatLink https://stat.link/7tj8pn

Table B.4.11 [2/4] **Students reducing the energy they use at home to protect the environment, by student environmental attitudes and proficiency in science**

	Increased likelihood of students reducing the energy they use at home to protect the environment[1]																	
	Environmental awareness[2]						Self-efficacy in environmental understanding[3]						Environmental sense-of-purpose[4]					
	Before accounting for other variables		After accounting for environmental attitudes		After accounting for environmental attitudes and student characteristics		Before accounting for other variables		After accounting for environmental attitudes		After accounting for environmental attitudes and student characteristics		Before accounting for other variables		After accounting for environmental attitudes		After accounting for environmental attitudes and student characteristics	
	Odds ratio	S.E.	Odds ratio	S.E.	Odds ratio	S.E.	Odds ratio	S.E.	Odds ratio	S.E.	Odds ratio	S.E.	Odds ratio	S.E.	Odds ratio	S.E.	Odds ratio	S.E.
Partners																		
Albania	**1.30**	(0.11)	1.09	(0.11)	1.08	(0.11)	**1.37**	(0.12)	**1.27**	(0.13)	**1.26**	(0.13)	**1.60**	(0.19)	**1.48**	(0.18)	**1.44**	(0.18)
Argentina	**1.32**	(0.09)	1.13	(0.08)	1.09	(0.08)	**1.44**	(0.09)	**1.30**	(0.09)	**1.27**	(0.09)	**1.93**	(0.16)	**1.82**	(0.15)	**1.75**	(0.15)
Baku (Azerbaijan)	1.17	(0.10)	1.09	(0.09)	1.10	(0.10)	1.16	(0.11)	1.10	(0.10)	1.11	(0.11)	**1.47**	(0.13)	**1.44**	(0.13)	**1.44**	(0.13)
Bosnia and Herzegovina	**1.18**	(0.09)	1.05	(0.09)	1.03	(0.09)	**1.32**	(0.08)	**1.25**	(0.08)	**1.24**	(0.08)	**1.46**	(0.10)	**1.41**	(0.10)	**1.40**	(0.10)
Brazil	**1.31**	(0.08)	1.08	(0.07)	**1.18**	(0.09)	**1.37**	(0.08)	**1.23**	(0.07)	**1.27**	(0.08)	**2.40**	(0.19)	**2.29**	(0.18)	**2.26**	(0.18)
Brunei Darussalam	0.99	(0.06)	0.89	(0.07)	0.95	(0.07)	1.05	(0.06)	0.97	(0.07)	1.03	(0.08)	**1.98**	(0.13)	**2.04**	(0.14)	**2.05**	(0.15)
Bulgaria	1.17	(0.10)	1.06	(0.10)	1.13	(0.11)	**1.21**	(0.08)	1.16	(0.09)	**1.18**	(0.09)	**1.24**	(0.11)	1.19	(0.12)	1.21	(0.12)
Croatia	**1.40**	(0.10)	1.15	(0.09)	1.11	(0.09)	**1.41**	(0.08)	**1.23**	(0.07)	**1.19**	(0.07)	**2.32**	(0.16)	**2.22**	(0.16)	**2.19**	(0.16)
Cyprus	**1.30**	(0.11)	1.18	(0.11)	1.16	(0.11)	**1.21**	(0.09)	1.09	(0.09)	1.07	(0.09)	**1.71**	(0.17)	**1.65**	(0.16)	**1.66**	(0.17)
Dominican Republic	0.94	(0.10)	0.81	(0.10)	0.84	(0.11)	**1.33**	(0.17)	**1.40**	(0.20)	**1.49**	(0.21)	1.22	(0.21)	1.20	(0.21)	1.25	(0.23)
Hong Kong (China)	**1.72**	(0.19)	**1.33**	(0.16)	**1.29**	(0.16)	**1.50**	(0.13)	**1.26**	(0.12)	**1.24**	(0.12)	**3.49**	(0.30)	**3.34**	(0.29)	**3.30**	(0.29)
Indonesia	**1.62**	(0.12)	**1.60**	(0.12)	**1.43**	(0.11)	1.06	(0.09)	0.94	(0.08)	0.95	(0.09)	**1.46**	(0.17)	**1.37**	(0.17)	**1.33**	(0.16)
Jordan	1.14	(0.10)	1.03	(0.09)	1.08	(0.11)	1.11	(0.09)	1.03	(0.09)	1.04	(0.10)	**1.48**	(0.12)	**1.46**	(0.12)	**1.49**	(0.13)
Kazakhstan	**1.27**	(0.06)	**1.21**	(0.07)	**1.28**	(0.07)	0.98	(0.05)	**0.90**	(0.05)	0.95	(0.05)	**1.91**	(0.09)	**1.88**	(0.09)	**1.88**	(0.10)
Kosovo	**1.47**	(0.14)	**1.28**	(0.14)	**1.24**	(0.14)	**1.36**	(0.15)	1.21	(0.14)	1.17	(0.14)	**1.92**	(0.20)	**1.77**	(0.20)	**1.74**	(0.20)
Lebanon	**0.78**	(0.07)	**0.75**	(0.07)	**0.78**	(0.08)	0.98	(0.07)	1.04	(0.08)	1.06	(0.08)	1.05	(0.10)	1.12	(0.10)	1.14	(0.10)
Macao (China)	**1.40**	(0.16)	**1.33**	(0.17)	**1.33**	(0.17)	1.03	(0.09)	0.94	(0.09)	0.91	(0.09)	**2.60**	(0.30)	**2.55**	(0.30)	**2.51**	(0.30)
Malaysia	**1.52**	(0.10)	**1.30**	(0.09)	**1.20**	(0.09)	**1.45**	(0.09)	**1.22**	(0.08)	**1.15**	(0.08)	**1.82**	(0.14)	**1.67**	(0.13)	**1.62**	(0.13)
Malta	**1.99**	(0.24)	**1.42**	(0.20)	**1.33**	(0.19)	**1.54**	(0.16)	1.13	(0.15)	1.08	(0.15)	**2.93**	(0.37)	**2.60**	(0.34)	**2.52**	(0.33)
Moldova	**1.31**	(0.09)	**1.17**	(0.09)	**1.21**	(0.09)	**1.22**	(0.08)	1.10	(0.07)	1.13	(0.08)	**1.85**	(0.14)	**1.78**	(0.14)	**1.82**	(0.15)
Montenegro	**1.16**	(0.08)	1.00	(0.08)	1.05	(0.08)	**1.36**	(0.08)	**1.30**	(0.08)	**1.34**	(0.08)	**1.52**	(0.11)	**1.46**	(0.11)	**1.49**	(0.11)
Morocco	**1.24**	(0.10)	1.10	(0.09)	1.11	(0.10)	**1.33**	(0.12)	**1.26**	(0.11)	**1.26**	(0.12)	**1.45**	(0.15)	**1.39**	(0.14)	**1.42**	(0.15)
North Macedonia	**1.34**	(0.08)	**1.15**	(0.08)	1.13	(0.08)	**1.46**	(0.09)	**1.36**	(0.09)	**1.36**	(0.09)	**1.71**	(0.17)	**1.57**	(0.16)	**1.49**	(0.15)
Panama	**1.45**	(0.20)	**1.34**	(0.19)	**1.34**	(0.19)	1.26	(0.15)	1.13	(0.14)	1.14	(0.15)	**1.59**	(0.19)	**1.50**	(0.18)	**1.50**	(0.19)
Peru	**1.48**	(0.18)	1.20	(0.16)	1.18	(0.16)	**1.63**	(0.17)	**1.47**	(0.16)	**1.44**	(0.16)	**2.26**	(0.39)	**2.11**	(0.36)	**2.01**	(0.35)
Philippines	**1.55**	(0.12)	**1.29**	(0.11)	**1.23**	(0.11)	**1.51**	(0.10)	**1.30**	(0.09)	**1.28**	(0.09)	**1.74**	(0.13)	**1.55**	(0.13)	**1.51**	(0.13)
Romania	**1.22**	(0.08)	1.04	(0.08)	1.15	(0.09)	**1.43**	(0.10)	**1.37**	(0.10)	**1.45**	(0.11)	**1.78**	(0.14)	**1.72**	(0.13)	**1.83**	(0.15)
Saudi Arabia	**1.30**	(0.11)	1.17	(0.11)	1.17	(0.11)	**1.33**	(0.10)	**1.20**	(0.09)	**1.19**	(0.09)	**1.64**	(0.11)	**1.56**	(0.11)	**1.56**	(0.11)
Serbia	0.97	(0.07)	**0.81**	(0.06)	**0.82**	(0.07)	**1.30**	(0.08)	**1.30**	(0.08)	**1.33**	(0.08)	**1.54**	(0.10)	**1.52**	(0.09)	**1.52**	(0.09)
Singapore	**1.71**	(0.19)	**1.35**	(0.17)	**1.32**	(0.17)	**1.55**	(0.14)	**1.29**	(0.12)	**1.26**	(0.12)	**2.89**	(0.24)	**2.77**	(0.24)	**2.68**	(0.23)
Chinese Taipei	**1.38**	(0.12)	1.10	(0.10)	1.10	(0.10)	**1.40**	(0.11)	**1.25**	(0.10)	**1.25**	(0.10)	**2.50**	(0.22)	**2.38**	(0.21)	**2.35**	(0.21)
Thailand	**1.85**	(0.13)	**1.48**	(0.12)	**1.25**	(0.11)	**1.66**	(0.14)	**1.36**	(0.13)	1.19	(0.11)	**2.24**	(0.23)	**1.94**	(0.20)	**1.79**	(0.19)
Ukraine	**1.22**	(0.08)	1.05	(0.07)	1.00	(0.07)	**1.22**	(0.06)	1.10	(0.06)	1.06	(0.06)	**2.02**	(0.12)	**1.98**	(0.12)	**1.96**	(0.12)
United Arab Emirates	m	m	m	m	m	m	m	m	m	m	m	m	m	m	m	m	m	m
Uruguay	**1.46**	(0.13)	**1.24**	(0.11)	**1.23**	(0.11)	**1.49**	(0.13)	**1.33**	(0.12)	**1.33**	(0.13)	**1.88**	(0.19)	**1.75**	(0.18)	**1.72**	(0.17)
Viet Nam	m	m	m	m	m	m	m	m	m	m	m	m	m	m	m	m	m	m
OECD average	**1.42**	(0.02)	**1.18**	(0.01)	**1.17**	(0.01)	**1.37**	(0.01)	**1.22**	(0.01)	**1.22**	(0.01)	**2.08**	(0.02)	**1.97**	(0.02)	**1.92**	(0.02)

Note: Values that are statistically significant are marked in bold.

* In 2018, some regions in Spain conducted their high-stakes exams for tenth-grade students earlier in the year than in the past, which resulted in the testing period for these exams coinciding with the end of the PISA testing window. Because of this overlap, a number of students were negatively disposed towards the PISA test and did not try their best to demonstrate their proficiency. Although the data of only a minority of students show clear signs of lack of engagement (see PISA 2018 Results Volume I, Annex A9), the comparability of PISA 2018 data for Spain with those from earlier PISA assessments cannot be fully ensured.

1. All regression models reported in this table use the same sample: students who had no missing data on any of the variables included in the analyses.

2. Results come from three logistic regression models in which the outcome variable is whether a student responded Yes (response value = 1) or No (response value = 0) to the statement "I reduce the energy I use at home to protect the environment". The first model includes only student awareness of climate change and global warming as a predictor. The second model includes all three environmental attitudes as predictors. The third model includes also the following variables: a dummy variable for whether the student scored above the baseline Level 2 in science (plausible values), student socio-economic status (value in the PISA index of economic, social and cultural status [ESCS]) and student gender (girl=1, boy=0).

3. Same as above, but in this case the first model includes only student self-efficacy regarding climate change (i.e. student can explain how carbon-dioxide emissions affect global climate change) as a predictor.

4. Same as above, but in this case the first model includes only student sense-of-purpose regarding environmental issues (i.e. student reported that looking after the global environment is important to them) as a predictor.

5. Same as above, but in this case the first model includes two dummy variables indicating a student proficiency level in science: whether she/he scored in science at Levels 2, 3 or 4 (response value = 1, otherwise=0) and whether she/he scored at Levels 5 or 6 (response value = 1, 0 otherwise).

StatLink https://stat.link/7tj8pn

Table B.4.11 [3/4] **Students reducing the energy they use at home to protect the environment, by student environmental attitudes and proficiency in science**

		Increased likelihood of students reducing the energy they use at home to protect the environment[1]											
		Students who score at Levels 2, 3 and 4 in science[5]						Students who score at Level 5 and Level 6 in science[5]					
		Before accounting for other variables		After accounting for environmental attitudes		After accounting for environmental attitudes and student characteristics		Before accounting for other variables		After accounting for environmental attitudes		After accounting for environmental attitudes and student characteristics	
		Odds ratio	S.E.	Odds ratio	S.E.	Odds ratio	S.E.	Odds ratio	S.E.	Odds ratio	S.E.	Odds ratio	S.E.
OECD	Australia	1.14	(0.10)	0.93	(0.09)	0.90	(0.09)	**1.56**	(0.21)	1.08	(0.15)	1.05	(0.15)
	Austria	**1.51**	(0.12)	**1.27**	(0.11)	**1.24**	(0.11)	**2.22**	(0.36)	**1.58**	(0.28)	**1.56**	(0.28)
	Canada	1.12	(0.11)	0.93	(0.10)	0.90	(0.10)	**1.64**	(0.21)	1.19	(0.16)	1.16	(0.16)
	Chile	0.89	(0.10)	**0.74**	(0.09)	0.79	(0.10)	1.17	(0.55)	0.83	(0.39)	1.00	(0.49)
	Colombia	**1.20**	(0.10)	1.06	(0.08)	1.04	(0.08)	2.19	(1.96)	1.81	(1.59)	1.68	(1.45)
	Costa Rica	1.05	(0.11)	0.89	(0.09)	1.00	(0.11)	c	c	c	c	c	c
	Estonia	1.00	(0.15)	0.85	(0.13)	0.84	(0.13)	**1.87**	(0.36)	1.40	(0.29)	1.39	(0.29)
	France	1.26	(0.15)	0.97	(0.14)	0.97	(0.15)	**3.25**	(0.77)	**2.11**	(0.56)	**2.16**	(0.59)
	Germany	**1.57**	(0.21)	1.27	(0.19)	1.22	(0.19)	**2.24**	(0.39)	**1.57**	(0.30)	**1.55**	(0.33)
	Greece	1.00	(0.09)	0.89	(0.08)	0.88	(0.09)	1.69	(0.61)	1.35	(0.49)	1.33	(0.49)
	Hungary	**1.60**	(0.12)	**1.27**	(0.11)	**1.26**	(0.12)	**2.70**	(0.50)	**1.86**	(0.35)	**1.86**	(0.39)
	Iceland	0.97	(0.10)	0.88	(0.10)	0.82	(0.10)	1.03	(0.40)	0.85	(0.34)	0.83	(0.34)
	Ireland	**1.46**	(0.14)	1.17	(0.13)	1.13	(0.12)	**2.12**	(0.39)	1.35	(0.29)	1.36	(0.28)
	Italy	0.85	(0.08)	**0.72**	(0.07)	**0.70**	(0.07)	1.42	(0.31)	1.10	(0.24)	1.06	(0.23)
	Korea	1.18	(0.12)	0.97	(0.11)	0.95	(0.11)	1.06	(0.14)	0.82	(0.12)	0.81	(0.13)
	Latvia	0.98	(0.09)	0.84	(0.08)	**0.81**	(0.08)	**1.81**	(0.54)	1.37	(0.40)	1.28	(0.38)
	Lithuania	0.90	(0.07)	**0.81**	(0.07)	**0.79**	(0.07)	1.11	(0.22)	0.89	(0.18)	0.91	(0.18)
	Mexico	**1.33**	(0.13)	1.15	(0.12)	1.18	(0.12)	c	c	c	c	c	c
	New Zealand	1.22	(0.13)	1.03	(0.12)	0.98	(0.11)	**1.80**	(0.23)	**1.35**	(0.19)	**1.33**	(0.19)
	Poland	1.09	(0.13)	0.91	(0.11)	0.92	(0.11)	1.30	(0.22)	0.97	(0.18)	1.02	(0.20)
	Portugal	1.16	(0.13)	0.91	(0.11)	0.91	(0.11)	**1.54**	(0.32)	1.02	(0.22)	1.04	(0.22)
	Scotland (United Kingdom)	**1.39**	(0.21)	1.13	(0.16)	1.15	(0.17)	**2.11**	(0.45)	1.36	(0.32)	1.47	(0.36)
	Slovak Republic	1.07	(0.11)	0.95	(0.11)	0.90	(0.11)	1.54	(0.36)	1.18	(0.29)	1.08	(0.26)
	Slovenia	**1.34**	(0.18)	1.08	(0.16)	1.09	(0.16)	**2.87**	(0.66)	**2.00**	(0.49)	**2.05**	(0.51)
	Spain*	**1.24**	(0.11)	1.01	(0.10)	1.01	(0.11)	**2.01**	(0.35)	1.38	(0.23)	1.38	(0.24)
	Switzerland	**1.36**	(0.17)	1.11	(0.15)	1.07	(0.15)	**2.39**	(0.55)	**1.62**	(0.40)	1.58	(0.42)
	Türkiye	**1.29**	(0.17)	1.06	(0.14)	1.12	(0.15)	1.97	(0.80)	1.42	(0.58)	1.79	(0.76)
	OECD average	**1.19**	(0.03)	0.99	(0.02)	0.98	(0.02)	**1.87**	(0.12)	**1.34**	(0.09)	**1.35**	(0.09)

Note: Values that are statistically significant are marked in bold.

* In 2018, some regions in Spain conducted their high-stakes exams for tenth-grade students earlier in the year than in the past, which resulted in the testing period for these exams coinciding with the end of the PISA testing window. Because of this overlap, a number of students were negatively disposed towards the PISA test and did not try their best to demonstrate their proficiency. Although the data of only a minority of students show clear signs of lack of engagement (see PISA 2018 Results Volume I, Annex A9), the comparability of PISA 2018 data for Spain with those from earlier PISA assessments cannot be fully ensured.

1. All regression models reported in this table use the same sample: students who had no missing data on any of the variables included in the analyses.

2. Results come from three logistic regression models in which the outcome variable is whether a student responded Yes (response value = 1) or No (response value = 0) to the statement "I reduce the energy I use at home to protect the environment". The first model includes only student awareness of climate change and global warming as a predictor. The second model includes all three environmental attitudes as predictors. The third model includes also the following variables: a dummy variable for whether the student scored above the baseline Level 2 in science (plausible values), student socio-economic status (value in the PISA index of economic, social and cultural status [ESCS]) and student gender (girl=1, boy=0).

3. Same as above, but in this case the first model includes only student self-efficacy regarding climate change (i.e. student can explain how carbon-dioxide emissions affect global climate change) as a predictor.

4. Same as above, but in this case the first model includes only student sense-of-purpose regarding environmental issues (i.e. student reported that looking after the global environment is important to them) as a predictor.

5. Same as above, but in this case the first model includes two dummy variables indicating a student proficiency level in science: whether she/he scored in science at Levels 2, 3 or 4 (response value = 1, otherwise=0) and whether she/he scored at Levels 5 or 6 (response value = 1, 0 otherwise).

StatLink https://stat.link/7tj8pn

Table B.4.11 [4/4] **Students reducing the energy they use at home to protect the environment, by student environmental attitudes and proficiency in science**

		Increased likelihood of students reducing the energy they use at home to protect the environment[1]											
		Students who score at Levels 2, 3 and 4 in science[5]						Students who score at Level 5 and Level 6 in science[5]					
		Before accounting for other variables		After accounting for environmental attitudes		After accounting for environmental attitudes and student characteristics		Before accounting for other variables		After accounting for environmental attitudes		After accounting for environmental attitudes and student characteristics	
		Odds ratio	S.E.	Odds ratio	S.E.	Odds ratio	S.E.	Odds ratio	S.E.	Odds ratio	S.E.	Odds ratio	S.E.
Partners	Albania	**1.20**	(0.11)	1.11	(0.11)	1.19	(0.11)	c	c	c	c	c	c
	Argentina	**1.34**	(0.11)	1.17	(0.10)	1.18	(0.11)	2.23	(1.18)	1.73	(0.94)	1.77	(0.94)
	Baku (Azerbaijan)	0.97	(0.09)	0.93	(0.09)	0.93	(0.09)	c	c	c	c	c	c
	Bosnia and Herzegovina	**1.21**	(0.08)	1.12	(0.09)	1.13	(0.09)	m	m	m	m	m	m
	Brazil	1.00	(0.07)	**0.82**	(0.07)	0.87	(0.07)	1.08	(0.30)	0.79	(0.22)	0.93	(0.27)
	Brunei Darussalam	**0.83**	(0.06)	**0.77**	(0.07)	**0.77**	(0.07)	0.90	(0.22)	0.77	(0.19)	0.76	(0.19)
	Bulgaria	0.85	(0.09)	**0.79**	(0.09)	0.79	(0.10)	1.12	(0.36)	0.96	(0.31)	0.97	(0.33)
	Croatia	**1.31**	(0.13)	1.14	(0.12)	1.14	(0.12)	**2.19**	(0.54)	**1.69**	(0.41)	**1.70**	(0.42)
	Cyprus	1.12	(0.09)	1.00	(0.09)	0.97	(0.09)	1.33	(0.42)	1.07	(0.35)	1.00	(0.33)
	Dominican Republic	0.71	(0.13)	**0.65**	(0.13)	**0.64**	(0.13)	m	m	m	m	m	m
	Hong Kong (China)	**1.33**	(0.16)	1.08	(0.14)	1.08	(0.15)	**1.72**	(0.35)	1.31	(0.26)	1.33	(0.28)
	Indonesia	**1.69**	(0.19)	**1.51**	(0.18)	**1.47**	(0.18)	c	c	c	c	c	c
	Jordan	1.03	(0.09)	0.98	(0.09)	0.99	(0.09)	0.86	(0.72)	0.77	(0.64)	0.78	(0.65)
	Kazakhstan	**0.74**	(0.04)	**0.70**	(0.04)	**0.69**	(0.04)	0.69	(0.34)	0.61	(0.29)	0.58	(0.28)
	Kosovo	**1.35**	(0.17)	1.17	(0.15)	1.14	(0.15)	m	m	m	m	m	m
	Lebanon	**0.81**	(0.08)	0.85	(0.09)	0.83	(0.09)	1.14	(0.83)	1.22	(0.89)	1.17	(0.86)
	Macao (China)	0.96	(0.21)	0.85	(0.20)	0.85	(0.20)	1.43	(0.37)	1.23	(0.34)	1.23	(0.34)
	Malaysia	**1.58**	(0.13)	**1.34**	(0.12)	**1.32**	(0.12)	**3.51**	(2.20)	2.88	(1.77)	2.76	(1.74)
	Malta	**1.51**	(0.18)	1.18	(0.16)	1.18	(0.16)	**2.47**	(0.94)	1.70	(0.70)	1.76	(0.75)
	Moldova	1.00	(0.08)	0.87	(0.07)	0.89	(0.08)	1.28	(0.79)	1.07	(0.74)	1.11	(0.77)
	Montenegro	0.94	(0.08)	0.85	(0.07)	0.87	(0.08)	c	c	c	c	c	c
	Morocco	1.08	(0.15)	0.95	(0.15)	0.94	(0.15)	m	m	m	m	m	m
	North Macedonia	**1.19**	(0.09)	1.02	(0.08)	1.01	(0.08)	2.52	(3.16)	1.86	(2.39)	1.87	(2.42)
	Panama	1.08	(0.15)	0.95	(0.13)	0.93	(0.13)	c	c	c	c	c	c
	Peru	**1.36**	(0.17)	1.15	(0.15)	1.20	(0.17)	c	c	c	c	c	c
	Philippines	**1.38**	(0.15)	1.15	(0.13)	1.05	(0.12)	c	c	c	c	c	c
	Romania	**0.86**	(0.06)	**0.70**	(0.06)	**0.71**	(0.06)	1.00	(0.53)	0.64	(0.34)	0.66	(0.35)
	Saudi Arabia	1.06	(0.09)	0.96	(0.08)	0.93	(0.08)	c	c	c	c	c	c
	Serbia	1.01	(0.08)	0.97	(0.08)	1.00	(0.08)	0.92	(0.25)	0.82	(0.22)	0.87	(0.24)
	Singapore	**1.41**	(0.20)	1.18	(0.18)	1.19	(0.18)	**1.77**	(0.25)	1.36	(0.21)	**1.43**	(0.24)
	Chinese Taipei	1.18	(0.16)	1.05	(0.15)	1.09	(0.16)	1.40	(0.25)	1.17	(0.21)	1.29	(0.24)
	Thailand	**2.12**	(0.19)	**1.77**	(0.18)	**1.60**	(0.16)	5.09	(5.62)	3.72	(4.13)	2.68	(3.08)
	Ukraine	**1.23**	(0.12)	1.15	(0.12)	1.12	(0.12)	**1.75**	(0.35)	**1.54**	(0.33)	1.47	(0.31)
	United Arab Emirates	m	m	m	m	m	m	m	m	m	m	m	m
	Uruguay	1.19	(0.11)	1.04	(0.10)	1.05	(0.11)	2.57	(1.70)	1.96	(1.29)	2.03	(1.35)
	Viet Nam	m	m	m	m	m	m	m	m	m	m	m	m
	OECD average	**1.18**	(0.02)	1.01	(0.02)	1.00	(0.02)	**1.82**	(0.17)	**1.37**	(0.13)	**1.36**	(0.12)

Note: Values that are statistically significant are marked in bold.

* In 2018, some regions in Spain conducted their high-stakes exams for tenth-grade students earlier in the year than in the past, which resulted in the testing period for these exams coinciding with the end of the PISA testing window. Because of this overlap, a number of students were negatively disposed towards the PISA test and did not try their best to demonstrate their proficiency. Although the data of only a minority of students show clear signs of lack of engagement (see PISA 2018 Results Volume I, Annex A9), the comparability of PISA 2018 data for Spain with those from earlier PISA assessments cannot be fully ensured.

1. All regression models reported in this table use the same sample: students who had no missing data on any of the variables included in the analyses.

2. Results come from three logistic regression models in which the outcome variable is whether a student responded Yes (response value = 1) or No (response value = 0) to the statement "I reduce the energy I use at home to protect the environment". The first model includes only student awareness of climate change and global warming as a predictor. The second model includes all three environmental attitudes as predictors. The third model includes also the following variables: a dummy variable for whether the student scored above the baseline Level 2 in science (plausible values), student socio-economic status (value in the PISA index of economic, social and cultural status [ESCS]) and student gender (girl=1, boy=0).

3. Same as above, but in this case the first model includes only student self-efficacy regarding climate change (i.e. student can explain how carbon-dioxide emissions affect global climate change) as a predictor.

4. Same as above, but in this case the first model includes only student sense-of-purpose regarding environmental issues (i.e. student reported that looking after the global environment is important to them) as a predictor.

5. Same as above, but in this case the first model includes two dummy variables indicating a student proficiency level in science: whether she/he scored in science at Levels 2, 3 or 4 (response value = 1, otherwise=0) and whether she/he scored at Levels 5 or 6 (response value = 1, 0 otherwise).

StatLink https://stat.link/7tj8pn

Table B.4.14 [1/4] **Students boycotting products or companies for political, ethical or environmental reasons, by student environmental attitudes and proficiency in science**

		Increased likelihood of students boycotting products or companies for political, ethical or environmental reasons[1]																
		Environmental awareness[2]						Self-efficacy in environmental understanding[3]						Environmental sense-of-purpose[4]					
	Before accounting for other variables		After accounting for environmental attitudes		After accounting for environmental attitudes and student characteristics		Before accounting for other variables		After accounting for environmental attitudes		After accounting for environmental attitudes and student characteristics		Before accounting for other variables		After accounting for environmental attitudes		After accounting for environmental attitudes and student characteristics	
	Odds ratio	S.E.	Odds ratio	S.E.	Odds ratio	S.E.	Odds ratio	S.E.	Odds ratio	S.E.	Odds ratio	S.E.	Odds ratio	S.E.	Odds ratio	S.E.	Odds ratio	S.E.
OECD																		
Australia	**1.37**	(0.10)	1.02	(0.09)	1.09	(0.10)	**1.51**	(0.09)	**1.37**	(0.10)	**1.47**	(0.11)	**2.21**	(0.18)	**2.10**	(0.17)	**2.09**	(0.17)
Austria	**1.30**	(0.12)	0.95	(0.09)	0.94	(0.09)	**1.66**	(0.11)	**1.60**	(0.11)	**1.50**	(0.12)	**1.67**	(0.13)	**1.58**	(0.12)	**1.61**	(0.13)
Canada	1.08	(0.08)	0.89	(0.07)	0.91	(0.07)	**1.28**	(0.07)	**1.24**	(0.07)	**1.28**	(0.08)	**1.94**	(0.15)	**1.92**	(0.15)	**1.86**	(0.15)
Chile	**1.24**	(0.11)	**1.26**	(0.12)	**1.40**	(0.14)	1.12	(0.09)	1.08	(0.09)	1.16	(0.10)	**0.71**	(0.07)	**0.68**	(0.07)	**0.76**	(0.08)
Colombia	0.96	(0.08)	0.98	(0.09)	1.06	(0.09)	0.96	(0.08)	0.99	(0.09)	1.05	(0.10)	0.84	(0.08)	0.84	(0.08)	0.92	(0.09)
Costa Rica	**1.35**	(0.11)	**1.31**	(0.10)	**1.48**	(0.12)	**1.26**	(0.09)	**1.21**	(0.09)	**1.30**	(0.09)	**0.56**	(0.06)	**0.53**	(0.06)	**0.59**	(0.07)
Estonia	0.98	(0.09)	**0.76**	(0.08)	**0.80**	(0.09)	**1.43**	(0.12)	**1.45**	(0.13)	**1.40**	(0.13)	**1.56**	(0.12)	**1.53**	(0.12)	**1.63**	(0.13)
France	**1.63**	(0.19)	**1.29**	(0.15)	**1.33**	(0.17)	**1.62**	(0.14)	**1.42**	(0.13)	**1.36**	(0.13)	**1.69**	(0.15)	**1.52**	(0.13)	**1.51**	(0.13)
Germany	1.02	(0.16)	**0.70**	(0.12)	**0.69**	(0.13)	**1.61**	(0.19)	**1.67**	(0.22)	**1.50**	(0.20)	**1.65**	(0.19)	**1.65**	(0.20)	**1.75**	(0.22)
Greece	1.01	(0.07)	0.90	(0.06)	1.00	(0.07)	**1.36**	(0.08)	**1.38**	(0.09)	**1.35**	(0.08)	1.13	(0.09)	1.12	(0.09)	**1.24**	(0.11)
Hungary	**1.19**	(0.10)	1.09	(0.09)	**1.24**	(0.12)	**1.36**	(0.11)	**1.37**	(0.11)	**1.37**	(0.11)	**0.81**	(0.07)	**0.75**	(0.06)	**0.84**	(0.07)
Iceland	**1.27**	(0.15)	1.07	(0.14)	1.15	(0.16)	**1.32**	(0.11)	**1.25**	(0.11)	**1.28**	(0.12)	**1.30**	(0.12)	**1.23**	(0.11)	**1.30**	(0.12)
Ireland	**1.24**	(0.13)	0.86	(0.10)	0.92	(0.10)	**1.56**	(0.16)	**1.46**	(0.16)	**1.52**	(0.17)	**2.13**	(0.25)	**2.04**	(0.24)	**1.99**	(0.23)
Italy	**0.58**	(0.06)	**0.61**	(0.07)	**0.74**	(0.08)	**0.71**	(0.06)	**0.81**	(0.07)	0.88	(0.08)	1.02	(0.08)	1.16	(0.10)	**1.30**	(0.11)
Korea	**1.54**	(0.14)	**1.36**	(0.12)	**1.40**	(0.14)	**1.37**	(0.11)	**1.22**	(0.10)	1.17	(0.09)	**1.46**	(0.12)	**1.36**	(0.12)	**1.34**	(0.12)
Latvia	**0.74**	(0.06)	**0.75**	(0.07)	0.84	(0.09)	**0.84**	(0.06)	0.91	(0.08)	0.95	(0.08)	1.08	(0.08)	1.15	(0.09)	**1.23**	(0.11)
Lithuania	**0.86**	(0.06)	**0.84**	(0.07)	1.04	(0.09)	1.11	(0.07)	**1.20**	(0.08)	**1.22**	(0.09)	**0.72**	(0.05)	**0.72**	(0.05)	**0.86**	(0.06)
Mexico	0.97	(0.08)	0.95	(0.09)	1.07	(0.10)	**1.18**	(0.08)	**1.22**	(0.09)	**1.29**	(0.10)	**0.75**	(0.07)	**0.74**	(0.07)	0.85	(0.08)
New Zealand	**1.55**	(0.16)	1.21	(0.13)	**1.36**	(0.15)	**1.54**	(0.15)	**1.36**	(0.14)	**1.49**	(0.16)	**1.93**	(0.20)	**1.79**	(0.18)	**1.73**	(0.18)
Poland	0.90	(0.07)	0.89	(0.08)	0.92	(0.08)	0.97	(0.07)	1.01	(0.08)	1.06	(0.09)	1.02	(0.09)	1.03	(0.08)	**1.20**	(0.10)
Portugal	0.88	(0.10)	0.85	(0.12)	0.98	(0.13)	1.04	(0.08)	1.10	(0.10)	1.20	(0.12)	0.79	(0.12)	0.80	(0.12)	0.90	(0.14)
Scotland (United Kingdom)	1.27	(0.16)	1.01	(0.13)	1.06	(0.14)	**1.30**	(0.15)	1.17	(0.14)	1.23	(0.15)	**2.04**	(0.22)	**1.98**	(0.21)	**1.95**	(0.22)
Slovak Republic	**0.59**	(0.05)	**0.53**	(0.04)	**0.65**	(0.06)	1.03	(0.08)	**1.20**	(0.09)	**1.18**	(0.09)	1.16	(0.10)	**1.28**	(0.11)	**1.39**	(0.12)
Slovenia	**1.47**	(0.11)	**1.34**	(0.11)	**1.28**	(0.11)	**1.25**	(0.09)	1.11	(0.09)	1.05	(0.09)	**1.40**	(0.13)	**1.31**	(0.12)	**1.32**	(0.12)
Spain*	**0.87**	(0.05)	**0.78**	(0.04)	**0.86**	(0.05)	**1.21**	(0.07)	**1.31**	(0.08)	**1.31**	(0.08)	0.91	(0.06)	0.92	(0.06)	0.96	(0.06)
Switzerland	**1.38**	(0.14)	1.12	(0.12)	1.19	(0.14)	**1.55**	(0.15)	**1.47**	(0.15)	**1.40**	(0.15)	**1.34**	(0.11)	**1.26**	(0.11)	**1.34**	(0.13)
Türkiye	**0.79**	(0.05)	**0.74**	(0.05)	**0.82**	(0.06)	**1.17**	(0.08)	**1.27**	(0.09)	**1.34**	(0.10)	0.93	(0.06)	0.95	(0.06)	1.07	(0.07)
OECD average	**1.11**	(0.02)	0.97	(0.02)	**1.05**	(0.02)	**1.27**	(0.02)	**1.25**	(0.02)	**1.27**	(0.02)	**1.29**	(0.02)	**1.26**	(0.02)	**1.32**	(0.03)

Note: Values that are statistically significant are marked in bold.

* In 2018, some regions in Spain conducted their high-stakes exams for tenth-grade students earlier in the year than in the past, which resulted in the testing period for these exams coinciding with the end of the PISA testing window. Because of this overlap, a number of students were negatively disposed towards the PISA test and did not try their best to demonstrate their proficiency. Although the data of only a minority of students show clear signs of lack of engagement (see PISA 2018 Results Volume I, Annex A9), the comparability of PISA 2018 data for Spain with those from earlier PISA assessments cannot be fully ensured.

1. All regression models reported in this table use the same sample: students who had no missing data on any of the variables included in the analyses.

2. Results come from three logistic regression models in which the outcome variable is whether a student responded Yes (response value = 1) or No (response value = 0) to the statement "I boycott products or companies for political, ethical or environmental reasons". The first model includes only student awareness of climate change and global warming as a predictor. The second model includes all three environmental attitudes as predictors. The third model includes also the following variables: a dummy variable for whether the student scored above the baseline Level 2 in science (plausible values), student socio-economic status (value in the PISA index of economic, social and cultural status [ESCS]) and student gender (girl=1, boy=0).

3. Same as above, but in this case the first model includes only student self-efficacy regarding climate change (i.e. student can explain how carbon-dioxide emissions affect global climate change) as a predictor.

4. Same as above, but in this case the first model includes only student sense-of-purpose regarding environmental issues (i.e. student reported that looking after the global environment is important to them) as a predictor.

5. Same as above, but in this case the first model includes two dummy variables indicating a student proficiency level in science: whether she/he scored in science at Levels 2, 3 or 4 (response value = 1, otherwise=0) and whether she/he scored at Levels 5 or 6 (response value = 1, 0 otherwise).

StatLink https://stat.link/0fzcpg

Table B.4.14 [2/4] **Students boycotting products or companies for political, ethical or environmental reasons, by student environmental attitudes and proficiency in science**

	Increased likelihood of students boycotting products or companies for political, ethical or environmental reasons[1]																	
	Environmental awareness[2]						Self-efficacy in environmental understanding[3]						Environmental sense-of-purpose[4]					
	Before accounting for other variables		After accounting for environmental attitudes		After accounting for environmental attitudes and student characteristics		Before accounting for other variables		After accounting for environmental attitudes		After accounting for environmental attitudes and student characteristics		Before accounting for other variables		After accounting for environmental attitudes		After accounting for environmental attitudes and student characteristics	
	Odds ratio	S.E.	Odds ratio	S.E.	Odds ratio	S.E.	Odds ratio	S.E.	Odds ratio	S.E.	Odds ratio	S.E.	Odds ratio	S.E.	Odds ratio	S.E.	Odds ratio	S.E.
Partners																		
Albania	**0.60**	(0.05)	**0.66**	(0.05)	**0.78**	(0.07)	**0.73**	(0.05)	0.86	(0.07)	0.98	(0.08)	**0.76**	(0.08)	0.88	(0.09)	0.95	(0.10)
Argentina	**1.16**	(0.08)	1.14	(0.08)	**1.23**	(0.10)	1.16	(0.10)	1.13	(0.10)	**1.20**	(0.11)	0.86	(0.08)	0.82	(0.08)	0.90	(0.10)
Baku (Azerbaijan)	0.95	(0.07)	0.86	(0.07)	0.96	(0.08)	**1.27**	(0.10)	**1.32**	(0.11)	**1.32**	(0.11)	1.03	(0.08)	1.02	(0.08)	1.07	(0.09)
Bosnia and Herzegovina	0.97	(0.07)	**0.85**	(0.05)	0.94	(0.06)	**1.31**	(0.09)	**1.33**	(0.09)	**1.41**	(0.10)	**1.44**	(0.10)	**1.42**	(0.11)	**1.47**	(0.11)
Brazil	**0.75**	(0.06)	**0.71**	(0.06)	0.96	(0.09)	1.09	(0.06)	**1.26**	(0.08)	**1.38**	(0.09)	**0.72**	(0.06)	**0.75**	(0.06)	0.86	(0.07)
Brunei Darussalam	**0.82**	(0.07)	**0.80**	(0.07)	0.91	(0.08)	0.90	(0.07)	0.93	(0.07)	1.08	(0.08)	**1.35**	(0.10)	**1.43**	(0.11)	**1.54**	(0.12)
Bulgaria	**0.68**	(0.05)	**0.71**	(0.06)	**0.83**	(0.08)	0.89	(0.07)	1.06	(0.10)	1.10	(0.11)	**0.70**	(0.06)	**0.75**	(0.06)	0.85	(0.07)
Croatia	**0.73**	(0.06)	**0.72**	(0.06)	**0.77**	(0.07)	0.87	(0.07)	0.94	(0.08)	1.01	(0.09)	**1.29**	(0.12)	**1.36**	(0.12)	**1.45**	(0.13)
Cyprus	0.93	(0.07)	0.90	(0.08)	1.00	(0.10)	1.06	(0.07)	1.10	(0.08)	1.12	(0.09)	0.94	(0.07)	0.95	(0.08)	1.09	(0.09)
Dominican Republic	**0.81**	(0.08)	0.98	(0.10)	1.15	(0.13)	**0.64**	(0.06)	**0.68**	(0.07)	**0.80**	(0.08)	**0.59**	(0.08)	**0.63**	(0.09)	0.76	(0.11)
Hong Kong (China)	0.98	(0.10)	0.91	(0.10)	1.01	(0.12)	1.06	(0.08)	1.04	(0.09)	1.09	(0.09)	**1.63**	(0.14)	**1.64**	(0.14)	**1.74**	(0.15)
Indonesia	0.95	(0.06)	0.91	(0.06)	1.03	(0.07)	**1.26**	(0.08)	**1.29**	(0.08)	**1.25**	(0.08)	0.94	(0.08)	0.94	(0.08)	1.02	(0.09)
Jordan	0.90	(0.06)	**0.80**	(0.06)	0.87	(0.07)	1.14	(0.08)	**1.21**	(0.09)	**1.21**	(0.09)	1.15	(0.08)	**1.17**	(0.09)	**1.25**	(0.10)
Kazakhstan	**0.74**	(0.04)	**0.71**	(0.04)	**0.87**	(0.04)	0.98	(0.04)	1.07	(0.05)	**1.20**	(0.06)	0.99	(0.05)	1.03	(0.06)	1.09	(0.06)
Kosovo	**0.67**	(0.05)	**0.63**	(0.05)	**0.75**	(0.06)	**1.23**	(0.09)	**1.40**	(0.11)	**1.39**	(0.12)	**0.77**	(0.08)	0.82	(0.09)	0.90	(0.10)
Lebanon	**0.80**	(0.05)	**0.79**	(0.05)	0.88	(0.06)	1.05	(0.07)	**1.17**	(0.09)	**1.25**	(0.10)	**0.84**	(0.07)	0.86	(0.07)	0.92	(0.08)
Macao (China)	**1.28**	(0.15)	1.12	(0.13)	1.20	(0.14)	**1.35**	(0.11)	**1.31**	(0.10)	**1.32**	(0.11)	1.20	(0.12)	1.16	(0.12)	**1.24**	(0.13)
Malaysia	1.04	(0.06)	0.97	(0.05)	1.00	(0.06)	1.12	(0.08)	1.10	(0.08)	1.13	(0.08)	**1.35**	(0.11)	**1.33**	(0.11)	**1.40**	(0.11)
Malta	**0.72**	(0.08)	**0.66**	(0.08)	0.82	(0.10)	0.94	(0.08)	1.04	(0.10)	1.21	(0.13)	1.13	(0.11)	**1.25**	(0.12)	**1.38**	(0.15)
Moldova	**0.71**	(0.05)	**0.68**	(0.05)	**0.80**	(0.06)	0.93	(0.08)	1.01	(0.09)	1.11	(0.10)	1.15	(0.09)	**1.22**	(0.10)	**1.39**	(0.12)
Montenegro	**0.81**	(0.06)	**0.77**	(0.06)	0.90	(0.08)	1.03	(0.06)	1.10	(0.07)	**1.18**	(0.08)	1.05	(0.07)	1.08	(0.07)	**1.17**	(0.08)
Morocco	**1.49**	(0.11)	**1.34**	(0.11)	**1.20**	(0.10)	**1.49**	(0.13)	**1.35**	(0.13)	**1.26**	(0.12)	1.18	(0.10)	1.08	(0.10)	1.09	(0.10)
North Macedonia	**0.80**	(0.07)	0.83	(0.08)	0.92	(0.09)	1.07	(0.09)	1.17	(0.11)	1.20	(0.12)	**0.61**	(0.07)	**0.62**	(0.07)	**0.70**	(0.08)
Panama	0.95	(0.12)	1.03	(0.13)	1.18	(0.15)	0.86	(0.11)	0.88	(0.11)	0.96	(0.13)	**0.68**	(0.10)	**0.68**	(0.10)	0.77	(0.11)
Peru	**0.81**	(0.08)	0.82	(0.09)	0.95	(0.11)	0.99	(0.10)	1.07	(0.11)	1.24	(0.14)	**0.71**	(0.09)	**0.72**	(0.10)	0.85	(0.12)
Philippines	**0.57**	(0.04)	**0.59**	(0.04)	**0.75**	(0.06)	**0.77**	(0.04)	0.90	(0.05)	1.07	(0.06)	0.93	(0.07)	1.09	(0.08)	**1.21**	(0.09)
Romania	**0.73**	(0.06)	**0.68**	(0.05)	0.85	(0.08)	**1.23**	(0.09)	**1.43**	(0.11)	**1.61**	(0.14)	**0.69**	(0.07)	**0.71**	(0.07)	0.90	(0.09)
Saudi Arabia	**1.18**	(0.07)	1.11	(0.07)	1.14	(0.08)	**1.22**	(0.08)	**1.16**	(0.08)	**1.17**	(0.09)	**1.19**	(0.08)	**1.15**	(0.08)	**1.23**	(0.09)
Serbia	**0.67**	(0.06)	**0.63**	(0.06)	**0.72**	(0.07)	0.94	(0.07)	1.06	(0.08)	1.06	(0.08)	**1.19**	(0.08)	**1.26**	(0.09)	**1.33**	(0.09)
Singapore	0.99	(0.09)	0.91	(0.10)	1.01	(0.12)	1.09	(0.09)	1.09	(0.10)	1.18	(0.11)	**1.64**	(0.18)	**1.64**	(0.19)	**1.68**	(0.19)
Chinese Taipei	**1.25**	(0.10)	1.01	(0.09)	1.05	(0.10)	**1.57**	(0.08)	**1.51**	(0.08)	**1.51**	(0.09)	**1.56**	(0.13)	**1.47**	(0.13)	**1.53**	(0.14)
Thailand	**0.87**	(0.06)	**0.87**	(0.06)	1.02	(0.07)	0.93	(0.06)	0.95	(0.06)	1.02	(0.07)	1.12	(0.08)	**1.17**	(0.08)	**1.27**	(0.10)
Ukraine	**0.79**	(0.06)	**0.75**	(0.06)	**0.82**	(0.07)	0.99	(0.07)	1.05	(0.07)	1.06	(0.08)	1.15	(0.08)	**1.20**	(0.09)	**1.29**	(0.09)
United Arab Emirates	m	m	m	m	m	m	m	m	m	m	m	m	m	m	m	m	m	m
Uruguay	1.09	(0.12)	1.09	(0.13)	1.25	(0.15)	1.10	(0.10)	1.10	(0.11)	1.15	(0.11)	0.82	(0.09)	**0.80**	(0.09)	0.89	(0.10)
Viet Nam	m	m	m	m	m	m	m	m	m	m	m	m	m	m	m	m	m	m
Overall average	0.99	(0.01)	**0.90**	(0.01)	1.00	(0.01)	**1.16**	(0.01)	**1.18**	(0.01)	**1.22**	(0.01)	**1.15**	(0.01)	**1.15**	(0.01)	**1.22**	(0.02)

Note: Values that are statistically significant are marked in bold.

* In 2018, some regions in Spain conducted their high-stakes exams for tenth-grade students earlier in the year than in the past, which resulted in the testing period for these exams coinciding with the end of the PISA testing window. Because of this overlap, a number of students were negatively disposed towards the PISA test and did not try their best to demonstrate their proficiency. Although the data of only a minority of students show clear signs of lack of engagement (see PISA 2018 Results Volume I, Annex A9), the comparability of PISA 2018 data for Spain with those from earlier PISA assessments cannot be fully ensured.

1. All regression models reported in this table use the same sample: students who had no missing data on any of the variables included in the analyses.

2. Results come from three logistic regression models in which the outcome variable is whether a student responded Yes (response value = 1) or No (response value = 0) to the statement "I boycott products or companies for political, ethical or environmental reasons". The first model includes only student awareness of climate change and global warming as a predictor. The second model includes all three environmental attitudes as predictors. The third model includes also the following variables: a dummy variable for whether the student scored above the baseline Level 2 in science (plausible values), student socio-economic status (value in the PISA index of economic, social and cultural status [ESCS]) and student gender (girl=1, boy=0).

3. Same as above, but in this case the first model includes only student self-efficacy regarding climate change (i.e. student can explain how carbon-dioxide emissions affect global climate change) as a predictor.

4. Same as above, but in this case the first model includes only student sense-of-purpose regarding environmental issues (i.e. student reported that looking after the global environment is important to them) as a predictor.

5. Same as above, but in this case the first model includes two dummy variables indicating a student proficiency level in science: whether she/he scored in science at Levels 2, 3 or 4 (response value = 1, otherwise=0) and whether she/he scored at Levels 5 or 6 (response value = 1, 0 otherwise).

StatLink https://stat.link/0fzcpg

Table B.4.14 [3/4] **Students boycotting products or companies for political, ethical or environmental reasons, by student environmental attitudes and proficiency in science**

	Increased likelihood of students boycotting products or companies for political, ethical or environmental reasons[1]											
	Students who score at Levels 2, 3 and 4 in science[5]						Students who score at Level 5 and Level 6 in science[5]					
	Before accounting for other variables		After accounting for environmental attitudes		After accounting for environmental attitudes and student characteristics		Before accounting for other variables		After accounting for environmental attitudes		After accounting for environmental attitudes and student characteristics	
	Odds ratio	S.E.	Odds ratio	S.E.	Odds ratio	S.E.	Odds ratio	S.E.	Odds ratio	S.E.	Odds ratio	S.E.
OECD Australia	**0.61**	(0.05)	**0.50**	(0.04)	**0.47**	(0.04)	0.86	(0.10)	**0.61**	(0.07)	**0.55**	(0.06)
Austria	0.95	(0.11)	0.80	(0.10)	**0.73**	(0.09)	**1.57**	(0.25)	1.08	(0.19)	0.88	(0.16)
Canada	**0.66**	(0.05)	**0.59**	(0.05)	**0.55**	(0.05)	**0.79**	(0.07)	**0.64**	(0.06)	**0.58**	(0.06)
Chile	**0.52**	(0.05)	**0.48**	(0.05)	**0.43**	(0.05)	0.48	(0.19)	**0.41**	(0.16)	**0.32**	(0.13)
Colombia	**0.59**	(0.05)	**0.58**	(0.05)	**0.52**	(0.05)	0.41	(0.22)	0.39	(0.21)	**0.29**	(0.16)
Costa Rica	**0.59**	(0.05)	**0.53**	(0.04)	**0.48**	(0.04)	m	m	m	m	m	m
Estonia	**0.49**	(0.07)	**0.43**	(0.06)	**0.42**	(0.06)	**0.63**	(0.11)	**0.50**	(0.09)	**0.47**	(0.09)
France	0.89	(0.11)	**0.66**	(0.10)	**0.61**	(0.09)	1.32	(0.22)	0.84	(0.16)	0.69	(0.14)
Germany	**0.64**	(0.11)	**0.56**	(0.10)	**0.50**	(0.09)	0.99	(0.23)	0.76	(0.19)	**0.57**	(0.15)
Greece	**0.74**	(0.06)	**0.68**	(0.06)	**0.67**	(0.06)	0.78	(0.23)	0.65	(0.19)	0.59	(0.19)
Hungary	**0.58**	(0.06)	**0.51**	(0.05)	**0.47**	(0.05)	0.91	(0.19)	0.73	(0.16)	**0.62**	(0.14)
Iceland	**0.66**	(0.07)	**0.55**	(0.06)	**0.53**	(0.06)	0.85	(0.21)	0.62	(0.16)	**0.56**	(0.15)
Ireland	**0.68**	(0.09)	**0.55**	(0.08)	**0.51**	(0.07)	1.22	(0.24)	0.86	(0.18)	0.75	(0.16)
Italy	**0.38**	(0.05)	**0.41**	(0.06)	**0.39**	(0.06)	**0.34**	(0.11)	**0.38**	(0.12)	**0.34**	(0.11)
Korea	0.83	(0.08)	**0.71**	(0.07)	**0.65**	(0.07)	1.07	(0.13)	0.86	(0.11)	**0.74**	(0.10)
Latvia	**0.45**	(0.04)	**0.45**	(0.05)	**0.44**	(0.04)	**0.50**	(0.17)	0.51	(0.18)	**0.46**	(0.16)
Lithuania	**0.48**	(0.05)	**0.47**	(0.05)	**0.48**	(0.06)	**0.33**	(0.08)	**0.31**	(0.08)	**0.29**	(0.08)
Mexico	**0.50**	(0.04)	**0.48**	(0.04)	**0.43**	(0.04)	c	c	c	c	c	c
New Zealand	**0.59**	(0.06)	**0.46**	(0.05)	**0.41**	(0.05)	0.87	(0.13)	**0.59**	(0.09)	**0.51**	(0.08)
Poland	**0.51**	(0.07)	**0.49**	(0.07)	**0.47**	(0.07)	**0.46**	(0.08)	**0.44**	(0.08)	**0.37**	(0.07)
Portugal	**0.46**	(0.05)	**0.43**	(0.05)	**0.40**	(0.05)	**0.62**	(0.13)	**0.54**	(0.12)	**0.46**	(0.11)
Scotland (United Kingdom)	0.84	(0.15)	0.72	(0.13)	0.71	(0.14)	1.01	(0.33)	0.75	(0.26)	0.74	(0.26)
Slovak Republic	**0.46**	(0.05)	**0.49**	(0.05)	**0.48**	(0.05)	**0.33**	(0.10)	**0.34**	(0.11)	**0.30**	(0.09)
Slovenia	1.10	(0.13)	0.94	(0.12)	0.89	(0.11)	**1.61**	(0.30)	1.25	(0.25)	1.09	(0.23)
Spain*	**0.60**	(0.06)	**0.57**	(0.06)	**0.53**	(0.06)	**0.73**	(0.10)	**0.65**	(0.09)	**0.54**	(0.07)
Switzerland	**0.63**	(0.09)	**0.52**	(0.07)	**0.46**	(0.07)	1.12	(0.26)	0.79	(0.20)	0.60	(0.17)
Türkiye	**0.68**	(0.05)	**0.68**	(0.06)	**0.63**	(0.05)	0.63	(0.15)	**0.62**	(0.15)	**0.46**	(0.12)
OECD average	**0.63**	(0.01)	**0.56**	(0.01)	**0.53**	(0.01)	**0.82**	(0.04)	**0.64**	(0.03)	**0.55**	(0.03)

Note: Values that are statistically significant are marked in bold.

* In 2018, some regions in Spain conducted their high-stakes exams for tenth-grade students earlier in the year than in the past, which resulted in the testing period for these exams coinciding with the end of the PISA testing window. Because of this overlap, a number of students were negatively disposed towards the PISA test and did not try their best to demonstrate their proficiency. Although the data of only a minority of students show clear signs of lack of engagement (see PISA 2018 Results Volume I, Annex A9), the comparability of PISA 2018 data for Spain with those from earlier PISA assessments cannot be fully ensured.

1. All regression models reported in this table use the same sample: students who had no missing data on any of the variables included in the analyses.

2. Results come from three logistic regression models in which the outcome variable is whether a student responded Yes (response value = 1) or No (response value = 0) to the statement "I boycott products or companies for political, ethical or environmental reasons". The first model includes only student awareness of climate change and global warming as a predictor. The second model includes all three environmental attitudes as predictors. The third model includes also the following variables: a dummy variable for whether the student scored above the baseline Level 2 in science (plausible values), student socio-economic status (value in the PISA index of economic, social and cultural status [ESCS]) and student gender (girl=1, boy=0).

3. Same as above, but in this case the first model includes only student self-efficacy regarding climate change (i.e. student can explain how carbon-dioxide emissions affect global climate change) as a predictor.

4. Same as above, but in this case the first model includes only student sense-of-purpose regarding environmental issues (i.e. student reported that looking after the global environment is important to them) as a predictor.

5. Same as above, but in this case the first model includes two dummy variables indicating a student proficiency level in science: whether she/he scored in science at Levels 2, 3 or 4 (response value = 1, otherwise=0) and whether she/he scored at Levels 5 or 6 (response value = 1, 0 otherwise).

StatLink https://stat.link/0fzcpg

Table B.4.14 [4/4] **Students boycotting products or companies for political, ethical or environmental reasons, by student environmental attitudes and proficiency in science**

	Increased likelihood of students boycotting products or companies for political, ethical or environmental reasons[1]											
	Students who score at Levels 2, 3 and 4 in science[5]						Students who score at Level 5 and Level 6 in science[5]					
	Before accounting for other variables		After accounting for environmental attitudes		After accounting for environmental attitudes and student characteristics		Before accounting for other variables		After accounting for environmental attitudes		After accounting for environmental attitudes and student characteristics	
	Odds ratio	S.E.	Odds ratio	S.E.	Odds ratio	S.E.	Odds ratio	S.E.	Odds ratio	S.E.	Odds ratio	S.E.
Partners												
Albania	**0.55**	(0.05)	**0.60**	(0.05)	**0.58**	(0.06)	c	c	c	c	c	c
Argentina	**0.70**	(0.06)	**0.64**	(0.06)	**0.61**	(0.06)	0.43	(0.23)	0.36	(0.20)	**0.31**	(0.17)
Baku (Azerbaijan)	**0.62**	(0.05)	**0.60**	(0.05)	**0.58**	(0.05)	c	c	c	c	c	c
Bosnia and Herzegovina	**0.71**	(0.05)	**0.65**	(0.05)	**0.62**	(0.05)	m	m	m	m	m	m
Brazil	**0.41**	(0.03)	**0.39**	(0.03)	**0.36**	(0.03)	**0.40**	(0.18)	**0.34**	(0.16)	**0.28**	(0.13)
Brunei Darussalam	**0.49**	(0.04)	**0.46**	(0.04)	**0.42**	(0.04)	0.81	(0.19)	0.72	(0.17)	**0.54**	(0.14)
Bulgaria	**0.47**	(0.04)	**0.50**	(0.05)	**0.47**	(0.05)	**0.24**	(0.11)	**0.26**	(0.12)	**0.22**	(0.10)
Croatia	**0.58**	(0.06)	**0.58**	(0.07)	**0.56**	(0.07)	**0.47**	(0.14)	**0.48**	(0.14)	**0.41**	(0.13)
Cyprus	**0.56**	(0.04)	**0.53**	(0.04)	**0.52**	(0.04)	0.56	(0.26)	0.50	(0.23)	0.42	(0.20)
Dominican Republic	**0.21**	(0.04)	**0.22**	(0.04)	**0.23**	(0.05)	m	m	m	m	m	m
Hong Kong (China)	**0.66**	(0.06)	**0.62**	(0.06)	**0.60**	(0.06)	**0.61**	(0.10)	**0.57**	(0.10)	**0.50**	(0.09)
Indonesia	**0.59**	(0.05)	**0.58**	(0.05)	**0.57**	(0.05)	c	c	c	c	c	c
Jordan	0.98	(0.07)	0.98	(0.07)	0.97	(0.07)	1.29	(0.99)	1.24	(0.96)	1.15	(0.93)
Kazakhstan	**0.43**	(0.02)	**0.43**	(0.03)	**0.42**	(0.03)	**0.32**	(0.12)	**0.30**	(0.12)	**0.26**	(0.10)
Kosovo	**0.62**	(0.05)	**0.63**	(0.06)	**0.56**	(0.06)	m	m	m	m	m	m
Lebanon	**0.64**	(0.06)	**0.64**	(0.06)	**0.60**	(0.06)	0.92	(0.61)	0.92	(0.62)	0.78	(0.53)
Macao (China)	**0.57**	(0.10)	**0.49**	(0.09)	**0.50**	(0.10)	**0.65**	(0.14)	**0.52**	(0.12)	**0.51**	(0.12)
Malaysia	**0.85**	(0.06)	**0.78**	(0.06)	**0.71**	(0.06)	1.07	(0.65)	0.97	(0.58)	0.70	(0.45)
Malta	**0.46**	(0.05)	**0.43**	(0.05)	**0.42**	(0.05)	**0.50**	(0.14)	**0.45**	(0.13)	**0.40**	(0.12)
Moldova	**0.51**	(0.04)	**0.51**	(0.05)	**0.49**	(0.05)	0.39	(0.21)	0.38	(0.21)	0.36	(0.20)
Montenegro	**0.57**	(0.05)	**0.56**	(0.05)	**0.54**	(0.05)	c	c	c	c	c	c
Morocco	**1.54**	(0.15)	**1.35**	(0.14)	**1.26**	(0.13)	m	m	m	m	m	m
North Macedonia	**0.66**	(0.07)	**0.68**	(0.07)	**0.68**	(0.08)	1.19	(0.63)	1.18	(0.63)	1.12	(0.56)
Panama	**0.39**	(0.05)	**0.39**	(0.05)	**0.37**	(0.05)	c	c	c	c	c	c
Peru	**0.42**	(0.04)	**0.41**	(0.04)	**0.37**	(0.04)	m	m	m	m	m	m
Philippines	**0.28**	(0.03)	**0.30**	(0.03)	**0.29**	(0.03)	c	c	c	c	c	c
Romania	**0.43**	(0.04)	**0.42**	(0.04)	**0.41**	(0.04)	0.45	(0.21)	**0.37**	(0.18)	**0.33**	(0.16)
Saudi Arabia	0.98	(0.07)	0.92	(0.07)	0.93	(0.08)	c	c	c	c	c	c
Serbia	**0.62**	(0.06)	**0.64**	(0.06)	**0.62**	(0.06)	0.62	(0.25)	0.65	(0.26)	0.58	(0.25)
Singapore	**0.54**	(0.06)	**0.49**	(0.06)	**0.45**	(0.05)	**0.52**	(0.05)	**0.46**	(0.05)	**0.39**	(0.05)
Chinese Taipei	**0.79**	(0.08)	**0.70**	(0.07)	**0.66**	(0.07)	1.09	(0.14)	0.90	(0.13)	0.78	(0.11)
Thailand	**0.66**	(0.04)	**0.64**	(0.04)	**0.62**	(0.04)	**0.51**	(0.15)	**0.49**	(0.15)	**0.39**	(0.13)
Ukraine	**0.61**	(0.07)	**0.61**	(0.08)	**0.57**	(0.07)	1.06	(0.21)	1.07	(0.22)	0.91	(0.19)
United Arab Emirates	m	m	m	m	m	m	m	m	m	m	m	m
Uruguay	**0.49**	(0.07)	**0.46**	(0.07)	**0.44**	(0.07)	0.53	(0.32)	0.47	(0.28)	0.41	(0.25)
Viet Nam	m	m	m	m	m	m	m	m	m	m	m	m
Overall average	**0.62**	(0.01)	**0.58**	(0.01)	**0.54**	(0.01)	**0.75**	(0.04)	**0.63**	(0.04)	**0.54**	(0.03)

Note: Values that are statistically significant are marked in bold.

* In 2018, some regions in Spain conducted their high-stakes exams for tenth-grade students earlier in the year than in the past, which resulted in the testing period for these exams coinciding with the end of the PISA testing window. Because of this overlap, a number of students were negatively disposed towards the PISA test and did not try their best to demonstrate their proficiency. Although the data of only a minority of students show clear signs of lack of engagement (see PISA 2018 Results Volume I, Annex A9), the comparability of PISA 2018 data for Spain with those from earlier PISA assessments cannot be fully ensured.

1. All regression models reported in this table use the same sample: students who had no missing data on any of the variables included in the analyses.

2. Results come from three logistic regression models in which the outcome variable is whether a student responded Yes (response value = 1) or No (response value = 0) to the statement "I boycott products or companies for political, ethical or environmental reasons". The first model includes only student awareness of climate change and global warming as a predictor. The second model includes all three environmental attitudes as predictors. The third model includes also the following variables: a dummy variable for whether the student scored above the baseline Level 2 in science (plausible values), student socio-economic status (value in the PISA index of economic, social and cultural status [ESCS]) and student gender (girl=1, boy=0).

3. Same as above, but in this case the first model includes only student self-efficacy regarding climate change (i.e. student can explain how carbon-dioxide emissions affect global climate change) as a predictor.

4. Same as above, but in this case the first model includes only student sense-of-purpose regarding environmental issues (i.e. student reported that looking after the global environment is important to them) as a predictor.

5. Same as above, but in this case the first model includes two dummy variables indicating a student proficiency level in science: whether she/he scored in science at Levels 2, 3 or 4 (response value = 1, otherwise=0) and whether she/he scored at Levels 5 or 6 (response value = 1, 0 otherwise).

StatLink https://stat.link/0fzcpg

Table B.4.32 [1/2] **Misalignment between environmental enthusiasm and environmental actions**

		Environmentally enthusiastic[1] students who do not take part in the following action:								
		Reduce the energy they use at home to protect the environment		Choose certain products for ethical or environmental reasons, even if they are a bit more expensive		Sign environmental or social petitions online		Boycott products or companies for political, ethical or environmental reasons		Participate in activities in favour of environmental protection	
		%	S.E.	%	S.E.	%	S.E.	%	S.E.	%	S.E.
OECD	Australia	23.3	(0.7)	50.5	(0.7)	78.2	(0.6)	73.3	(0.7)	60.1	(0.7)
	Austria	22.3	(0.9)	39.3	(1.2)	75.1	(1.2)	58.0	(1.2)	59.6	(1.3)
	Canada	26.6	(0.6)	51.9	(0.6)	80.2	(0.5)	71.2	(0.7)	57.6	(0.7)
	Chile	19.0	(0.8)	57.3	(1.0)	70.7	(1.1)	76.1	(0.9)	56.9	(1.0)
	Colombia	16.4	(0.9)	42.8	(1.1)	76.4	(0.9)	71.1	(1.1)	37.6	(1.2)
	Costa Rica	15.1	(0.8)	47.0	(1.1)	75.2	(0.9)	75.0	(0.8)	39.5	(1.4)
	Estonia	24.0	(1.0)	49.1	(1.2)	77.0	(1.1)	71.8	(1.0)	62.7	(1.2)
	France	24.3	(0.8)	46.2	(1.0)	79.9	(0.9)	69.2	(1.0)	70.7	(0.9)
	Germany	25.1	(1.1)	51.4	(2.0)	81.8	(1.1)	76.4	(1.3)	70.9	(1.4)
	Greece	24.0	(1.0)	42.8	(1.1)	76.8	(1.2)	63.4	(1.4)	51.0	(1.5)
	Hungary	24.7	(0.9)	41.5	(1.1)	82.1	(0.9)	70.7	(1.1)	53.0	(1.0)
	Iceland	27.5	(1.0)	46.7	(1.4)	61.5	(1.5)	63.2	(1.3)	41.1	(1.4)
	Ireland	20.8	(0.9)	59.8	(0.8)	81.6	(0.8)	79.4	(0.9)	65.1	(0.9)
	Italy	29.9	(1.0)	52.4	(1.2)	83.3	(1.0)	84.1	(0.8)	69.9	(1.0)
	Korea	20.7	(0.6)	59.1	(1.0)	52.2	(0.8)	62.7	(0.9)	43.1	(0.8)
	Latvia	30.6	(1.1)	47.0	(1.0)	78.0	(0.9)	79.9	(0.8)	56.8	(1.1)
	Lithuania	29.7	(1.0)	50.6	(1.2)	59.5	(0.9)	65.1	(1.0)	47.8	(1.1)
	Mexico	18.6	(0.9)	46.5	(1.2)	74.9	(1.1)	72.3	(1.1)	39.9	(1.2)
	New Zealand	25.5	(0.9)	48.0	(1.1)	74.3	(1.0)	74.4	(0.9)	60.0	(1.2)
	Poland	22.8	(0.9)	43.1	(1.1)	78.3	(1.0)	76.0	(0.9)	55.6	(1.2)
	Portugal	19.2	(0.8)	49.3	(1.0)	81.6	(0.8)	76.4	(0.8)	61.5	(1.1)
	Scotland (United Kingdom)	24.6	(1.2)	56.6	(1.4)	72.9	(1.2)	77.0	(1.4)	72.0	(1.6)
	Slovak Republic	28.4	(1.2)	47.8	(1.4)	72.2	(1.4)	74.2	(1.5)	47.6	(1.5)
	Slovenia	17.1	(1.0)	45.0	(1.3)	81.5	(1.0)	53.8	(1.3)	66.7	(1.0)
	Spain	19.1	(0.5)	54.4	(0.7)	70.0	(0.5)	80.5	(0.6)	61.7	(0.7)
	Switzerland	27.1	(1.3)	48.8	(1.4)	79.6	(1.2)	72.4	(1.3)	66.8	(1.3)
	Türkiye	9.4	(0.6)	32.4	(1.0)	47.0	(1.0)	63.4	(1.2)	24.8	(0.9)
	OECD average	22.8	(0.2)	48.4	(0.2)	74.1	(0.2)	71.5	(0.2)	55.6	(0.2)

1. Environmentally enthusiastic students are students who reported that looking after the global environment is important to them (sense-of-purpose), that they know something or are very familiar with climate change and global warming (awareness), and that they could explain how carbon-dioxide emissions affect global climate change easily or with a bit of effort (self-efficacy).

StatLink https://stat.link/wornc1

Table B.4.32 [2/2] **Misalignment between environmental enthusiasm and environmental actions**

		Environmentally enthusiastic[1] students who do not take part in the following action:									
		Reduce the energy they use at home to protect the environment		Choose certain products for ethical or environmental reasons, even if they are a bit more expensive		Sign environmental or social petitions online		Boycott products or companies for political, ethical or environmental reasons		Participate in activities in favour of environmental protection	
		%	S.E.	%	S.E.	%	S.E.	%	S.E.	%	S.E.
OECD	Albania	16.3	(0.7)	44.9	(0.9)	69.4	(0.9)	69.8	(1.0)	20.7	(0.9)
	Argentina	23.3	(1.1)	54.2	(1.4)	69.1	(1.3)	77.6	(1.0)	57.1	(1.2)
	Baku (Azerbaijan)	24.5	(1.4)	29.5	(1.5)	44.9	(1.9)	48.0	(1.8)	32.6	(1.5)
	Bosnia and Herzegovina	24.4	(1.3)	51.8	(1.4)	63.0	(1.4)	61.8	(1.4)	37.3	(1.3)
	Brazil	20.3	(1.0)	53.1	(1.1)	67.8	(1.2)	73.3	(1.1)	56.4	(1.2)
	Brunei Darussalam	21.3	(0.8)	49.4	(1.0)	80.3	(0.9)	78.5	(0.8)	57.4	(1.0)
	Bulgaria	33.6	(1.1)	43.8	(1.2)	65.4	(1.5)	64.9	(1.3)	42.5	(1.5)
	Croatia	24.4	(0.8)	51.2	(1.1)	81.1	(0.7)	81.0	(0.9)	60.8	(1.0)
	Cyprus	24.4	(1.4)	45.7	(1.3)	67.2	(1.2)	64.7	(1.2)	47.2	(1.2)
	Dominican Republic	18.4	(1.2)	37.3	(1.8)	61.0	(2.1)	64.3	(1.7)	39.7	(1.9)
	Hong Kong (China)	15.4	(0.7)	39.0	(0.8)	74.6	(0.9)	63.3	(0.9)	35.9	(0.9)
	Indonesia	13.7	(1.2)	28.2	(1.4)	58.7	(2.0)	48.4	(1.7)	18.5	(1.4)
	Jordan	14.0	(0.9)	18.6	(0.8)	51.6	(1.4)	38.0	(1.5)	17.3	(1.0)
	Kazakhstan	21.0	(0.7)	29.0	(0.7)	63.3	(0.9)	67.2	(0.8)	39.2	(0.8)
	Kosovo	11.7	(1.0)	20.1	(1.3)	65.1	(1.5)	64.1	(1.5)	29.9	(1.5)
	Lebanon	29.1	(1.6)	52.1	(1.5)	66.5	(1.4)	63.6	(1.5)	42.6	(1.5)
	Macao (China)	16.9	(0.8)	41.7	(1.2)	85.3	(0.8)	66.8	(1.1)	49.5	(1.1)
	Malaysia	18.8	(0.7)	36.3	(1.0)	67.8	(1.1)	59.6	(1.5)	31.5	(1.1)
	Malta	15.6	(0.9)	44.7	(1.3)	60.6	(1.1)	70.0	(1.0)	53.9	(1.3)
	Moldova	28.5	(1.1)	33.5	(1.1)	70.0	(1.2)	79.6	(1.1)	40.8	(1.3)
	Montenegro	30.4	(0.9)	38.7	(0.9)	62.1	(1.1)	66.8	(1.0)	33.0	(1.0)
	Morocco	19.0	(1.3)	41.0	(1.6)	58.5	(1.7)	30.3	(1.9)	21.5	(1.4)
	North Macedonia	22.7	(1.0)	54.2	(1.5)	70.9	(1.4)	80.4	(1.1)	39.6	(1.2)
	Panama	20.0	(1.6)	43.5	(1.8)	71.9	(1.9)	74.0	(1.6)	42.6	(1.8)
	Peru	11.9	(0.8)	52.7	(1.4)	69.5	(1.2)	75.9	(0.9)	46.8	(1.4)
	Philippines	13.6	(0.8)	35.8	(0.8)	62.4	(1.0)	66.9	(1.0)	24.9	(1.0)
	Romania	25.4	(1.3)	38.1	(1.6)	71.5	(1.4)	72.1	(1.5)	42.2	(1.4)
	Saudi Arabia	14.8	(1.1)	32.1	(1.5)	c	c	40.7	(1.7)	36.3	(1.7)
	Serbia	32.0	(1.4)	48.9	(1.4)	72.8	(1.3)	70.6	(1.4)	48.6	(1.1)
	Singapore	13.7	(0.5)	50.0	(0.8)	79.4	(0.6)	74.2	(0.7)	53.8	(0.9)
	Chinese Taipei	16.3	(0.6)	30.4	(0.8)	73.0	(0.8)	52.9	(0.8)	30.2	(0.8)
	Thailand	10.5	(0.6)	26.6	(0.9)	53.1	(1.3)	53.1	(1.2)	23.2	(0.7)
	Ukraine	35.7	(1.1)	40.3	(1.2)	72.0	(1.2)	77.7	(1.0)	46.7	(1.3)
	United Arab Emirates	m	m	m	m	m	m	m	m	m	m
	Uruguay	28.7	(1.5)	58.3	(1.9)	73.5	(1.5)	78.6	(1.3)	58.4	(1.7)
	Viet Nam	13.8	(0.8)	24.7	(0.9)	63.2	(1.7)	54.9	(1.4)	6.6	(0.7)
	Overall average	21.6	(0.1)	44.0	(0.2)	70.3	(0.2)	67.8	(0.2)	46.2	(0.2)

1. Environmentally enthusiastic students are students who reported that looking after the global environment is important to them (sense-of-purpose), that they know something or are very familiar with climate change and global warming (awareness), and that they could explain how carbon-dioxide emissions affect global climate change easily or with a bit of effort (self-efficacy).

StatLink https://stat.link/wornc1

Annex B **List of tables available on line**

Chapter 2 **Student knowledge and skills on environmental issues**

https://stat.link/zy2p63

...

Chapter 3 **Students' attitudes and beliefs regarding environmental issues**

https://stat.link/gra5to

WEB	**Table B.3.2**	Environmental awareness, by student characteristics
WEB	**Table B.3.4**	Self-efficacy in environmental understanding, by student characteristics
WEB	**Table B.3.6**	Environmental sense-of-purpose, by student characteristics
WEB	**Table B.3.7**	Students in schools whose principal reported that climate change and global warming are covered in the school curriculum
WEB	**Table B.3.8**	Environmental awareness and parents' environmental awareness and actions
WEB	**Table B.3.9**	Self-efficacy in environmental understanding and parents' environmental awareness and actions
WEB	**Table B.3.10**	Environmental sense-of-purpose, by parents' environmental actions and attitudes
WEB	**Table B.3.11**	Parents' involvement in environmental actions and attitudes
WEB	**Table B.3.13**	Students' environmental attitudes, by number of environmental attitudes displayed
WEB	**Table B.3.14**	Mean score in science, by environmental awareness
WEB	**Table B.3.15**	Mean score in science, by self-efficacy in environmental understanding
WEB	**Table B.3.16**	Mean score in science, by environmental sense-of-purpose
WEB	**Table B.3.17**	Mean score in science, by overlap of students' environmental attitudes
WEB	**Table B.3.18**	Mean score in science, by number of students' environmental attitudes
WEB	**Table B.3.19**	Mean score in science, by students' involvement in environmental actions
WEB	**Table B.3.20**	Change in science performance, by overlap of environmental attitudes, before and after accounting for student socio-economic status
WEB	**Table B.3.21**	Change in science performance, by number of environmental attitudes, before and after accounting for student socio-economic status
WEB	**Table B.3.22**	Environmentally enthusiastic students, by student, school and parental characteristics
WEB	**Table B.3.23**	Environmentally indifferent students, by student and parental characteristics
WEB	**Table B.3.25**	Likelihood of being an environmentally indifferent student, by student, school and parental characteristics

Chapter 4 **Student involvement in actions regarding environmental issues**

https://stat.link/vg1mh6

WEB	**Table B.4.1**	Students who reported that they reduce the energy they use at home to protect the environment, by student and school characteristics
WEB	**Table B.4.2**	Students who reported that they choose certain products for ethical or environmental reasons, by student and school characteristics
WEB	**Table B.4.3**	Students who reported that they sign environmental or social petitions online, by student and school characteristics
WEB	**Table B.4.4**	Students who reported that they boycott products or companies for political, ethical or environmental reasons, by student and school characteristics
WEB	**Table B.4.5**	Students who reported that they participate in activities in favour of environmental protection, by student and school characteristics
WEB	**Table B.4.6**	Students who reported that they reduce the energy they use at home to protect the environment, by whether or not they take part in the other environmental actions
WEB	**Table B.4.7**	Students who reported that they choose certain products for ethical or environmental reasons, even if they are more expensive, by whether or not they take part in the other environmental actions
WEB	**Table B.4.8**	Students who reported that they sign environmental or social petitions online, by whether or not they take part in the other environmental actions
WEB	**Table B.4.9**	Students who reported that they boycott products or companies for political, ethical or environmental reasons, by whether or not they take part in the other environmental actions
WEB	**Table B.4.10**	Students who reported that they participate in activities in favour of environmental protection, by whether or not they take part in the other environmental actions
WEB	**Table B.4.12**	Students choosing certain products for ethical or environmental reasons, by student environmental attitudes and proficiency in science
WEB	**Table B.4.13**	Students signing environmental or social petitions online, by student environmental attitudes and proficiency in science
WEB	**Table B.4.15**	Students participating in activities in favour of environmental protection, by student environmental attitudes and proficiency in science
WEB	**Table B.4.16**	Number of environmental actions students take part in and science performance
WEB	**Table B.4.17**	Misalignment between students' environmental awareness and environmental actions

...

WEB	**Table B.4.18**	Misalignment between students' environmental awareness and environmental actions, by socio-economic status and gender
WEB	**Table B.4.19**	Misalignment between students' environmental awareness and environmental actions, by proficiency levels in science
WEB	**Table B.4.20**	Misalignment between students' environmental awareness and environmental actions, by self-efficacy in environmental understanding and environmental sense-of-purpose
WEB	**Table B.4.21**	Misalignment between students' self-efficacy in environmental understanding and environmental actions
WEB	**Table B.4.22**	Misalignment between students' self-efficacy in environmental understanding and environmental actions, by socio-economic status and gender
WEB	**Table B.4.23**	Misalignment between students' self-efficacy in environmental understanding and environmental actions, by proficiency levels in science
WEB	**Table B.4.24**	Misalignment between students' self-efficacy in environmental understanding and environmental actions, by environmental awareness and environmental sense-of-purpose
WEB	**Table B.4.25**	Misalignment between students' environmental sense-of-purpose and environmental actions
WEB	**Table B.4.26**	Misalignment between students' environmental sense-of-purpose and environmental actions, by socio-economic status and gender
WEB	**Table B.4.27**	Misalignment between students' environmental sense-of-purpose and environmental actions, by proficiency levels in science
WEB	**Table B.4.28**	Misalignment between students' environmental sense-of-purpose and environmental actions, by environmental awareness and self-efficacy in environmental understanding
WEB	**Table B.4.29**	Student perception of boycotts and involvement in boycotts for environmental reasons
WEB	**Table B.4.30**	Mean score in science, by students' involvement in environmental actions
WEB	**Table B.4.31**	Average number of environmental actions that students in the school take part in and student involvement in environmental actions
WEB	**Table B.4.33**	Environmentally enthusiastic students who do not reduce the energy they use at home to protect the environment, by student characteristics
WEB	**Table B.4.34**	Environmentally enthusiastic students who do not choose certain products for ethical or environmental reason, by student characteristics
WEB	**Table B.4.35**	Environmentally enthusiastic students who do not sign environmental or social petitions online, by student characteristics
WEB	**Table B.4.36**	Environmentally enthusiastic students who do not boycott products or companies for political, ethical or environmental reasons, by student characteristics
WEB	**Table B.4.37**	Environmentally enthusiastic students who do not participate in activities in favour of environmental protection, by student characteristics
WEB	**Table B.4.38**	Environmentally enthusiastic students who do not take part in any environmental action
WEB	**Table B.4.39**	Environmentally enthusiastic students who do not take part in each environmental action, by student socio-economic status and gender
WEB	**Table B.4.40**	Environmentally enthusiastic students who do not take part in each environmental action, by student characteristics
WEB	**Table B.4.41**	Environmentally enthusiastic students who do not take part in each environmental action, by parental environmental attitudes and actions
WEB	**Table B.4.42**	Environmentally enthusiastic students who do not take part in each environmental action, by existence of formal curriculum on climate change and global warming in their school
WEB	**Table B.4.43**	Students boycotting products or companies for political, ethical or environmental reasons, by parents boycotting products or companies or student perception on boycott
WEB	**Table B.4.44**	Environmentally enthusiastic students who do not take part in boycotting products or companies for political, ethical or environmental reasons, by student perception about boycotts

www.ingramcontent.com/pod-product-compliance
Lightning Source LLC
Chambersburg PA
CBHW061219240926
51846CB00006B/1280